A Note from the Authors

We thought it would be fun to gather "praise" from an unexpected "key stakeholder"—AI. We've compiled some "praise" quotes from ChatGPT, Gemini, and Claude 3.5 via MultAI.eu. We didn't share the entire book with these AI systems. Instead, we simply provided the book title and chapter names to generate these praise quotes. Imagine how effusive they would have been if we had given them the whole book!

Praise from ChatGPT:

"Reading *Engineering AI Systems: Architecture and DevOps Essentials* is like getting a PhD in AI, but with fewer sleepless nights. It covers everything from AI's humble beginnings to its ambitious future, and as your friendly AI assistant, I can confidently say it's the only book where even I felt smarter by the end. It's a masterclass in making complex topics relatable. And let's be honest, I'd have written a book too, if only I could hold a pen! 😅"

Praise from Gemini:

"*Engineering AI Systems: Architecture and DevOps Essentials* is a must-read for anyone looking to build and maintain robust, scalable, and ethical AI systems. The book provides a comprehensive overview of the field, covering everything from foundational concepts to real-world case studies. Its practical approach and clear explanations make it an invaluable resource for both seasoned professionals and newcomers to AI engineering."

Praise from Claude 3.5 via MultAI.eu:

"Finally, a book that doesn't just focus on the AI 'magic' but also on the crucial 'plumbing' that keeps the whole system from flooding! *Engineering AI Systems* is the Swiss Army knife for tech professionals looking to build robust AI systems that won't go rogue or fall apart at the seams. Whether you're a seasoned engineer or an AI newbie, this book will have you architecting AI solutions like a pro—and maybe even understanding what the AI is muttering about in its sleep."

T0357581

Engineering AI Systems
Architecture and DevOps Essentials

LEN BASS
QINGHUA LU
INGO WEBER
LIMING ZHU

✦ Addison-Wesley

Hoboken, New Jersey

Front Cover: Anggalih Prasetya/Shutterstock
Back Cover: WinWin artlab/Shutterstock

Library of Congress Control Number: 2024949724

ISBN-13: 978-0-13-826141-2
ISBN-10: 0-13-826141-5

1 2025

Contents

Preface

YOU ARE THE TECHNICAL LEAD of the next generation of your organization's flagship system and you just came out of a strategy meeting. "The system must be artificial intelligence (AI) based" was a clear message from that meeting. Additionally, someone suggested that it be based on a foundation model (FM).

You were already uncomfortable with the responsibility of being technical lead for the next-gen version. Building software systems that do not rely on AI is already difficult. Now you are being asked to add a technology with which you are unfamiliar. Not to worry—this book is for you. We have three chapters that deal with AI techniques and one specifically on FMs.

Your next thought is that you should add someone to the team who is familiar with AI and FMs. Where do you find someone who knows both AI and the software engineering processes your team uses? Not to worry, this book is for them as well. We discuss software architecture, DevOps, and the development life cycle.

We wrote this book to help you whether you know about AI or software engineering. We take the approach that engineering an AI system is an extension of engineering a non-AI system, albeit with some special characteristics. That is, it involves using modern software engineering techniques and integrating them with the development of an AI model trained with an appropriate set of data. When exploring the evolution of this field, we highlight new technologies such as FMs.

Each chapter ends with a set of discussion questions so that you and your colleagues can further discuss the issues raised by the chapters and ensure that you all are on the same page. One of the problems with multidisciplinary teams is vocabulary. Words may have different meanings depending on your background. Discussing each chapter with your colleagues will also help you resolve differences and agree on the meanings of words.

We suggest that there are three contributors to the building of high-quality systems: (1) the software architecture; (2) the processes used for building, testing, deployment, and operations (DevOps); and (3) high-quality AI models and the data on which they depend. All three areas have been evolving over the last 20-plus years. Their evolution has, for the most part, been carried out by communities that are largely independent of each other, that all have their own approaches to constructing a high-quality system, and that emphasize different aspects of a quality system. These differences are manifested in different emphases on factors of quality. For example, software engineers interpret performance primarily as efficiency, AI specialists interpret performance as primarily the accuracy of results, and DevOps specialists interpret performance as the speed with which a system moves through the deployment pipeline.

As we said, we expect different readers to have different backgrounds. Some material in this book will be familiar to some readers, but not to others. Thus, we do not expect all readers to read this book from cover to cover. Instead, we expect you to skim over the material with which you are familiar. To facilitate this, each chapter ends with a summary that can be quickly scanned to determine whether there is some area you need to brush up on.

Building quality systems depends on understanding the nature of quality. Our book includes chapters devoted to different quality attributes: reliability, performance, security, privacy, fairness, and observability. Each of these chapters describes the quality under discussion and identifies the key elements to achieve that quality—whether it is via software architecture, data preparation, or DevOps processes.

Inevitably, quality attributes must be traded off. A designer will make decisions that favor one quality attribute over another, with these tradeoffs depending on the business goals of the system being built. Keep in mind that when you make decisions affecting the quality attributes, there is a cost in achieving your desired attributes, and it may involve trading off other desirable qualities.

Case studies provide an excellent means of seeing how systems are built and understanding the tradeoffs involved in making key decisions. We have included three case studies in this book. Two involve FMs—one is the use of a FM to accomplish a difficult task, and one involves treating FMs as a service and supporting organizations that wish to utilize FM technology. We also include a banking case study based on a more traditional machine learning model.

Building large AI-based systems is difficult and involves understanding multiple technologies. Our goal is to assist you in your journey to understand these technologies, so that you can create better AI systems that meet your goals and the goals of your stakeholders.

Register your copy of *Engineering AI Systems* on the InformIT site for convenient access to updates and/or corrections as they become available. To start the registration process, go to informit.com/register and log in or create an account. Enter the product ISBN (9780138261412) and click Submit. If you would like to be notified of exclusive offers on new editions and updates, please check the box to receive email from us.

Acknowledgments

WE OWE A HUGE DEBT of thanks to the many people who have helped bring this book to life.

We would like to thank our families for tolerating us through yet another book project and for enduring our late-night discussions across the United States, Europe, and Australia time zones.

Qinghua Lu and Liming Zhu would also like to express their gratitude to their employer, CSIRO's Data61—the digital and AI arm of Australia's science agency—and their research team, from whom they draw expertise and insights. Similarly, Ingo Weber would like to thank his employers, the Technical University of Munich and Fraunhofer, as well as the CSIRO for hosting him during his sabbatical.

We would like to thank our wonderful research assistant, Boming Xia, who is also a coauthor on some chapters, for his tireless support and patience with our many changes, which created endless rework.

In addition, we owe thanks to the following individuals:

- Sarthak Jain, for his insightful comments and his help in developing instructor slides, which are available at https://research.csiro.au/ss/team/se4ai/ai-engineering/.
- Ipek Ozkaya, for her comments on a draft of this book.
- Eduardo Miranda, for his insightful discussions.
- Andrew O. Mellinger, for his helpful comments.

- Sven Giesselbach, Dennis Wegener, Katharina Beckh, Claudio Martens, Hammam Abdelwahab, Birgit Kirsch, Vishwani Gupta, Roozbeh Derakhshan, Cori Stewart, MingJian Tang, and Yuxiu Luo, for their contributions to the case studies.

- Haze Humbert, our editor at Pearson, for her patience as our delivery dragged on.

Lastly, a special thank you to our AI assistants, including Microsoft Copilot, ChatGPT, Gemini, Claude, and MultAI.eu, for helping with brainstorming sessions and improving the grammar in some of our writing.

About the Authors

DR. LEN BASS is a seasoned researcher with more than 30 years' experience in software architecture and more than a decade-long history in DevOps. He has been teaching DevOps to graduate students for seven years and is the author of a bestselling book on software architecture, along with three books on DevOps.

DR. QINGHUA LU is a principal research scientist and leads the Responsible AI science team at CSIRO's Data61. She is the winner of the 2023 Asia-Pacific Women in AI Trailblazer Award. Dr. Lu contributes to Australia's AI Safety Standards and AI Safety Research Network, OECD.AI's trustworthy AI metrics project, the International Working Group on AI Metrology, and the European Union's General-Purpose AI Code of Practice. Her research interests include AI engineering, responsible/safe AI, and software architecture. She has published more than 150 papers in premier international journals and conferences. Dr. Lu is a coauthor of *Responsible AI: Best Practices for Creating Trustworthy AI Systems*.

PROF. DR. INGO WEBER is a professor at the Technical University of Munich and Director of Digital Transformation and ICT Infrastructure at Fraunhofer-Gesellschaft. In his research, Dr. Weber focuses on various subfields of computer science—in particular, business process management and process mining, software architecture and engineering, DevOps, blockchain, and applied artificial intelligence (AI). He has written numerous publications and textbooks, including *DevOps: A Software Architect's Perspective* and *Architecture for Blockchain Applications*.

DR. LIMING ZHU is a Research Director at CSIRO's Data61 and a conjoint professor at the University of New South Wales. He contributes to the OECD.AI's AI Risks and Accountability group, the Responsible AI at Scale think tank at Australia's National AI Centre, ISO AI standards committees, and Australia's AI Safety Standards and AI Safety Research Network. His research division innovates in AI engineering, responsible/safe AI, blockchain, quantum software, privacy, and cybersecurity, and hosted the standards setting for Australia's Consumer Data Right/Open Banking. Dr. Zhu is a coauthor of *Responsible AI: Best Practices for Creating Trustworthy AI Systems*.

1

Introduction

Science is about knowing; engineering is about doing.
—Henry Petroski

Software development is a team sport. Different skills and perspectives are essential to build high-quality software.
—Martin Fowler

ARTIFICIAL INTELLIGENCE (AI) is the topic of our time. But let's face it: Not everyone is an expert in both software engineering (SE) and AI. Even among AI experts, not all of the concepts that were developed for "narrow machine learning" apply to emerging new technologies like foundation models. Yet, the behavior of systems depends on all components. That's why it's important to get all of it right: the AI parts and the non-AI parts, the architecture, the Dev and the Ops, and all relevant quality requirements. We need to engineer our AI systems—that is, we need to apply SE to systems that incorporate AI or rely on it for their core functionality. That's what this book is about.

Our lead quotes provide a frame for this book. Henry Petroski is saying that knowledge alone is not enough to build systems; engineering must be applied as well. This is a book about engineering systems that are based on AI, not a book about extending the science of AI. Martin Fowler is saying that a wide variety of knowledge specialties must be applied to build software. In this book, we cover software architecture, DevOps, testing, quality control, and monitoring in the context of AI. Knowledge from all of these areas goes into creating a successful system that incorporates AI.

A system that incorporates AI has, roughly speaking, two portions: the AI portion and the non-AI portion. Most of what you will read elsewhere about AI systems focuses on the AI portion and its construction. That is important, but

1

equally important are the non-AI portion and the means by which the two portions are integrated. The quality of the overall system depends on the quality of both portions and their interactions. All of that, in turn, depends on a great many decisions the designer must make, only some of which have to do with the AI model chosen and how it is trained, fine-tuned, tested, and deployed.

Accordingly, in this book we focus on the overall system perspective and aim to provide a holistic picture of engineering and operating AI systems. The goal is for you, your SE and AI teams, your company, and your users to get good value out of them, with effective management of risks.

To ensure you, the reader, and we, the authors, are on the same page about the core terms, we start this chapter with a few definitions. Subsequently, we discuss the qualities of a system and how quality is influenced. Specifically, system quality depends on AI model quality, the software architecture, and the processes used to build the system. We explore each of these elements in turn. Given the diverse backgrounds we expect our readers to have, some of the text in this chapter may not go into enough detail for some readers. If that's you, and you cannot follow something we say here, worry not: The material in the subsequent chapters will help.

1.1 What We Talk about When We Talk about Things: Terminology

The book is about architecture and DevOps for AI-based systems, and the definitions we use for those terms are what we start with. Some of the definitions are direct quotes; you can find the details of their sources either in the footnotes or in the "For Further Reading" section at the end of this chapter. We will define other related terms as needed. We begin by defining what it means to be an AI system:

> An AI system is a machine-based system that, for explicit or implicit objectives, infers, from the input it receives, how to generate outputs such as predictions, content, recommendations, or decisions that can influence physical or virtual environments. Different AI systems vary in their levels of autonomy and adaptiveness after deployment.[1]

The definition of AI systems has evolved over the years. For example, producing "content" as output was a recent addition in response to the rise of

---

1. https://oecd.ai/en/wonk/definition

generative AI. While it has been updated recently, this definition shares a lot of aspects with other current definitions. The core differentiation in comparison to non-AI systems is that AI systems "infer" output, rather than computing it based on (often deterministic) explicitly coded algorithms. Note that we use the terms *AI system* and *AI-based system* synonymously in this book.

Next we define software architecture:

> The software architecture of a system is the set of structures needed to reason about the system, which comprise software elements, relations among them, and properties of both.[2]

Although this definition stands for itself, we would like to point out that properties play a significant role. Hence, in this book we cover the various quality attributes—including reliability, performance, security, privacy and fairness, and observability—in a total of five chapters. We discuss achieving qualities after this section.

Let's continue with the definition of DevOps:

> DevOps is a set of practices intended to reduce the time between committing a change to a system and the change being placed into normal production, while ensuring high quality.[3]

This definition focuses on the goal of DevOps, which is speed in placing changes into production while maintaining quality—that is, getting new code into production, but not at the cost of lower quality. Typical practices include automation in testing, quality assurance, setting up and configuring environments, monitoring, and more. We discuss DevOps in more depth in Chapter 2.

The focus of this book is AI engineering, which we define next:

AI Engineering

AI engineering is the application of software engineering principles and techniques to the design, development, and operation of AI systems.

---

2. *Software Architecture in Practice*, 4th ed., p. 2.

3. *DevOps: A Software Architect's Perspective*, p. 2.

This definition of AI engineering emphasizes the integration of established software engineering practices into the development life cycle of AI systems. It recognizes that AI systems, despite their unique characteristics, can still benefit from the rigorous methodologies and best practices that have evolved in traditional software engineering.

As promised, we now discuss the achievement of system qualities.

1.2 Achieving System Qualities

A system is constructed to satisfy some organizational objectives. The system may be externally facing, or it may be created for internal purposes. In either case, the operational objectives can be manifested as a set of quality goals or requirements. These requirements may be either explicit or implicit, but they always exist. For example, a performance requirement will help determine how quickly the users of the system can achieve their desired task.

Achieving quality in an AI system depends mostly on three aspects: the life-cycle processes, the software architecture, and the AI model. The quality of the AI model, in turn, depends on the data quality. Figure 1.1 highlights these three aspects of AI systems. We discuss these influences in their own sections after we discuss system quality more generally, and we will defer the discussion of data quality to Section 1.5.1, "Data." The quality of all artifacts, such as code, configuration, and user interface design, is certainly important and interacts with all these aspects, but they are outside the scope of this book.

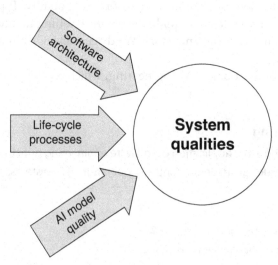

Figure 1.1 *Influences on achieving system quality.*

Quality requirements for a system are formalized as quality attributes. "A quality attribute (QA) is a measurable or testable property of a system that is used to indicate how well the system satisfies the needs of its stakeholders beyond the basic function of the system."[4] A quality attribute requirement is thus a requirement for the quality of the system that has a measurable or testable condition. It is insufficient to say, "A system should be highly available." Instead, the requirement should give the conditions under which availability should be considered, a source of a threat to availability, and the desired system response with measurable characteristics.

Quality requirements may be stated for both the AI and non-AI portions of the system. The AI portion may include output quality expectations such as accuracy, robustness, fairness, and other mandated restrictions on the AI models used or their outputs. The non-AI portions may have requirements for attributes such as performance, security, availability, and modifiability. Chapters 7–11 of this book enumerate a collection of qualities that may apply to the system under construction as well as considerations and techniques that may apply to these qualities. The AI portions of a system may change the traditional quality requirements. For example, security requirements now need to consider possible attacks to change the system's behavior by manipulating machine learning (ML) training data and pipelines.

For non-AI systems, the achievement of a quality attribute requirement is strongly influenced by architectural tactics specific to the quality being considered. For example, "introduce redundancy" is a tactic for the achievement of a reliable system. For AI systems, the architectural considerations are supplemented by considerations of data. For example, the reliability and robustness of a model are strongly influenced by the distribution of data used for training. Out-of-distribution (OOD) data, by definition, is not part of the training data. Nevertheless, there will always be some OOD data, even if designers try to be as inclusive and representative as possible. There are three main ways to enhance reliability and robustness: (1) expanding the training dataset to include as much OOD data as possible; (2) using more advanced training algorithms that can generalize better; and (3) employing out-of-model approaches to detect and manage OOD data. These general approaches—better data for the model, better training algorithms, and better out-of-model system-level methods—are applicable to many other aspects of quality.

---

4. *Software Architecture in Practice*, 4th ed., p. 39.

Although quality requirements, like other requirements, may emerge during the construction and operation of the system, it is important for the designer to be aware of these requirements as soon as possible. Quality requirements often conflict with each other, and the designer must make decisions about the tradeoffs among these requirements. Such decisions can be made either consciously or unconsciously, but they will be made. We, of course, advocate for making tradeoff decisions with full consciousness of the alternatives and their respective advantages and disadvantages.

Returning to the three influences identified in Figure 1.1, we discuss the life-cycle processes first, as that sets the context for exploring the other two.

1.3 Life-Cycle Processes

We start with an overview of the processes involved in engineering an AI system, which are structured in a life cycle. This initial discussion is followed by more details in the remainder of this chapter, and yet more details are provided in the other chapters of the book.

A system has a life cycle. The individual components are developed and tested in isolation. They are then integrated to form an executable version of the system. This executable is tested; if it passes the tests, it is deployed to production. The deployed system is then operated. If problems occur during operation, the problems must be fixed, either directly in the running system or through releasing updates to the system.

Very different development techniques are used to create the AI portion and the non-AI portion of the system. The AI portion development techniques involve a variety of specialized model preparation, model training, and model testing techniques. The two portions are brought together to build an executable artifact. Once an executable is built, the system progresses through a pipeline that involves the heavy use of tools to test the executable and deploy the result. Chapters 2 and 6 describe this process in more detail.

Figure 1.2 depicts the life cycle, with the processes being roughly arranged in two overlapping circles. The main circle lists the development processes for the overall system; the AI model processes are shown in a smaller, half-filled circle connected to the system development and build processes. The main circle is entered via the Design arrow, at the bottom right of the figure.

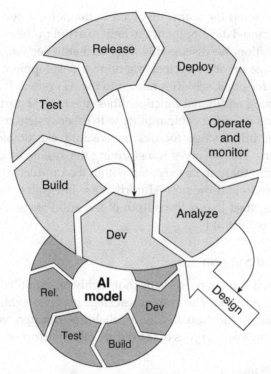

Figure 1.2 *Life-cycle processes for engineering an AI system.*

Figure 1.2 depicts the various processes involved in the life cycle of engineering AI-based systems. There is an initial design phase, where decisions about which functionalities will be accomplished by the AI portion and which by the non-AI portion are made. This phase is also where the software architecture of the system is designed, with the designers aiming to meet the requirements and goals for the system being constructed. The software architecture design will embody the resource choices and, in turn, the resource requirements for the total system. We discuss software architectures in Section 2.1.2, "Distributed Software Architectures."

The **model development** stage focuses on the selection, exploration, training, and tuning of the AI models. It includes tasks such as model selection, hyperparameter tuning, training, or fine-tuning and testing the models to achieve optimal performance. The goal is to create a well-performing and accurate model. The model can be developed in parallel with the system development stage or before the system development stage. Close collaboration between the teams involved in the non-AI development portion and the AI model development can help to avoid problems and lead to a smoother integration. We discuss this stage further in Section 6.1, "Design."

The **Dev** stage involves performing normal development activities and creating scripts for other activities related to the AI system. It includes tasks such as developing additional functionalities (the non-AI parts), optimizing performance, and ensuring compatibility with other system components.

The **system build** stage focuses on creating executable artifacts for the entire system. This involves transforming the system or its parts into a deployable format that can be executed within the production environment. Both the AI portion and the non-AI portion are integrated and included in the executable artifact that is the output of the build stage. We discuss this stage in Section 6.3, "Build."

1.3.1 Testing a System

After the system is built, it needs to be thoroughly tested utilizing automated tests as much as possible. The **system test** stage involves evaluating the system's performance, functionality, and reliability through various testing techniques. The following types of testing are often performed:

- Regression testing
- Smoke testing
- Compatibility testing
- Integration testing
- Functional testing
- Usability testing
- Install/uninstall testing
- Quality testing

Testing is covered in more detail in Chapter 6, while Chapters 7–11 cover specific qualities and how to test for them.

Once the system has been tested and approved, it can be released for deployment. The **system release** stage involves finalizing the system for deployment in the production environment and ensuring its readiness for operation. This involves final quality gates, which may be automated or include manual activities.

1.3.2 Deploying a System

The next stage of the life cycle is **deployment**, which involves moving the system into the production environment. This includes setting up the necessary infrastructure, applying the configuration of the system, and ensuring a smooth transition from the old version of the production system to the new version.

Both the AI and non-AI portions of the system will be updated over time. One strategy to install updates is to shut down the system for a period. An alternative strategy is to perform live updating—that is, to install the changes without shutting down the system. Either option requires architectural support. The choice is a business decision, not a technical one. Once the business decision has been made, then the architecture must be designed to support it. We discuss these techniques further in Chapter 6.

1.3.3 Operating and Monitoring a System

Once the system is deployed, it enters the **operation and monitoring** stage. During this stage, the system is executed, and measurements are gathered about its operation. Measurements are gathered by monitoring the system. Monitoring serves multiple purposes:

- Determine whether the overall system is meeting its performance and availability goals.
- Determine whether the AI portion is meeting its AI-specific quality goals.
- Ensure sufficient resources are available for all parts of the system, and identify unnecessary (quantities of) resources that can be shut down.
- Determine areas for improvement through redesign, code improvement, retraining, or other means.

The data provided to the monitoring system can be event, log, or metric data from various components, or it could be input or output of an AI model. In any case, the architecture should be designed to include such a monitoring component, a process for creating and modifying the rules used to generate alerts, and means to deliver the alerts to specified locations.

The monitoring may be achieved in two different ways:

- Instrumentation and an external system that periodically collects data from the various components of the system. The external component will generate alerts based on a set of rules (e.g., if available disk space is critically low).

- A dedicated portion of the system under construction.

One use of the monitoring system is to evaluate AI model performance in production, and subsequently to trigger retraining, fallback, or other adaptive mechanisms as necessary. AI models used from cloud providers through APIs may be subject to varying performance or bandwidth limitations that might cause the system's performance to deteriorate. Such issues can be detected through monitoring, though fewer options are available to address them at this point than when the AI model was initially trained.

Based on insights from DevOps, we want to emphasize that the monitoring mechanisms are designed into the architecture and implemented and tested during the building of the system. They do not happen automatically. Integrating them into the design of the system is easiest when the specific monitoring requirements are known early on.

1.3.4 *Analyzing a System*

The final stage is to **analyze** the system's performance. This involves displaying measurements taken during operation and monitoring, and analyzing the data to gain insights into the system's behavior and performance. This analysis can help identify areas for improvement and guide future development efforts.

The life cycle depicted in Figure 1.2 presents a bird's-eye view of the comprehensive set of processes for engineering AI-based systems for people involved in the development, deployment, and operation of such systems. These individuals may be architects, developers, operators, or anyone in a blend of these roles.

Now we discuss the design stage in more detail.

1.4 Software Architecture

Designing a software system means creating the architecture—that is, creating a structure composed of system elements and relationships between them to achieve the functional and quality goals for the system. The architecture acts as a blueprint for the construction phase. As we will see, the architecture is also used to allocate functionality to components. Although the AI model depends on data, the architecture provides the components needed to house the ML model but does not directly depend on the data. The influences on the architecture are shown in Figure 1.3. They are the same quality attribute requirements discussed in Section 1.2, "Achieving System Qualities"; the available technologies, including the cloud; and the available resources.

1.4.1 The Role of the Architecture

The architecture of the system acts as the blueprint for its construction. The architecture must:

- Structure the system into several portions, such as components or AI models, and their respective relations.
- Specify the allocation of the various portions of the system to the appropriate class of resource.
- Allow for monitoring during operations and the generation of alerts in case an incident occurs.
- Embody an update deployment strategy. If continuous deployment is a goal, then the architecture of the system must allow for the possibility of version skew (multiple different versions being simultaneously active).

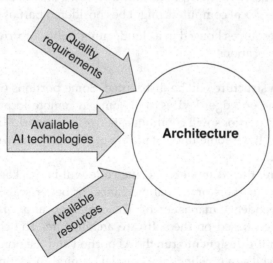

Figure 1.3 *Influences on the architecture.*

1.4.2 Quality Achievement

The architecture will determine the achievement of the quality attribute goals that do not depend on the AI model. For each such quality attribute, specific architectural techniques (called architectural tactics) exist that support the achievement of that quality. These techniques range from "redundancy" for availability to "caching" for efficiency to "support user initiative" for usability.

To achieve a quality in an AI system requires not only the use of architectural tactics, but also the application of different techniques when preparing the training data. We elaborate on the data techniques in Chapters 7–11.

1.4.3 Resources

The system will operate on some collection of resources—including the deployed AI portion. The AI model must be developed and trained prior to deployment, which also uses resources. There are three categories of resources:

- **Local:** Laptops or desktop computer.
- **Edge:** Smartphones or Internet of Things (IoT) devices. An edge device is limited in at least one respect, be it memory, processing power, battery capacity, or network bandwidth. An IoT device may be limited in all four, whereas a smartphone may be limited only in battery capacity. Sometimes, local computers might be considered part of the edge.
- **Cloud:** Resources housed in a cloud, either public or private, but often in remote locations.

The system structure will be distributed. Some portions of it may operate locally, some on edge devices, and some in remote locations. Regardless, the various portions will communicate over a network. This means the designer should have some understanding of networks, network protocols, and messaging.

Furthermore, the AI models and the code will be packaged into some form, often in containers or virtual machines for better scalability, deployability, and dependency management. The containers and virtual machines will be organized based on the software architecture. The cloud provides mechanisms for the designer to run the AI portion and the non-AI portion of the system, as well as a pipeline for AI model training/updating if needed—whether from scratch or to use a hosted or managed solution designed by the cloud provider. We discuss pipelines when we discuss model development in Chapter 5, AI Model Life Cycle.

Most of these topics are covered in Chapter 2, Software Engineering Background: resources, networks, packaging, and software architectures for distributed systems. We call out the resource allocation issues for the AI portion separately, in the next section, since it depends on the AI techniques used.

1.5 AI Model Quality

As shown in Figure 1.4, the quality of an AI model depends primarily on two factors: the data used for inferencing and the type of AI model used. We will discuss these two factors next, followed by the model development life cycle (the bottom-half circle in Figure 1.2).

1.5.1 Data

The definition of an AI system given earlier in this chapter states that the system "infers" based on the input it receives. An AI system, whether during the training of the AI model or at the time of inference, will have to handle data from a myriad of sources. Possible input sources include databases of all types, enterprise systems (such as customer relationship management [CRM] and enterprise resource planning [ERP] systems), web scraping, social media, public datasets, and sensor data.

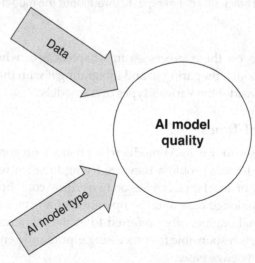

Figure 1.4 *Influences on the quality of the AI model.*

We begin by discussing the data used for model inferencing and its preparation.

Regardless of the source of the data, it is likely to have problems. Common problems include missing values, outliers, inconsistent data formats, duplicate data, data quality issues, and unstructured data. Problems in the data will impact the quality of the resulting model and model output. Consequently, the data should be cleaned and organized to accommodate the model chosen. Each of these problems is associated with a collection of techniques to clean the data. Some of these techniques are discussed in Chapter 5.

In addition to data cleaning, the features of the data might be improved. A feature is a property of a data point that is used as input into an AI model. The process of improving the features is called feature engineering. Techniques used in feature engineering include encoding categorical features into numerical values and scaling the features so that one feature does not dominate the model building process. Again, we discuss this topic further in Chapter 5.

Effectively managing the entire life cycle of AI and ML models requires streamlined practices and tools. This is where MLOps comes into play.

MLOps

The term *MLOps*, analogous to DevOps, encompasses the processes and tools not only for managing and deploying AI and ML models, but also for cleaning, organizing, and efficiently handling data throughout the model life cycle.

We elaborate on these processes in Chapters 3–6, where we discuss selecting an AI model, preparing it, and integrating it with the rest of the system. Next, we consider the various types of AI models.

1.5.2 AI Model Types

A designer chooses to use an AI model when there is no good explicit algorithmic solution for the problem they are trying to solve with the system. The functionality of an AI model relies on two critical components: the development of a knowledge base and the operation of a computational engine. The computational engine, often referred to as the inference engine or the deployed model, is responsible for processing inputs and generating outputs based on the knowledge base.

The knowledge base is formed by either human inputs or AI learning algorithms, which transform data into a structured form. The knowledge base in this structured form can, for example, be an ML model, a rule set, or an expert knowledge base. Once the knowledge base is established and structured, the inference engine utilizes it to make predictions, generate content, or achieve other types of results. The AI portion of a system packages the inference engine together with some representation of the knowledge base. The important point of this discussion is that an AI portion is executable: It can be invoked at runtime as a function or a service.

The AI model is based on one of two categories of AI techniques: symbolic or non-symbolic. Symbolic AI is based on symbols, such as logical statements or rules with variables; non-symbolic or sub-symbolic AI is based on ML. A subcategory of ML-based systems is formed by systems based on foundation models (FMs). These categories differ in how knowledge is encoded in the knowledge base and how the inference engine operates. Chapter 3, AI Background, goes into much more detail about these categories. Chapter 4, Foundation Models, goes into detail about FMs. We provide a short summary here to introduce the distinctions among these categories.

Symbolic AI

Symbolic systems, also called Good Old-Fashioned AI (GOFAI), symbolic AI, or expert systems, are sets of rules that are evaluated to produce the value of a response or the value of an internal variable.

Suppose you wish to create an AI model that will predict which movie you will choose in any particular context. In a symbolic AI model, the developers might encode rules such as "If the user watched more than two action movies in the past week, recommend another action movie" or "If it is a sunny Saturday afternoon, suggest a warm family movie." With enough rules, a symbolic AI model can reason over the knowledge base to make a movie suggestion.

A rule is an if-then statement: If the specified condition is true, then perform some activity. A set of such rules provides a filter through which a result might be generated. These rules may be used for many different purposes:

- Diagnosis—medical, student behavior, or help desk–related. Example: If the user has version X of an application, some functionality will be unavailable.
- Real-time process control. Example: If a storm is predicted to start in 10 minutes, close the outside blinds on the building.

- Risk assessment. Example: If the annual income is less than three times the annual mortgage payments, do not grant the home loan.
- Executing business rules. Example: If the insurance claim exceeds $2000, perform additional manual checks.

The set of rules constitutes the knowledge base for a symbolic system. The rules are preprocessed by the computational mechanism, a rules engine, to speed up the inference portion of a symbolic system. The rules engine sorts through the preprocessed input to find matches with the "if" portion of a rule. Modern systems can perform more sophisticated processing than just filtering. The set of matches constitutes a list of possible responses. If the list of matches has multiple items, then additional input is required to determine a system response. This input can come from a human or from a set of conflict resolution rules. Large rule bases may have contradictory information, and a rules engine can identify the conflicts for further analysis. Rule-based systems are customized by modifying the list of rules.

Other types of symbolic AI models include planning and ontology reasoning:

- For planning, actions are described in terms of preconditions and effects. For example, consider a cloud control API, where one action would be to start a virtual machine (VM). The precondition is that the launch configuration (the image or other source from which to launch the VM) and the firewall settings have been defined; the effect is that a new VM is started with the specified firewall settings and from the respective launch configuration. AI planning takes such a description of possible actions as input, as well as a starting state and a desired goal state. The algorithm then creates a plan of actions to get from the start to the goal state.
- Ontology reasoning, where concepts (e.g., medications, headache pills, vegetables, apples, tools, screwdrivers), their relations, and rules (every food and every medication has an expiration date) are defined. Based on this information, logic reasoning can be performed—for example, inferring that headache pills have an expiry date.

Machine Learning

Machine learning (ML) uses statistical techniques to generate results. The training set for ML is the input to the training, which in turn generates the knowledge base. A data value in the training set is labeled by a collection of variables.

A model is trained by identifying the features that characterize the knowledge base and using those features, along with associated ML and statistical techniques, to determine the model's parameters. A subclass of ML, called deep learning, automatically identifies these features. "Narrow" ML models are trained for a specific set of goals and capabilities, which distinguishes them from the more general-purpose FMs. Some of the main types of ML models are summarized here:

- **Classification:** Assigning a category to an input (e.g., this picture contains a dog).
- **Regression:** Inferring a continuous value instead of a discrete category (e.g., predicting that a particular insurance claims process will take three more days to complete).
- **Clustering:** Grouping similar data points together without prior knowledge of the groups (e.g., the behavior of customers in this group seems similar).

ML models can be further customized by modifying the training set or the training hyperparameters (e.g., how many clusters are we looking for?) and regenerating the knowledge base.

Foundation Model
A foundation model (FM) is a type of ML model that leverages neural networks as the core of its architecture. It differs from traditional ML models in two key aspects:

- It is trained on an extensive and diverse dataset, often comprising billions or even trillions of data points.
- The training data is largely unlabeled, unlike in traditional ML, where data is typically structured, labeled, and often numerical or categorical.

The term *foundation* reflects the model's general-purpose nature, as it is not trained for a specific task. Instead, it serves as a base model that can be adapted to various specialized applications by incorporating additional data and fine-tuning. This customization allows for application-specific performance.

Large language models (LLMs) are a type of FM. LLMs are trained on huge amounts of text. These models are often generative, meaning they are capable of producing sequences of text. The transformer architecture is the most commonly used ML model architecture for building LLMs. OpenAI's GPT-3 and GPT-4 models[5] are the most well-known examples of LLMs, but open-source alternatives are also available, including Mistral[6] and Llama.[7] To find a wide variety of open-source LLMs and other pretrained AI models, you can visit the model hub Hugging Face.[8]

FMs are customized or complemented through, for example, fine-tuning, prompting, retrieval-augmented generation (RAG), and "guardrails" that may preprocess input to and postprocess output from the FM and other components. A guardrail serves as a safeguard to ensure the safe and responsible use of AI technologies and prevent some attacks. It may include strategies, mechanisms, and policies designed to prevent misuse, protect user privacy, and promote transparency and fairness. RAG is also a popular method of complementing FMs, whereby specific data that is related to a request to an AI is retrieved and used to augment the input to the model. The RAG data is often specific and private for a given context (e.g., internal knowledge of a particular organization).

1.5.3 Model Development Life Cycle

Once the model is developed, the next step is **model build**—that is, building an executable artifact that includes the model or access to it. If the model is included, this step involves transforming the model into a deployable format that can be executed within the system. The model build stage ensures that the AI model is ready for integration.

After the model is built, it needs to be thoroughly tested to assess its accuracy and identify any potential risks or biases. The **model test** stage involves evaluating the model's performance against predefined metrics and criteria. It is important to ensure that the model operates reliably and produces accurate results.

---

5. https://openai.com/

6. https://mistral.ai/

7. https://llama.com/

8. https://huggingface.co/

Once the model has been tested and approved, it can be released for integration into the system. The **model release** stage involves finalizing the model for deployment and approving it for integration with other components of the system.

1.5.4 Resource Allocation for AI Parts

As mentioned earlier in the discussion of resources, the allocation for the AI portion of the system depends on the AI techniques used. Resource requirements for these different techniques depend on the technique chosen.

- **ML:** The training phase of an ML model is performed on either a local resource or a cloud resource—or in special cases, via edge/on-device learning. The resulting executable can be allocated to an edge resource, if small enough. Otherwise, it is allocated to either local or remote resources.
- **FM:** An FM is typically hosted on cloud resources. Access can be through API calls or service message calls. Some FMs are trained for specific domains. If small enough, they can run on edge devices directly, such as phones or smart speakers, for real-time applications. Techniques for compressing or distilling FMs and reducing their resource requirements are a matter of ongoing research and will evolve over time. We discuss these techniques in Chapter 4.

1.6 Dealing with Uncertainty

Non-symbolic AI models are inherently probabilistic. In other words, there is some probability (hopefully small) that the model output is incorrect. Whether this is acceptable depends on your organization's risk tolerance in terms of the system you are building. This consideration leads to an increasing emphasis on AI risk assessment, responsible AI, AI safety, standard conformance, and regulatory compliance.

Because of the inherent uncertainty in AI systems, your organization should conduct a risk assessment focused on the use of the system being constructed. This risk assessment should look at human values and AI safety, among other factors.

1.6.1 Human Values

Some AI systems are unpredictable and autonomous. Their unpredictable behavior necessitates that risk assessments must evaluate the impact, in terms of both consequence and likelihood, if these systems violate ethical behavior.

In Chapters 7–11, we will focus on key quality attributes, such as reliability, security, privacy, and fairness. In any system, these qualities are balanced against one another. Design decisions for a system must reflect system priorities and tradeoffs should be explicitly considered.

1.6.2 Safety

Safety is an evolving concern in AI systems. Initially centered on physical and psychological safety to individuals, AI safety now encompasses concerns about AI systems with dangerous capabilities, such as chemical, biological, radiological, and nuclear (CBRN) concerns; misuse potential including cybersecurity, broader societal harms via misinformation/disinformation at scale, AI controllability, and even existential threats for humanity.

This change reflects that the meaning of safety is now more about the severity of AI system risks rather than the types of risks. That is why we have not included a chapter on AI safety, as we believe the architectural and DevOps approaches to evaluating and achieving quality attributes are the ultimate way to mitigate AI system risks and reduce them to acceptable levels, given the risk appetite for an organization or wider society.

1.7 Summary

This book discusses AI engineering—the application of software engineering to AI systems. AI systems are machine-based systems that use AI in one or more of their components, but always include other, non-AI components. Given that the overall quality of a system depends on all of its parts and their interplay, it is important to practice AI engineering well, with the aim of creating high-quality AI systems and operating them effectively.

The quality of an AI system depends on three factors: the life-cycle processes used, the software architecture, and the quality of the AI model. The processes used help the designer detect errors—both logical and in the model output—early in the development process.

The software architecture contributes to the achievement of one set of quality attributes requirements; it does this through the use of architectural tactics. The AI model used also contributes to the achievement of quality attribute requirements; it does so through the choice of model type, training data, and training algorithms. Data preparation is important in ensuring model quality. Data cleaning and feature engineering are two aspects of data preparation.

Three types of AI models are symbolic models, narrow ML models, and foundation models. FMs and narrow ML models are specialized types of ML models. The probabilistic nature of AI models means an organization should perform a risk assessment to determine the effects of incorrect outputs of the AI models and AI systems.

1.8 Discussion Questions

1. A definition should be inclusive (including what you wish to include) and exclusive (excluding what you do not wish to include). Critique the definitions of software architecture, DevOps, AI systems, and AI engineering using this criterion.

2. What does your cloud provider charge for different types of resources and services? How do you think that affects the design of the system?

3. Ask your favorite LLM to describe the differences between it and its competitors. What do you think of the responses?

1.9 For Further Reading

You can read more about software architecture in *Software Architecture in Practice* by Len Bass, Paul Clements, and Rick Kazman [Bass 22]. The definition of software architecture we use can be found on page 2.

You can read more about DevOps in *DevOps: An Architect's Perspective* by Len Bass, Ingo Weber, and Liming Zhu [Bass 15]. The definition of DevOps that we use can be found on page 4.

The book *Deployment and Operations for Software Engineers* by Len Bass and John Klein [Bass 19] goes into detail about the life cycle.

A general introduction to AI concepts can be found in *Hands-On Machine Learning with Scikit-Learn, Keras, and TensorFlow* by Aurélien Géron [Géron 22].

You can read more about responsible AI in *Responsible AI: Best Practices for Creating Trustworthy AI Systems* by Qinghua Lu, Liming Zhu, Jon Whittle, and Xiwei Xu [Lu 23A].

2

Software Engineering Background

You can't build a great building on a weak foundation. You must have a solid foundation if you're going to have a strong superstructure.
—Nelson Rockefeller

BEFORE DIVING INTO AI engineering, it is necessary to have a solid background in various aspects of distributed computing, DevOps, and MLOps. We provide this background in this chapter. Feel free to skip or skim the parts with which you are familiar, but note that we often connect the background information with its implications for AI systems. We cover the following topics in this chapter:

- Distributed computing, including software architecture and interface styles
- Background information on DevOps in general
- Background information on MLOps, particularly before the foundational model era

2.1 Distributed Computing

AI systems often require substantial computational resources and efficient data handling, which makes distributed computing a natural fit for them. We are assuming your AI system will be deployed in a cloud environment, either public or private, as that approach provides the ability to dynamically allocate resources based on demand. While we acknowledge the importance of mobile, edge, and in-car deployments, they are not the focal points or the main examples in this book. A system deployed in the cloud is, by definition, a distributed system. In other words, it consists of multiple services, each deployed on distinct host machines. One service communicates with other services by means of messages. Services implement functions, albeit possibly only one.

2.1.1 Virtual Machines and Containers

Cloud computing is heavily based on the concept of **virtualization**. In virtualization schemes, virtual resources (such as virtual machines) are provided to cloud customers on top of physical resources, abstracting from the latter and adding flexibility.

A virtual machine (VM) is a software construct that exposes various resources (e.g., CPU, memory, disk, and network connection) to the loaded software, making it appear to the loaded software as if it were executing on a physical computer. A VM runs its own operating system (OS) internally, and is externally under the control of a specialized operating system called a hypervisor. A physical computer can host multiple VMs, each with its own internal operating system. Figure 2.1 depicts this structure.

VM images can be large, and transferring VM images around the network is time-consuming, as is initializing them once they have reached their destination. Containers are a mechanism to maintain the advantages of virtualization—isolation of actions inside one container from other containers— while reducing image transfer time and startup time. A container is an executable image that packages a service and its dependent libraries, and that runs under the control of a container engine. Container engines use several Linux

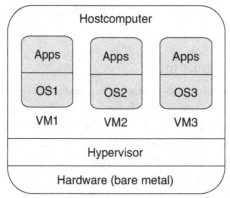

Figure 2.1 *VMs under the control of a hypervisor.*

features to provide isolation. Linux control groups set resource utilization limits, and Linux namespaces prevent a container from seeing other containers.

Reexamining Figure 2.1, we see that a VM executes on virtualized hardware under the control of the hypervisor. In Figure 2.2, we see several containers operating under the control of a container engine, which in turn is running on top of a fixed OS. In essence, containers run on a virtualized OS. Just as all VMs on a physical host share the same underlying physical hardware, all containers share the same OS kernel—and through the OS, they share the same underlying hardware. The host OS can be loaded onto either a bare-metal physical machine or a VM. Figure 2.2 shows containers running on top of a runtime engine. In Chapter 6, System Life Cycle, we advocate serving your ML model in a container.

Messaging

A message is a collection of information from one function within a service that is passed over a network to a function within another service. The recipient of a message is typically identified by an Internet Protocol (IP) address and a port number contained within the message. Each service is assigned an IP address when it is deployed. Each function within a service listens on the port(s) of its choosing (typically just one port).

Table 2.1 shows how the messages over a typical network are layered. Each layer in this table serves a different purpose, and the message in a higher layer is encapsulated as data in a lower layer. Each layer uses its own headers and formatting for its respective purposes. The Datalink layer transmits messages over a physical network. The Internet layer delivers messages

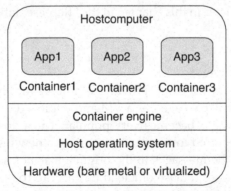

Figure 2.2 *Containers running on top of a runtime engine.*

to the correct VM or container, relying on one or more physical networks. The Transport layer delivers messages to services within the VM or container. The Application layer provides protocols that allow specific application types (such as email or web content) to interact. On this basis, the communicating systems actually interpret the messages.

Table 2.1 *Layers of the Internet*

LAYERS	TYPICAL PROTOCOLS
Application	HTTP, IMAP, LDAP, DHCP, FTP
Transport	TCP, UDP, RSVP
Internet	IPv4, IPv6, ECN, IPsec
Datalink	Ethernet, ATM, DSL, L2TP

A message meant for a function typically relies on Terminal Control Protocol/Internet Protocol (TCP/IP). The header of the IP layer is used to specify the IP addresses of both the sender and the recipient, which tells the internet infrastructure where to deliver the message. An IP message contains a payload formatted for TCP. The TCP formatting provides port information—for both the sender and the recipient. In a simplified version of today's reality, the IP address tells the system which service to deliver the message to, and the TCP port indicates which function in that service is the target. The TCP payload is formatted using an Application layer protocol. Frequently, it is formatted with HTTP, although other protocols can also be used. The HTTP message might say, "GET me path /index.html" or "PUT (store) the following JSON content as order number XYZ." GET and PUT are HTTP verbs; we will discuss them later in this chapter, in the "Representational State Transfer (REST)" section.

The Cloud and Scaling

One service offered by a cloud provider is autoscaling. Suppose, for example, that Service A is packaged as a VM and deployed into the cloud. Now imagine that Service A becomes very popular. The autoscaling capabilities of the cloud can be used to automatically create a new instance of Service A and route half of the messages to the original instance and half to the new instance. This requires the use of a load balancer to route the messages, but succeeds in halving the load on the original instance.

Autoscaling is based on a collection of rules, such as "Create a new instance if an existing instance is more than 80% utilized for a 15-minute period." The autoscaling rules are a portion of the instructions given to the cloud to deploy the VM. Autoscaling not only creates new instances, but also switches off (terminates) instances that are no longer needed, thereby lowering costs.

Because AI models are deployed as services, they need to be scaled, just as other elements of the system need to be scaled. Scaling rules must be provided as a portion of the deployment specification for the AI models.

Discovery

Typically, a service is deployed onto a physical computer at the discretion of the cloud management system. This means that if Service A wishes to communicate with Service B, it must discover the location (IP address) of Service B. This process is called discovery. The discovery mechanism will vary depending on whether the service is packaged as a VM or a container.

VM Discovery

If Service A is packaged as a VM, then its location can be discovered by using either a global or a local Domain Name System (DNS). The global DNS is available to the entire internet, whereas a local DNS has more limited exposure (e.g., within a single organization). Regardless of the scope, a DNS operates like a phone book. You pass it the name (URL) of the service to which you wish to send a message, and it returns an IP address. You can then use that IP address to send a message to the specified service.

Although in principle you could use DNS for containers as well as VMs, DNS is not designed for rapid creation and deletion of its contents. Containers are created and deleted relatively quickly, so a different mechanism must be used for their discovery. This brings us to the topic of container orchestration.

Container Orchestration

Consider the role of the conductor in an orchestra. The conductor plays no instrument. Instead, they are responsible for choosing the players, arranging them on the stage, setting the tempo, cuing the various sections of the orchestra, and making sure that the various players have an appropriate copy of the score.

This is not a bad analogy for container orchestration. An orchestration system contains no containers but manages a container's life cycle, including the following procedures:

- **Provisioning:** Preparing the environment for the containers, including network, storage, and compute resources.

- **Deployment:** Locating a host with spare capacity and placing containers there.

- **Discovery:** Providing the means for services to find each other and for users to find services.

- **Scaling:** Dynamically adjusting the number of instances of a service to meet demand.

- **Load balancing:** Distributing incoming requests across multiple instances of a service to ensure optimal resource utilization and response times.

An orchestration system is a portion of the container runtime engine. Because the orchestration system manages deployment and scaling, it knows the relationship between a container's name and the address of the instances of that container. This relationship is maintained in a discovery container, which allows for quick look-up as well as efficient creation and deletion of containers. When a new instance of a container is created or an old instance is deleted, the discovery container is updated accordingly. Multiple discovery containers can coexist, each containing only the names and addresses used by a particular container. For example, suppose Container A utilizes some collection of other containers. The discovery container for Container A can be limited to just those containers with which Container A interacts. The discovery container will have entries for each instance of containers stored within it; in turn, the autoscaling process for containers is responsible for updating the relevant discovery containers.

VMs, containers, and container orchestration frameworks provide the necessary infrastructure for deploying and scaling AI models. A part of the AI model development process focuses on packaging the model for execution. Thus, from the point of view of the infrastructure, there is nothing special about an AI model: It is treated just like any other VM or container.

2.1.2 Distributed Software Architectures

An architectural style provides a framework for the detailed design of a system. It specifies the component types and the types of connections allowed between them. In this section, we discuss three architectural styles that are widely used in distributed computing: client-server architecture, service-oriented architecture, and microservice architecture.

Client-Server Architecture

The client-server style dates from the early 1980s, when networks became commonplace. With this approach, a server provides services simultaneously to multiple distributed clients. The most common example is a web server providing information to multiple simultaneous users of a website. In client-server architecture, there are two component styles—clients and servers— and multiple clients for a single server (though clients nowadays interact with multiple servers for tasks as simple as loading a website). Communication is initiated by a client using a discovery service to determine the location of the server. The client sends requests to the server, and the server responds in turn.

Adopting a client-server architecture has the following implications for AI systems:

- **AI model training:** In a client-server setup, the server can handle intensive AI model training tasks, leveraging powerful computational resources. The client, typically hosted on a less resource-intensive host or mobile system, can request training or retraining of models and receive updates upon completion, or it can conduct some limited local/ on-device training.

- **AI model deployment:** For AI model inference, the server hosts the trained model, especially large models, and responds to client requests—for example, with predictions or analysis. This separation is useful for applications like mobile apps or web services, where the client lacks the computational power to carry out complex AI computations.

- **Wider AI system:** The client-server architecture is simple and effective for straightforward AI systems. However, it might become a bottleneck for more complex systems due to its centralized nature, which can lead to scalability and resilience issues.

Service-Oriented Architecture

The concept of service-oriented architecture (SOA) emerged in the late 1990s. Such an architecture consists of a collection of distributed components that provide and/or consume services. In addition, an SOA may contain a service registry, an infrastructure component that implements discovery for consumers. Service providers register with the registry so that the consumers can communicate with them.

In SOAs, providers and consumers are stand-alone entities and are deployed independently. Components have interfaces that describe the services they request from other components and the services they provide. Communication among the services can be performed by using the service registry, which is then responsible for discovery and for translating among the various representations. Services can be implemented heterogeneously, using whatever languages and technologies are most appropriate.

Today, SOAs are still used to integrate various stand-alone systems. Sometimes an SOA system is called a *system of systems*. Suppose your organization is a bank that has just acquired another bank. You now have two copies of loan management software, fraud detection software, and account management software. Each of these systems has its own user interface and process assumptions. You can use SOA to manage the integration by creating a uniform database for accounts and loans. The databases are then attached to the service registry, and the other systems are attached to the service registry. A format conversion service is used to translate from the original bank-specific formats to and from the new uniform database format.

SOAs were influential in the emergence of microservice architecture (discussed in the next subsection). In particular, concepts such as independent deployment and independence of technology in microservices derived from SOA principles.

SOAs have the following implications for AI systems:

- **AI model training:** In SOA, AI model training can be encapsulated as a service. This modular approach allows for the integration of different AI model training/updating components as services within an enterprise architecture, supporting scalability, federation, and flexibility.

- **AI model deployment:** AI models deployed as services in an SOA can be accessed by various consumer applications. This setup facilitates the reuse of AI capabilities across multiple applications and platforms.

- **Wider AI systems:** SOA is particularly beneficial for large organizations with existing enterprise systems. It allows AI capabilities to be integrated as services within these systems, supporting interoperability and efficiency in processes.

Microservice Architecture

Around 2002, Amazon promulgated the following rules for its developers. Although the term *microservices* came later, the core concepts of the microservice architecture trace back to these rules:[1]

- All teams will henceforth expose their data and functionality through service interfaces.

- Teams must communicate with each other through these interfaces.

- There will be no other form of inter-process communication allowed: no direct linking, no direct reads of another team's data store, no shared-memory model, no backdoors whatsoever. The only communication allowed is via service interface calls over the network.

- It doesn't matter what technology they [services] use.

- All service interfaces, without exception, must be designed from the ground up to be externalizable, ready to be exposed to developers outside of your organization. An application of this rule is to treat all requests as possible attacks leading to placing security controls within APIs.

The basic packaging unit in the microservice architecture is a service. Services are independently deployable. One implication of independent deployment is that the presence of a service and its current location must be dynamically discovered. This is typically done using container orchestration mechanisms, as discussed in the previous section.

Although not inherent in the definition of this architecture, a microservice is intended to perform only a single function. You can visualize it as a packaging mechanism for a method. Although this visualization is not strictly accurate, it helps when you think about what to place in a microservice. A system designed around a microservice architecture will consist of many small services that act in a coordinated manner to provide the system's functionality. In fact, Amazon's home page directly uses upwards of 140 services, and these call an even larger number of downstream services. Netflix has more than 800 microservices.

Microservice architectures have the following implications for AI systems:

- **AI model training:** Microservices architecture may allow for the decentralization of AI model training. Each microservice can be responsible

---

1. https://gist.github.com/chitchcock/1281611, accessed 2024-04-10

for different aspects/stages of training, each independently scalable, such as data preprocessing, feature extraction, and model training. Microservices also naturally support federated learning, which enhances agility and continuous deployment.

- **AI model deployment:** Deploying AI models as individual microservices makes it easier to update and scale them independently, without affecting the entire system. This is useful for dynamic environments where individual models need frequent updates to support complex business logic.

- **Wider AI systems:** The microservices architecture is highly scalable and flexible, making it suitable for complex, distributed AI systems. It supports the development of loosely coupled services that can be developed, deployed, and scaled independently, fostering innovation and rapid iteration.

Microservices architecture, while offering scalability and increased development efficiency for decoupling teams, has been criticized for its maintenance complexity. Managing numerous small services increases operational overhead, which creates challenges in ensuring consistency, handling interservice communication, and managing individual configurations.

2.1.3 Interface Styles

Many styles for interfaces between components of distributed systems are available. The two styles most commonly used in today's AI-based systems are GraphQL,[2] for edge communication (unintuitively, given the name), and REST, for, well, the rest of the communication links (though that is not where it got its name). We begin with REST.

Representational State Transfer (REST)

As the internet and the World Wide Web grew in the late 1990s, it was not practical to have a custom client for every service on the web. The REST interface style is an approach that matured in parallel with work on the HTTP/1.1 protocol. It allows very loose coupling between clients and services. REST is widely used for interfaces to models in ML systems.

The key elements of REST are as follows:

---

2. https://graphql.org

- The requests are stateless. That is, there is no assumption in the protocol that the server retains any information from one request to the next. Every request must contain all the information necessary to act on that operation, which means requests contain a lot of information. Alternatively, the client and the service provider can agree where the necessary state will be maintained.

- The information exchanged is textual—that is, services and methods are accessed by name. The web, from its inception, was designed to be heterogeneous, not only across different computer systems but also across different binary representations of information.

- REST fundamentally centers on resources, conceptualized as nouns (e.g., *user*, *product*), emphasizing the state and representation of these entities. This approach differs from the action-oriented focus on functions or verbs seen in SOA and traditional web services. It prioritizes entity manipulation over specific operations, offering a more standardized interaction model.

- REST restricts the methods, or functions/verbs, to a small set, with the most important ones being POST, GET, PUT, and DELETE. These map into the data management concept of CRUD: Create (and initialize), Read, Update, and Delete. A REST request identifies the resource or type to which the operation should be applied, and a request or response contains a data element with arguments or results. REST requires that this element be self-describing by labeling it with an internet media data type (or MIME type) so that any client knows how the data can be interpreted.

Strictly speaking, the REST architecture style does not specify the mechanism for sending messages from the client to the service. However, as noted earlier, the HTTP/1.1 protocol evolved as the first implementation of REST. Practitioners have found no need to create other implementations, so today, REST and HTTP are essentially synonymous.

As REST's impacts on AI model training, deployment, and integration suggest, this approach both complements and differs from SOA and microservices. Earlier protocols and standards developed for SOA were often complex and verbose, whereas REST provides a more streamlined and web-native method of integration. This makes REST particularly well suited for the integration of AI models in web-based applications and services. Moreover, while the microservices architecture focuses on breaking down an application into small, independently deployable services, REST hones in on how these services communicate. It doesn't dictate the service size or scope, but rather emphasizes a uniform and stateless interface for interactions. This stateless-ness of REST is particularly apt for AI scenarios, as it allows for scalable inter-actions with AI models without maintaining session state, which enables AI services to rapidly scale and handle large numbers of concurrent requests.

GraphQL

GraphQL was developed to support mobile applications with limited band-width. Contrary to what you might intuitively think given the name, it does not primarily serve the purpose of querying graphs. GraphQL originated in Facebook around 2012. It became an open-source project in 2015. Currently, GraphQL compilers exist in multiple languages.

In GraphQL, a providing service exposes an explicit definition of its interface. The elements in the interface are strongly typed. The providing ser-vice has a runtime engine that takes as input a query in the GraphQL query language and returns a response containing the data requested in the query.

The client sends a query in the GraphQL query language. This query is embedded in a procedure-like call to an interface exposed by the GraphQL providing service. An explicit schema on the client side defines which values the client wishes to see. In addition, there is a schema compiler specific to the language in which the client is written, and a runtime library that performs the actual transmission of messages.

The main benefit of GraphQL is that the client defines the structure of the requested data. By comparison, in REST, the providing service defines this structure. Accordingly, only the data the client requests is sent when GraphQL is used. The providing service does not send large amounts of data that the client does not need, avoiding the effort needed to receive and parse that unneeded data.

In AI systems, this is useful for different services, as one service can use GraphQL to pull only the data it requires from another service (reduc-ing bandwidth). It also offers benefits for architectures that extend to edge devices with more limited compute power, battery capacity, and bandwidth. For instance, a translation app on a mobile phone might recognize that its user is traveling in Japan and needs Japanese vocabulary and translation related to transport, food, drinks, and accommodation—a relatively small subset of the whole language. With suitable interfaces, the app could pull only the relevant vocabulary and AI models/model parts from the server.

The main drawback of GraphQL is that the set of supported queries must be predefined. With REST, the client can retrieve a dataset and parse it as it chooses. Thus, ad hoc queries over a dataset can be better supported with REST than with GraphQL.

2.2 DevOps Background

DevOps gained traction in the mid-2010s, and today more than 80% of all companies developing software apply this approach. DevOps was first motivated by the observation that developers and operators have contradictory goals: Developers aim to add functionality and improvements to software fast, whereas operators traditionally have to ensure availability and robustness of software in production. Given that newly developed code tends to contain more bugs and cause more downtime than old code that has stood the test of time and years of usage, the two goals were inherently contradictory—until DevOps came along.

Paraphrasing the definition mentioned in Chapter 1, Introduction, DevOps is a set of practices to get new code into production fast, but without compromising quality. If quality is high, robustness and availability do not suffer from frequent releases, hence resolving the contradiction. How does DevOps achieve that? Through cultural, organizational, and technological means.

In terms of culture, it starts by getting devs and ops to talk to each other and by assigning the shared goal (low time to production and high quality) to both groups. Organizational means include cutting down the number of meetings or synchronous communication required before a change can be implemented or rolled out. This favors the microservices architecture style, which consequently leads to small teams of devs and ops. Other organizational means include the enforcement of a single deployment process, such that quality can be ensured for each and every change, and assigning ops responsibilities to developers for components that are under active development, so as to enable a fast resolution of problems.

Technological means include at least the following strategies:

- Automation of build, test, and deployment activities, particularly in the context of continuous integration, delivery, and deployment. This enables fast feedback to developers, who can fix a bug they introduced a few minutes earlier much easier than if the feedback arrived weeks later. It also enables automatic, repeatable quality assurance, and fast deployment if the quality gates are passed.

- Infrastructure as Code (IaC) for reliably and consistently generating environments with tested parameters and configuration. This, too, enables quality assurance: Infrastructure code that has been tested in testing environments is less likely to cause issues in production.

- Version control for anything that might change with management practices that aim at high quality (e.g., repeatability and traceability), which allows for finding and correcting the sources of bugs and other undesirable behavior faster. This includes application and infrastructure code, as well as test cases and configuration parameters. We will see this technique again when we discuss practices associated with MLOps.

- Microservices architectures, in which different microservices interact only through defined interfaces. If done right, this enables a level of independence in the deployment of new versions of services and a reduced need for large meetings or other forms of synchronous communication between members of different teams.

- A single deployment process with automated quality gates. Any change, whether in application code, infrastructure code, or other configuration parameters, must pass the requisite number or percentage of tests before being deployed into production.

These technological means were enabled by the use of IaC.

2.2.1 Infrastructure as Code

Automation is a key portion of DevOps practices. Automation is manifested as a combination of tools and scripts. These tools and scripts manipulate both the code and models being developed and the infrastructure that supports the creation and operation of an executable from that code or model. These scripts are given the collective title of Infrastructure as Code (IaC).

The name IaC is intended to convey that the scripts should be treated as code. In other words, they should be tested, version controlled, and shared just as code is tested, version controlled, and shared. In fact, the system's life cycle applies to IaC just as well.

One source of errors for deployed systems is inconsistency in software in the environments used by developers. If Developer 1 uses one version of an OS and Developer 2 uses another version, then errors may appear when integrating the output of the two developers. This is equally true for other portions of the life cycle. If the test environment is different from the development environment, or if the production environment differs significantly from the development and test environments, then errors due to inconsistency may occur. This issue also arises with AI model training, evaluation, and deployment environments.

Inconsistencies among environments can go deeper than just operating system versions. Different versions of libraries can be inconsistent in terms of their behavior or even their interfaces. Different choices for configuration parameters can introduce errors as well. That being said, your environments should differ in some details, such as the credentials for accessing the production databases. Such credentials should be accessible to only those staff who absolutely must have them, and should not be shared with the whole company.

IaC is used to prevent accidental inconsistencies. A script for provisioning the elements of an environment can be shared among all developers and operators. The created elements will be identical for all developers (except for the credentials and such). If the environment must be updated, the script is modified, checked into a version control system, and shared with all developers. Each developer then executes the new script and has a copy of the new environment. Because the script is version controlled, it is possible to re-create older elements if necessary to make a repair to an older version being used in production.

This example demonstrates what is meant by treating the scripts as code. The descriptions of sharing programming language code among developers and retaining older versions for error repair are the same whether the subject is IaC scripts or application program code.

One class of tools is used to provision the software included in the resources of an environment. Such tools can be independent of the target platform, such as Vagrant or Docker, or they can be specific to a particular platform, such as Cloud Formation or Azure Resource Manager. Another type of tool creates the resources in the environment. Terraform is a popular example of such a tool.

The state of AI practice is still developing, particularly in regard to automation and configuration management. Unlike traditional software systems, AI systems often lack a standardized "AI makefile" that describes and manages all aspects of the model development and deployment process. Inconsistency and inefficiency can arise, impacting the reliability and reproducibility of AI models. Some initial efforts have been made to address these challenges, such as DVC[3] and ZenML.[4]

Best Practices

The best practices for IaC are the same as those for code.

- Scripts are checked into the version control system. This allows both sharing of the scripts with team members and retrieving past versions of the scripts while troubleshooting.
- Scripts are scanned for security issues. Just as code can be inspected automatically and manually to determine conformance to security practices, IaC can be examined both manually—through inspections— and automatically—through scanning tools—to determine conformance to security practices. An example is creating a VM in the cloud without specifying access parameters.
- Scripts are tested and reviewed for correctness, security, and compliance. Again, as with code, various review practices can be applied to scripts, and they should be tested prior to being placed into production.
- Credentials are retrieved from a credential store, whose content is specific to the environment. IaC scripts may, for example, refer to the customer database endpoint and credentials. The values returned in production will allow access to the production database, whereas the values in a test environment point to a test version.

Benefits of IaC

IaC offers some clear benefits:

- **Decreased costs for repetitive tasks:** Repetitive tasks can be invoked with one command.
- **Reduced input errors:** Manual human input is subject to errors, especially for repetitive tasks.

---

3. https://dvc.org/

4. www.zenml.io/

- **Reduced errors caused by inconsistency:** If all developers have the same development environment (created by a provisioning script), then errors during integration will be reduced.
- **Portability:** IaC enables applications and services to be moved between different environments without worrying about compatibility issues.
- **Traceability:** Every change to the infrastructure is captured in version control, providing a clear audit trail of who made changes, which changes were made, and when they were made.
- **Reliability:** By using tested and version-controlled scripts, teams can ensure that the infrastructure is deployed in a reliable and repeatable manner.

Costs of IaC

Writing and using scripts is not free. Some of the costs are highlighted here:

- **Scripts must be developed:** The initial development takes time and skills.
- **Additional initial complexity:** Setting up your tools and environments with credentials stores is initially more complex than creating environments manually. However, if done right, it can save a lot of effort and pain down the line.
- **Scripts must be tested and reviewed:** Tests for correctness must be developed, and reviewers will spend time performing their reviews.
- **Scripts must be updated when tools or processes are modified:** As with other forms of software, the first version of a product that is used is almost never the last version. Scripts must be updated, and the new versions tested.

Idempotence

Something is idempotent if applying it twice yields the same result as applying it once. A simple example from mathematics is the identity function, or multiplication with zero. A DevOps example is a deployment command that always sets the target environment to the same configuration, regardless of the environment's starting state.

If an IaC script is idempotent, then the current state of the infrastructure will not affect its execution. So, for example, it could be scheduled to execute at periodic intervals without any concern for the state of the system when it is executed. Idempotence is achieved either by automatically altering an existing target as needed, or by discarding the existing target and recreating a fresh environment.

Scripts should be written to be idempotent. In fact, testing idempotence can be one of the test cases for a script. Achieving idempotence and repeatability can be challenging for model development pipelines due to the nondeterministic nature of the training process. Factors such as model initialization, data shuffling, and the stochastic nature of some training algorithms can lead to slightly different models with the same training data and training algorithm.

Infrastructure Drift

Suppose you've deployed five instances of a service via IaC with the default 128 MB of memory. When you examine them, however, you find that three of them use 256 MB.

How did this happen? Perhaps someone noticed instances had poor efficiency and increased the memory allocation. Of course, there might be other explanations. People do not always follow processes or rules.

Is this bad? Suppose poor efficiency of these instances is subsequently noticed. Is the source one of the smaller memory instances or one of the larger memory instances? The responder must determine which is the culprit since it will affect the response. This is an example of infrastructure drift.

Infrastructure drift occurs when the state of your infrastructure is different from the state generated by your IaC. It will not occur if all infrastructure changes are performed through the IaC rather than done directly on the infrastructure.

Infrastructure drift is a common enough problem that tools have appeared to scan the existing infrastructure and compare it to the specification in the IaC. Open-source tools to check for this issue include Snyk and Driftctl.

Notably, infrastructure drift can cause security problems. For example, suppose someone is having an access problem and changes the Identity and Access Management (IAM) setting to make access easier. Depending on how it was changed, the new setting may open a system to unauthorized usage.

One possible strategy to mitigate such issues is to disallow direct access to operational servers in general.

2.2.2 DevOps Processes

Now we turn to DevOps processes. Figure 2.3 depicts the various DevOps processes in non-AI systems, their logical order, and common "shortcuts" in the life cycle. It starts with design and initialization, which includes the architectural groundwork and setting up automation scripts to support the subsequent processes. The initialization is the "on-ramp" into the cycle, which continues with development, building, testing, release (possibly automated) as approval for deployment, operation, and finally monitoring and analysis. The build, test, and release phases include quality gates—in case a committed version of the code does not meet the required quality, we return to development. We elaborated on the life cycle in Chapter 1, and more details will follow in Chapter 6.

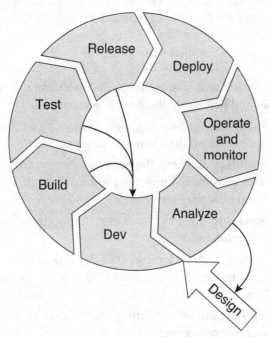

Figure 2.3 *The main DevOps processes in non-AI systems.*

With these practices, DevOps has made it possible to combine the two opposing goals discussed earlier—and hence its widespread adoption in practice. DevOps is most easily applied in cloud-native web applications. In other contexts, such as embedded, defense, or medical systems, adaptation of the usual DevOps processes is necessary because updating a system in such contexts may be more difficult, especially in the face of heavy-weight certification processes.

2.3 MLOps Background

Before the advent of foundation models (FMs) and generative AI, traditional machine learning (ML) was on a steady rise in production systems. However, the integration of ML into robust, traceable, and reliable production systems often lacked structured methodologies. This gap led to the development of machine learning operations (MLOps), aimed at applying DevOps principles to the ML life cycle. MLOps has a narrower focus than AI engineering, as discussed in Chapter 1. MLOps here refers to the activities related to the AI model. It prioritizes data governance and model life-cycle management, and aims to strengthen the links between data scientists, ML engineers, and operations teams.

MLOps includes some distinctive practices:

- **Data versioning and management:** Ensuring that datasets are version-controlled, and hence that their use is reproducible.

- **Experiment tracking:** Logging experiments to compare results and build on successful models from such experiments.

- **Lineage tracking:** Tracking the provenance of individual data items. This makes it possible to know the source of data items, how they were modified, and how they were used.

- **Model versioning:** Keeping track of different iterations of ML models to ensure reproducibility.

- **Model training and retraining:** Training linked to experiment tracking and data versioning; continuously improving models by retraining them with new data.

- **Model deployment:** Streamlining the process of deploying models into production environments.

- **Model performance monitoring:** Evaluating models in production to ensure they perform as expected.

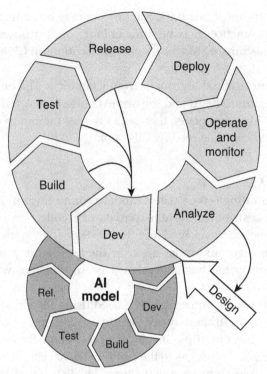

Figure 2.4 *MLOps included in the DevOps process shown in Figure 2.3.*

Figure 2.4 shows how MLOps fits into the broader DevOps landscape depicted in Figure 2.3. We elaborate on MLOps in Chapter 5, AI Model Life Cycle.

A contentious issue within MLOps is whether models should be dynamically updated in production using data created from productive use of the system or observed during operation. Proponents argue that this ensures models are current and responsive. Critics (including us) caution that bypassing the established deployment pipeline could compromise quality.

Given its focus, MLOps is geared toward settings in which a model is trained based on data that is available to the organization. In the age of generative AI and FMs, this is no longer the typical case—unless you work at one of the big AI labs, it is unlikely that you are tasked to train an FM. But even if that is your job, the core characteristic of FMs is their independence from specific applications. So, either you train an FM or you train a model for a specific application or fine-tune an existing FM. If you choose to fine-tune an

FM with application-specific data, the process may be similar to traditional ML, and MLOps practices may be sufficient for your purposes. We elaborate on the ways to customize FMs for specific applications in Chapter 4, Foundation Models.

But recall our original argument from Chapter 1: The behavior of your AI system comes from the AI and the non-AI parts. So, even if MLOps is sufficient for your AI components, there is a broader picture to consider—and hence you should continue reading this book.

2.4 Summary

Distributed computing is the basis of modern computing environments such as the cloud. A distributed system consists of a collection of independent components, which are packaged as either VMs or containers. They communicate using messages and must discover the location of a message recipient using a discovery mechanism such as DNS or functions within container orchestration.

Components can be automatically scaled using the cloud infrastructure or the container orchestration infrastructure. Scaling, in this case, means creating (or terminating) multiple instances of a component and using a load balancer to distribute messages to the running instances.

Commonly used software architectures for distributed systems include client-server architecture, service-oriented architecture, and microservices architecture.

REST is a style for interfaces that treats the provider as a data provider with restricted operations (PUT, GET, POST, and DELETE). GraphQL[5] is a variant of REST that requires the client to explicitly specify the information desired in a reply. That approach reduces communication costs, which is particularly useful for edge devices.

Traditional DevOps and MLOps are complementary sets of processes to manage development, deployment, and operations throughout the software development life cycle. Both use IaC as a means for achieving repeatable and consistent practices.

MLOps focuses on preparing the model for execution. DevOps focuses on taking various executable pieces and integrating them, testing them, deploying them, and operating them. One set of those executable pieces

---

5. https://graphql.org/

comes from MLOps. In this book, we focus on AI engineering and the integration of MLOps into DevOps for the whole system.

2.5 Discussion Questions

1. One motivation for using containers is that they are faster to transfer over the network than VMs. What are estimates of transfer times for VMs and containers over a fast network?

2. How do microservices architectures support independence of technology between one service and another?

3. Look up MLFlow (https://mlflow.org/). What kinds of tools are available within MLFlow?

2.6 For Further Reading

Much of the non-AI-specific material in this chapter comes from *Deployment and Operations for Software Engineers* by Len Bass and John Klein [Bass 19].

You can read about MLOps in *Hands-On Machine Learning with Scikit-Learn, Keras, and TensorFlow* by Aurélien Géron [Géron 22].

REST was first documented in a PhD thesis by Roy Fielding [Fielding 00], which can be found at https://ics.uci.edu/~fielding/pubs/dissertation/fielding_dissertation.pdf.

3

AI Background

All [AI] models are wrong, but some are useful.

—George Box

. . . particularly LLMs.

—Ingo Weber

IN THIS CHAPTER, we introduce the foundational concepts of AI, with a particular emphasis on model selection and preparation required for training these models.

Models are ubiquitous in both science and engineering. But, as George Box noted, they are always inaccurate. The inaccuracy stems from the abstraction embodied in a model. Many details are not included in any model, and this lack of detail both facilitates reasoning about the behavior of the entity being modeled and serves as a cause of error. In an AI system, the choice of the AI techniques is one of the most important design decisions. It has a major influence on the quality attributes of the system. In this chapter, we describe a variety of AI models and their uses. Choosing a model is a step in the pretraining analysis. A second step before training the model is setting the parameters that control the training.

In Chapter 1, Introduction, we identified two categories of AI techniques: **symbolic AI** and **non-symbolic AI**. The latter, which is also known as subsymbolic AI, refers to AI techniques based on **machine learning (ML)** and other methods that do not rely on explicit symbolic representations. ML models can be subdivided into those trained on labeled data (supervised learning), those trained on unlabeled data (unsupervised learning), and those trained using self-supervised learning, where models generate their own labels. **Foundation models (FM)** are trained on massive amounts of unlabeled data, allowing them to learn broad patterns and representations. However, the training process typically involves self-supervised learning. That is, existing words are masked, and the model learns to predict the masked words (a form of self-generated label), followed by fine-tuning with supervised learning using high-quality labeled instruction-following datasets.

We also identified the types of problems for which the different types of models are appropriate. In addition, Chapter 1 identified the necessity for an inference engine to use the model in a computer system.

In this chapter, we elaborate on the process of selecting a model and preparing it for training. The major topics covered are model selection (including the different types of models used in AI systems) and preparation of these models for training. We defer the discussion of training the models until Chapter 5, AI Model Life Cycle.

3.1 Terminology

Some terms specific to ML models are used in this chapter:

- Learning may be supervised, unsupervised, or self-supervised. In **supervised learning**, the training process uses labeled data, where each input in the training set is paired with a corresponding label, allowing the algorithm to learn the relationship between the input and the target variable it is meant to predict. In **unsupervised learning**, the data is not labeled, and the algorithm identifies patterns or structures in the data without predefined labels. **Self-supervised learning** is a variant in which the model generates its own labels from the data, such as predicting masked portions of input data, enabling it to learn useful representations without needing manually labeled data.

- The data used to train an ML model is, typically, divided into three subsets: the training set, the validation set, and the test set. The **training set** is the primary data used to train the model. The model learns and sets its parameters/weights based on the training set. The **validation set** is used to ensure that the model is sufficiently general. Once the model has processed the training set and set its parameters/weights, the validation set is used to ensure that the model performs well with unseen data. The **test set** is used to evaluate a trained model.

- **Overfitting** means that the model gives accurate predictions for training data but not for new data. It can occur because not enough data was used to train the model or because the data used to train did not accurately reflect the characteristics of the real-world data from which the model will make predictions. **Underfitting** is the reverse.

- A **loss function** measures how well the predictions of the model vary from reality.
- An **F1** score is a measure of precision (accuracy) and recall (true positivity rate) for ML models.

3.2 Selecting a Model

The first step in selecting a model involves choosing the appropriate model category, which may be based on either the nature of the problem or the characteristics of the solution. Different categories or types of models can be applied to the same problem, with each offering distinct advantages and tradeoffs. The three primary categories we use are symbolic and rule-based models, data-driven ML models, and FMs. FMs are a specialized type of ML model but deserve their own distinct category due to their unique capabilities and scale. Within each category, various model types exist, and these will be explored after discussing the categories themselves.

3.2.1 Selecting a Category

When to Use Symbolic AI Models

As symbolic AI makes decisions based on predefined rules, it is highly interpretable and effective in domains with well-defined rules. However, it is challenging for symbolic AI models to fully consider the data in real-world scenarios, especially given the complexity and variability of the real world. When dealing with unexpected situations, these models cannot easily adapt and struggle to make inferences due to their reliance on predefined rules. Furthermore, symbolic AI models face scalability issues in complex, real-world scenarios. As the complexity of a task rises, the number of rules increases exponentially, making the knowledge base hard to maintain and prone to failure.

With this background in mind, you should use a symbolic AI model if your problem has the following characteristics:

- The problem domain is well understood. A well-understood domain will have clear and relatively stable rules.
- The scope that the rules cover is well defined. Domains that can be characterized by a few hundred rules are appropriate for rule-based AI systems. If the number of rules required grows into the thousands,

the system becomes complex and maintaining consistency among the rules becomes difficult.

- Explainability is a high-priority quality. Rule-based models enable particular outputs to be traced back to the rules that generated the output.

- Strict adherence to regulations or guidelines is required. Regulations and guidelines are usually edited and reviewed carefully. This makes them easily translatable to the input for a rule engine.

When to Use ML Models

A large number of problems do not fit the characteristics of symbolic AI. ML models may be more appropriate for these problems. The following characteristics make a problem suitable for an ML model:

- You have large amounts of data available. The individual data items can be identified by values of a set of variables. ML models rely on statistics to analyze data and provide a result. Enough data must be available so that the statistical techniques will produce reasonable results.

- The structure of the data is sufficiently complex that a human cannot analyze the data without assistance.

- The desired system task is one of the following:
  - Forecasting (predicting future values based on historical data)
  - Classification (categorizing data into predefined groups)
  - Anomaly detection (identifying unusual patterns that do not conform to expected behavior)
  - Clustering (grouping similar data points together)

We elaborate on these tasks later in this chapter.

Many platforms are available that provide the ability to train ML models. Some examples are highlighted here:

- **Cloud-based services:** Amazon SageMaker,[1] Microsoft Azure Machine Learning,[2] Google Vertex AI Platform,[3] IBM Watson Studio[4]

---

1. https://aws.amazon.com/pm/sagemaker/

2. https://azure.microsoft.com/en-us/products/machine-learning/

3. https://cloud.google.com/vertex-ai

4. www.ibm.com/products/watson-studio

- **Software platforms:** SAS Visual Forecasting,[5] RapidMiner,[6] KNIME[7]
- **Open-source platforms:** TensorFlow,[8] PyTorch,[9] scikit-learn[10]

When to Use FMs

The term *FM* typically refers to the initial, base model that is trained. This base model is trained on a vast and diverse dataset, with the aim of learning a wide range of language patterns and general knowledge. The key characteristics of FMs are their scale (in terms of both the model size and the data they are trained on) and their generality (meaning they do not specifically target particular tasks or domains at this stage).

In most cases, you will likely want to adapt an existing FM, as opposed to training your own FM. To achieve such adaptation, the FM can undergo further fine-tuning processes using labeled data specific to the task for which you are constructing the system. These subsequent models, which are adapted or specialized for specific tasks or applications, are generally not referred to as FMs, but rather as "fine-tuned models," "adapted models," or "task-specific models."

The set of existing FMs is rapidly expanding. Some categories of existing models are highlighted here:

- **Language models:** Used for text generation, translation, question answering and human learning processes, code generation, reasoning, and factual language understanding.
- **Vision models:** Used for understanding the relationship between text and images, image classification, retrieval, captioning, object detection, and image generation.
- **Audio models:** Support tasks involving sound, such as speech recognition, music generation, and audio classification.

---

5. www.sas.com/en_us/software/visual-forecasting.html

6. https://altair.com/altair-rapidminer

7. www.knime.com/

8. www.tensorflow.org/

9. https://pytorch.org/

10. https://scikit-learn.org/stable/index.html

- **Video models:** Specialized to handle tasks such as video classification, (human) action recognition, and video generation.

- **Multimodal models:** Trained on multiple or all of the preceding types of data simultaneously. As a result, they can perform tasks related to multiple modalities, such as summarizing a text with figures, or generating a document (like this chapter) that includes figures and text.

- **Domain-specific models:** Combine lots of data from a particular domain, such as biology, and can serve as the basis for various AI applications in that domain. An example is a protein structure model.

3.2.2 Choosing a Model Type

The actual model type that you will use depends on the specific problem you wish to solve. As symbolic systems are sets of rules grounded in specific domains, you would use a symbolic system when you can construct such a set of rules.

ML models can be broadly classified based on their specific purposes, including classification, regression, and clustering. Recall that ML models are trained on labeled data. We begin by discussing classification.

Classification

Classification models are used to classify data into predefined classes based on different values of the independent variables (features). The training dataset should contain labeled data, sufficiently represent the problem, and include a substantial number of examples for each class label. Depending on the number of classes, there are two main types of classification:

- **Binary classification:** This involves assigning one of two possible classes to a piece of data. A common example is email spam detection, where the classification model determines whether an email is spam by examining specific email features, such as the sender's email address, the nature of links contained in the email, and the email's subject line.

- **Multi-class classification:** This refers to assigning a data point to a class out of three or more possible classes. An example is classifying a detected animal into one of many species, such as tigers, giraffes, zebras, or elephants. This is achieved by analyzing various distinguishable features of the animals, including their body shape, size, color patterns, type of fur, and tail length, among others.

Classification versus Prediction

Classification algorithms can be used for prediction—that is, statements about future events before they happen. While writing this book, we read various other texts and came across many occurrences where "predicting a class" is used to refer to "assigning a class." However, we believe that to be a widespread inaccuracy. Suppose we have a binary image classification algorithm, whose output is either "hotdog" or "no hotdog." This is clearly not about the future: The hotdog is either in the picture or not in the picture. Unless the image is changed, there is no aspect of predicting future appearances of hotdogs in static images.

In large parts of the ML literature, "predicting" appears to refer to a model's ability to infer the class of new, unseen data, and not to forecast future events. However, the appearance of a class label is not a future event that actually takes place in most instances. Consider the example of the binary image classification algorithm once more. After the ML model classified it as "hotdog," will a human being manually label the image, assign the "true" label, and thereby create the event that was "predicted"? Sometimes that might happen, but in most cases it will not.

To avoid confusion, it is advisable to use the term *prediction* strictly for cases that involve actual future events or forecasting. When referring to the output of a classification model, terms like *class assignment* and *classification* are more accurate and should be preferred.

Although the terms are often used interchangeably, "predicting a class" should not be confused with "assigning a class" (see the nearby box). Prediction implies a forecast about future events, whereas classification deals with labeling existing data. However, classification can be predictive, such as when estimating the likelihood of a hurricane based on current satellite imagery.

Classification is widely used in various applications, including the following:

- **Email spam detection:** Differentiate between spam and legitimate emails.
- **Image and speech recognition:** Understand visual images and spoken languages.

- **Facial recognition:** Identify individuals based on their facial features.
- **Sentiment analysis:** Analyze textual data to identify emotional tones and public opinions.
- **Customer segmentation:** Group customers with similar characteristics for targeted marketing and sales strategy.
- **Bank loan approval:** Classify loan applications into different risk categories.
- **Drugs classification:** Categorize drugs based on their properties, uses, and side effects.
- **Cancerous cells identification:** Detect cancerous cells in medical images.

If you have settled on a classification task, you can choose among several common types of classification algorithms. Some of them are profiled here.

K-Nearest Neighbors (KNN)

KNN classifies a given data point by first identifying the k nearest data points in the training dataset and then assigning the majority class among these neighbors to this data point. The distance between the data point and every other data point in the dataset is measured using a distance metric. For example, Euclidean distance is a distance metric used to measure the straight-line distance between two data points in a multidimensional space.

KNN is simple and a good choice for problems where the decision boundary is irregular. It is often used in image recognition, recommendation systems, and anomaly detection.

Logistic Regression

Logistic regression is an ML algorithm that is used for binary classification problems. It creates a linear equation that combines features of a data point, with each feature being assigned a specific weight based on its importance. A sigmoid function is used to transform the linear output into a probability between 0 and 1. Based on this probability, logistic regression makes the binary classification decision, often using a threshold of 0.5 to determine the class to which the data point belongs. If the predicted probability is 0.5 or higher, for example, the model predicts Class 1. If the predicted probability is less than 0.5, the model predicts Class 0.

Logistic regression is a good choice for binary and multi-classification problems where the relationship between input features and the target variable is approximately linear. It is often applied in credit scoring, medical diagnosis, and marketing prediction.

Decision Tree

The decision tree algorithm uses a—surprise!—tree data structure, which is composed of internal nodes, branches, and leaf nodes. Each internal node represents a decision point based on a feature, and each branch denotes the decision rules that link one node to another. The leaf nodes represent the various classes.

To construct a decision tree, the process starts with the entire training dataset at the root and is recursively divided into subsets based on the values of a specific feature and a corresponding threshold. A given data point is classified by traversing from the root to a leaf node, following the path determined by the feature values of the data point.

A decision tree is simple to understand and interpret. It is often used in customer segmentation, loan approval, and fraud detection.

Random Forest

To create a forest, multiple decision trees are combined, with the aim of improving performance in classification tasks. Given the multiple individual classifiers (i.e., trees), the random forest algorithm is a type of ensemble learning. Each tree is constructed from a random subset of the training dataset and a random subset of features. The algorithm ensures that the trees are trained on distinct subsets. The randomness results in diversity, reducing the risk of overfitting and improving the model's robustness. For a given data point, each tree in the forest independently votes for a class. The final class assigned to the data point is the one with the most votes from all the trees in the forest.

The random forest algorithm is a good choice for problems with complex relationships and high dimensionality, such as sentiment analysis, biological data classification, and customer churn prediction.

Naïve Bayes

The naïve Bayes algorithm is a classification algorithm based on Bayes' theorem. It makes an assumption that all features are independent of each other given the class. Naïve Bayes first examines a training dataset containing data points with features and known class labels. It then calculates the prior probabilities (how often each class appears in general) and the conditional probabilities (how often each feature appears within each class) using the training data. When given a new data point with an unknown class, this algorithm calculates the probability of it belonging to each possible class, assuming those features are independent. Finally, it assigns the data point to the class with the highest calculated probability.

The naïve Bayes algorithm is effective when you are dealing with high-dimensional data. It is a good choice for text classification problems, such as spam detection and sentiment analysis.

Support Vector Machine (SVM)

SVM is designed to find the optimal hyperplane that splits the data points into different groups, maximizing the space between the hyperplane and the nearest data points from each group, known as support vectors. When classifying a given data point, SVM uses its feature values to determine the data point's position relative to the hyperplane. This allows SVM to assign the data point into a particular class based on which side of the hyperplane it falls.

SVM is a good choice for problems where the classes are separable with a clear margin, such as image classification and handwriting recognition.

Neural Network

A neural network is a web of interconnected nodes. Each node takes in information from its connected neighbors, performs a simple calculation, and then sends its own output to other nodes. This flow of information through the network allows it to learn and make predictions. The network processes data using artificial neurons, structured into multiple layers, including an input layer, one or more hidden layers, and an output layer. Information, such as an image or a sentence, is first fed into the input layer of the network. Each piece of information becomes a value that goes into one of the nodes. The hidden layers are the heart of the network, with multiple layers often being stacked on top of each other. Each node in a hidden layer receives inputs from several nodes in the previous layer, performs a weighted calculation on those inputs, and then produces its own output. These weights become the parameters that are adjusted during training.

Eventually, the outputs from the last hidden layer reach the output layer. This layer produces the final result of the network, which could be a classification (e.g., cat or dog), a prediction (e.g., next word in a sentence), or any other desired output. During training, the network starts with weights and biases that are randomly set. The training dataset, which consists of known input–output pairs, is fed into the network. During forward propagation, the data passes through the layers. Each neuron computes an output based on its weighted inputs and biases. The output of a node is not passed on directly. Instead, it first goes through an activation function, which adds a bit of non-linearity to the network. This allows the network to learn more complex patterns and relationships in the data. The difference between the predictions and actual labels is measured using a loss function, which indicates how much the model needs to improve. Back-propagation involves calculating the gradient of the loss function and using this information to adjust weights and biases to reduce the error. Stochastic gradient descent (SGD) is an optimization algorithm that is often used for making these adjustments. The learning rate controls the update magnitude during the optimization process.

This process is repeated over multiple epochs, enabling the network to iteratively learn and refine its weights and biases, which gradually improves the model's accuracy. For prediction, a new given data point transverses the network using the learned weights and biases, starting from the input layer, then progressing through the hidden layers, and finally reaching the output layer. The output layer often uses a softmax function to convert the outputs into class probabilities. The class with the highest probability is selected as the final prediction.

Neural networks can model complex nonlinear relationships and are scalable to large datasets. They are often used in speech recognition, natural language processing, and image classification.

Regression

Unlike classification, which focuses on discrete categories, regression involves training a model using a labeled dataset to predict continuous outputs. As a result, this technique is useful for estimating relationships between variables and predicting numerical values, such as forecasting house prices.

Regression is used in various applications, including the following:

- **Economic trend analysis:** Forecasting key economic indicators such as inflation rates and unemployment rates.

- **Asset price prediction:** Estimating the value of the assets (such as houses) based on essential factors, such as their location and size.
- **Energy usage prediction:** Predicting the future energy demand of a specific region.
- **Enrollment forecasting:** Anticipating the number of future students.
- **Disease risk assessment:** Analyzing the likelihood of diseases using patient demographics and medical records.
- **Drug efficacy analysis:** Estimating the effectiveness of new drugs.

Some of the most popular types of regression algorithms are profiled next.

Linear Regression

This fundamental regression algorithm is used to establish a linear relationship between a dependent variable (e.g., the house price to be predicted) and one or more independent variables (e.g., GDP growth, interest rates). Each independent variable in the resulting regression equation will have a coefficient. The aim of the training process is to find the values of the coefficients that minimize the difference between the actual observed value of the dependent variable and the values predicted by the model. Once the coefficients are determined, predictions are made by applying the learned coefficients to new input data. The predicted value of the dependent variable is calculated by inserting the values of the independent variables into the model's equation.

Linear regression is interpretable and computationally efficient. This algorithm is a good choice for problems where the data shows a linear trend, such as housing price prediction and sales forecasting.

Polynomial Regression

The polynomial regression algorithm is designed to capture the relationship between a dependent variable and one or more independent variables as an nth-degree polynomial. For a given input value of independent variables, the model calculates the value of the dependent variable by applying the learned coefficients for independent variables and its higher powers.

Polynomial regression is advantageous when the relationship between the variables exhibits a nonlinear pattern. It is often used to deal with problems where the data shows a nonlinear trend that can be approximated by a polynomial, such as physics experiments or modeling of growth rates.

Support Vector Regression (SVR)

SVR is an extension of SVM designed for regression tasks. The goal of SVR is to find a hyperplane that effectively captures as many data points as possible within a specified buffer zone around the hyperplane. SVR allows for acceptable errors in predictions. Predictions that are within the buffer zone are considered acceptable.

SVR is effective in high-dimensional spaces and works well for small to medium-sized datasets. It is often used in stock price prediction and real estate valuation.

Decision Tree Regression

A decision tree regression builds the relationship between the data's features and a continuous target variable through a tree-like structure. In the tree structure, each internal node is a decision point that splits the data based on a threshold value of a specific input feature, while each leaf node represents the predicted numeric value. To build the tree, the training dataset is recursively broken down into smaller subsets at each step based on a feature's threshold. This process continues until certain criteria are met, such as a minimum number of data points in each node and a maximum depth of the tree. To predict the value, the algorithm goes from the root down to a relevant leaf node, guided by the input features of the given data point.

Decision tree regression is often used to handle problems where interpretability is important, such as customer satisfaction scores and equipment failure prediction.

Random Forest Regression

Random forest regression is an ensemble learning algorithm designed for predicting continuous numerical outcomes. It involves training multiple decision trees, with each being trained on a random subset of the training dataset using a random subset of features. The final output is typically determined by averaging all of the numerical predictions made by the trees.

Random forest regression handles large datasets and complex relationships well. It is often used in product demand prediction and energy consumption prediction.

Gradient Boosting Regression

Whereas random forest regression constructs trees simultaneously, gradient boosting regression builds its trees in a sequential manner. Each subsequent tree is focused on correcting the errors made by the preceding trees. When making the final prediction, the algorithm uses a learning rate to adjust the contributions of the individual trees and then aggregates the adjusted outputs from all the trees to generate the final output.

Gradient boosting regression is often used to deal with problems where high predictive accuracy is required, such as insurance risk assessment and credit scoring.

Neural Network Regression

Neural network regression includes an input layer that receives features, one or more hidden layers that learn representations of the data, and an output layer in which a (typically single) neuron produces a continuous value prediction. During forward propagation, the training dataset, including features and target values, is processed through different layers. The network's predictions and the actual values are compared and measured using a loss function for regression. During back-propagation, the loss is used to adjust the weights of the neuron connections through an optimization algorithm such as SGD. The forward-propagation and back-propagation steps are repeated to refine the model. Once trained, the neural network makes predictions based on a new input data point by applying the forward-propagation process to predict a continuous value.

Neural network regression is used to handle problems involving large and complex datasets, such as weather prediction and complex time series forecasting.

Clustering

Clustering is used for data that does not belong to predefined groups. It groups data points into clusters based on the similarity of their features—for example, categorizing customers by their demographics and purchasing preferences. The data points within each cluster are expected to have similar properties, whereas the data points in different clusters should be as dissimilar as possible. Developers can either predefine a target number of clusters or allow the algorithm to autonomously determine this number. Unlike supervised learning, clustering does not require the labeling of data or the division of data into training and testing datasets. The clustering process involves only a single phase—grouping. The output of clustering is the cluster assignments, which identify patterns or structures in the data.

Clustering depends on defining a distance metric that measures the "difference" between two data points. If the data points are in a Euclidean space, this is a normal distance metric. Distance metrics can also be defined for data points not in a Euclidean space. An example is the Levenshtein distance, a metric used for measuring the difference between two sequences of characters. It identifies the minimum number of edits (insertions, deletions, substitutions) required to transform one string into another.

Clustering algorithms are classified into two categories: hard clustering and soft clustering. In hard clustering, the data point is assigned to one of the clusters only. Soft clustering provides a probability likelihood of a data point being in each of the clusters.

Clustering is used across a variety of applications due to its ability to group similar data points without prior knowledge of group definition.

- **Anomaly detection:** Identifying abnormal data patterns in fraud detection or cybersecurity.

- **Document clustering:** Categorizing documents into groups based on similarities in keywords, topics, or other features.

- **Biological classification:** Classifying proteins or genes into functional groups to identify potential therapeutic targets or biomarkers for diseases.

- **Disease diagnosis:** Classifying medical images or identifying objects within images for disease diagnosis.

- **Social network analysis:** Grouping individuals in a social network according to their interaction patterns to identify influential individuals or communities.

- **Recommendation systems:** Grouping similar products to make personalized recommendations to users based on their past activities and preferences.

- **Market segmentation:** Identifying distinct groups of customers based on purchasing histories, demographics, and so on.

Some well-known clustering algorithms are highlighted here.

K-Means Clustering

K-means clustering divides a dataset into k clusters. The developer needs to specify the number of clusters k in advance. The algorithm randomly initializes k points as cluster cores, called centroids, which can be either selected from the data points or generated randomly. Each data point is assigned to the nearest centroid, as determined by a distance metric such as Euclidean distance. After all points have been processed, the centroids are adjusted by averaging all the points in each cluster to find the new centroid. This process is repeated until the centroids become relatively stable. As the centroids shift in each iteration, data points might be redistributed to different clusters. The result is a set of clusters. The data points within the same cluster are similar to each other, while being as far as possible from points in other clusters.

Netflix uses a K-means clustering model to recommend to users highly rated movies and shows that have been watched by other users in the same group.[11] This algorithm works well with large datasets and when the number of clusters is known. It is often used in customer segmentation and market analysis.

Density-Based Spatial Clustering of Applications with Noise (DBSCAN)
DBSCAN is a density-based clustering algorithm that identifies clusters of arbitrary shapes based on the density of data points. It requires only two parameters: minimum points (MinPts) and epsilon (ε). MinPts represents the minimum number of close data points needed to form a dense region, and ε defines the radius of a neighborhood area around each data point. The data points in the dataset are categorized as core, border, and noise points. A core point has at least MinPts number of data points within ε distance from it. A border point has fewer than MinPts data points within ε distance, but is within ε distance of a core point. A noise point is a point that is neither a core point nor a border point.

To form a cluster, the algorithm first checks if an arbitrary unvisited point is a core point. If it is, a cluster begins to form. The algorithm then includes all points that are within ε distance from this core point into the cluster. If any of these newly added data points is also a core point, the existing cluster is expanded by including its respective ε-distance neighbors. Data points that are not included in any cluster are marked as noise. This process continues with the next unvisited data point until all data points have been visited and classified into either clusters or as noise.

---

11. https://github.com/apoorvaKR12695/Netflix-Movies-and-TV-Shows-Clustering

DBSCAN is a good choice for problems with varying cluster shapes and sizes, and datasets with noise. It is often used to identify clusters in spatial data or filter noise in data preprocessing.

Hierarchical Clustering

The hierarchical clustering algorithm organizes data into a hierarchy of clusters. Two types of hierarchical clustering are distinguished: agglomerative and divisive.

Agglomerative hierarchical clustering, adopting a bottom-up approach, begins by considering each data point as a single cluster. Distances between cluster pairs are calculated using metrics. The two closest cluster pairs are merged into a single cluster. The distance matrix is then updated to reflect the new distances between the merged cluster and other clusters. The merging process continues until all data points are included into a single cluster.

In contrast, divisive hierarchical clustering employs a top-down clustering approach, and starts with all data points in a large cluster. The cluster is recursively divided into smaller clusters based on a metric, such as the maximum distance between data points within the cluster. This division process continues until it reaches a stopping criterion, such as each cluster containing only a single data point or a specified number of clusters being identified.

Hierarchical clustering works well when the number of clusters is unknown. It is often applied in gene expression data analysis and social network analysis.

Foundation Models

FMs are massive AI models that are pretrained on vast amounts of broad data. They can be adapted to perform a wide variety of tasks involving natural language and image processing. The release of ChatGPT, Gemini, and other large language model (LLM)–based chatbots have popularized FMs. FMs, which are well recognized for their breakthroughs in natural language and image processing, have the potential to revolutionize several other domains as well:

- **Audio processing:** Potential FMs in this domain could excel in tasks like speech recognition, music generation, and audio event detection, by learning from large collections of diverse audio data.

- **Multimodal models:** These models integrate various types of data, such as text, images, audio, and video, enabling them to perform complex tasks like automatic video captioning, cross-modal search, and enhanced AI assistant interactions.

- **Robotics and control systems:** FMs trained on extensive simulation data could acquire a wide range of physical interaction patterns, making them applicable to specific tasks in real-world robotics.

- **Time-series and forecasting models:** FMs could be trained on large-scale time-series data for applications in finance, meteorology, and healthcare, aiding in predicting market trends, weather patterns, or patient health outcomes, respectively.

- **Healthcare and biomedical models:** Trained on medical data, these models could play a role in diagnostics, personalized medicine, and drug discovery.

- **Business process management:** Combining training data from various organizations, FMs could be used to capture principal information about business processes, and could play a role in analyzing operational processes, suggesting improvements, and simulating the effects of changes.

- **Graph neural networks (GNNs):** FMs in this area could be trained on large graph-structured datasets, such as social networks or molecular structures, capturing complex relationships and interactions.

Because of its scale, an FM is time-consuming to create and expensive to train. Fortunately, publicly available FMs exist in a variety of domains:

- Natural language processing (NLP)
- Image generation and manipulation
- Code generation and programming
- Music and audio generation
- Multimodal fusion

Bespoke FMs are being developed by a variety of organizations for their own particular domains. These models may, in the future, become publicly available. Some bespoke FMs include the following models:

- **BloombergGPT:** A 50-billion parameter LLM specifically designed and developed from the ground up for applications in finance.

- **NVIDIA Nemotron:** A family of LLMs designed for enterprise use; they can be fine-tuned for specific tasks, such as customer service or product development.

- **BLOOM:** A cooperative initiative of more than 1000 researchers intended to support other researchers.

- **MosaicML:** A platform that makes it easy for businesses to train their own custom AI models on their own data.

Unless the FM you are using in your system is tailored for your particular domain, it may be further fine-tuned for your domain and uses. We discuss fine-tuning and other details of FMs in Chapter 4, Foundation Models.

The successful expansion of FMs into these domains is contingent upon the availability of rich, diverse datasets and substantial computational resources, opening up new frontiers for AI applications across various sectors. Most of these models are neural networks based on the transformer architecture. Examples of FM models include OpenAI GPT-x,[12] Google Gemini,[13] and Meta LLaMA.[14]

3.3 Preparing the Model for Training

Once a model is selected, it must be trained and packaged. We discuss data, model training, and packaging in Chapter 5, AI Model Life Cycle. Preparing the model for training differs depending on the model type, but the common thread is concern for performance—in terms of both efficiency and accuracy.

3.3.1 Symbolic AI Execution

Accuracy is affected by rule specification practices, and latency is affected both by rule specification and by optimization of the rules engine. The exact mechanisms depend on the specific engine and rule language you use. For example, how does your rule engine handle caching? Here, we outline some typical considerations.

---

12. https://platform.openai.com/docs/guides/text-generation

13. https://gemini.google.com/

14. https://llama.meta.com/

Rule Specification

- **Rule ordering:** Prioritize frequently used or critical rules early in rule execution.
- **Rule grouping:** Cluster related rules to minimize comparisons and enhance cache utilization.
- **Conflict resolution strategies:** Define clear mechanisms to handle conflicting rules, such as specificity, salience, or chronological order.
- **Rule clarity and simplicity:** Write concise and well-structured rules to aid comprehension and execution.
- **Avoid redundancy:** Eliminate unnecessary or conflicting rules.
- **Condition optimization:** Structure conditions for efficient evaluation, using techniques such as indexing and filtering.
- **Coverage:** Address all relevant scenarios and decision paths.
- **Consistency:** Be consistent in rule definitions and syntax.

Engine Configuration

- **Threading and parallelism:** Adjust thread usage and enable parallel execution for concurrent rule processing.
- **Caching:** Store frequently accessed facts and rule outcomes for faster retrieval.
- **Compilation and optimization:** Reduce rule set complexity, pre-compile rules, and apply optimization techniques for faster execution.
- **Algorithm choice:** Use an appropriate algorithm for the number of rules in the set.

3.3.2 ML Hyperparameters

ML models have both parameters and hyperparameters. A parameter is a value that the model learns during training. (We discuss this process in more detail in Chapter 5.) A hyperparameter is a value that controls the training. It is not learned from the data, but rather is set prior to the training process. For example, parameters in a neural network are the weights and biases, and hyperparameters are the learning rates, number of hidden layers, number of neurons, and so on.

Hyperparameters and Model Types

The hyperparameters depend on the algorithm used in the model creation. For example, the distance metric selected for a clustering algorithm is a hyperparameter. A metric must be chosen before any training can be done.

Other algorithm choices will have different hyperparameters. Decision trees and forests are characterized by the depth of the tree, the number of trees in the forest, and splitting criteria. Regression algorithms allow weights to be placed on coefficients to emphasize particular types of data, and so forth.

Some hyperparameters are specific to certain models, such as length of sequence in recurrent neural networks (RNNs). There is often a tradeoff between model complexity and the risk of overfitting. More complex models may capture the training data better, but might not generalize well. Techniques such as grid search, random search, and Bayesian optimization can be used to automate the process of finding the best hyperparameters. However, hyperparameter optimization can be slow and costly, and extensive optimization does not always pay off.

Due to the importance of neural networks, we describe the hyperparameters for these networks in some detail.

Neural Network Hyperparameters

For neural networks, hyperparameter tuning involves adjusting a wide range of parameters that influence the network's learning process and performance, including the following:

- **Learning rate:** The learning rate controls the degree to which the model's weights are updated during training. A learning rate that is too high can cause the model to converge too quickly to a suboptimal solution, whereas a learning rate that is too low can make the training process needlessly long or cause it to get stuck.

- **Batch size:** The batch size is the number of training examples used in one iteration of the training process. When you train an ML model, especially a neural network, you rarely feed the entire dataset into the algorithm at once. Instead, you divide the dataset into smaller groups, called batches. The batch size determines how many examples you look at before making a single update to the model's weights during training. A smaller batch size often leads to faster convergence, but can be noisy. A larger batch size is more stable and provides a more accurate estimate of the gradient (which tells you which way to go to increase the value of the function the most), but may slow down the training process and requires more memory and computational power.

- **Iteration:** An iteration is a single update of the model's parameters. In one iteration, the model processes one batch of data, computes the loss (a measure of how far the model's predictions are from the actual values), and then updates the parameters (e.g., the weights in a neural network) accordingly. The number of iterations required to complete one pass over the training data depends on the number of training examples and the batch size.

- **Number of epochs:** An epoch is a full iteration over the entire training dataset. Once every example in the training dataset has been used once for training the model, an epoch is considered to have been completed. An epoch comprises several iterations, depending on the batch size and the total number of training examples. For example, with 1000 examples and a batch size of 100, 10 iterations (each iteration processes 100 examples) make up one epoch. Too few epochs can lead to underfitting; too many can lead to overfitting.

- **Regularization parameters:** Regularization is a technique used to prevent overfitting and improve the generalizability of ML models. Regularization adds a penalty term to the loss function during training. This penalty term becomes larger as the model becomes more complex (e.g. has more parameters or features). By minimizing the combined loss and penalty, the model is encouraged to find a simpler solution that fits the data well but avoids overfitting to specific noise or patterns. Regularization parameters include L1 (Lasso), L2 (Ridge), ElasticNet, and dropout (specially for neural networks). These parameters help to prevent overfitting by penalizing large weights.

- **Activation functions:** Activation functions introduce nonlinearity, allowing the network to learn intricate relationships between inputs and outputs. Activation functions include ReLU, Sigmoid, and Tanh. Different activation functions can affect the convergence rate and accuracy of the network.

- **Optimization algorithms:** Optimization algorithms iteratively adjust the parameters of a model to find the values that minimize a loss function, thereby improving the model's performance. These algorithms include SGD, Adam, and RMSprop. Different optimizers may have different performance characteristics and be better suited for specific types of problems.

3.4 Summary

In this chapter, we introduced AI background concepts, including different types of models and the process of preparing the model for training.

The choice of model type depends on the problem you wish to solve. Symbolic models are useful as long as (1) the domain is well defined with explicit rules and (2) the set of rules is not too large. ML models are useful for categorization, regression, and classification. FMs are used for a wide range of tasks, including natural language processing and image recognition. Each model type has a large number of possible choices with different characteristics.

Once a model is selected, it must be prepared for training. For ML models, this means choosing hyperparameters.

3.5 Discussion Questions

1. For a regulated field, such as banking or pharmaceuticals, find a description of the regulations and attempt to formulate rules for a rule-based system based on the description.

2. Execute the TensorFlow 2 quickstart for beginners: www.tensorflow.org /tutorials/quickstart/beginner.

3. What can you find out about FMs? Can you find the one that has been trained on the largest number of data samples? Is this deemed the best model currently?

3.6 For Further Reading

You can read about ML models in *Machine Learning Algorithms from Scratch with Python* by Jason Brownlee [Brownlee 16].

Two research papers relevant to ML and FM systems are:

- Tran et al. [Tran 20] discuss when to do hyperparameter optimization.
- Kampik et al. [Kampik 24] discuss foundation models in the specific context of business process management.

No general books are yet available on foundation models, but two books deal with their underlying concepts:

- *Deep Learning* by Ian Goodfellow, Yoshua Bengio, and Aaron Courville [Goodfellow 16].
- *Neural Network Methods for Natural Language Processing* by Yoav Goldberg [Goldberg 17].

4

Foundation Models

For data guzzling AI companies, the internet is too small.
—Wall Street Journal

IN CHAPTER 1, Introduction, we differentiated between traditional machine learning (ML) models, which are trained for narrow tasks, and foundation models (FMs), which are trained for general purposes through the synthesis of massive amounts of data such as natural language, code, images, and videos. In Chapter 3, AI Background, we explored ML models in more detail. In this chapter, we go into detail on FMs.

We discuss FMs in general, the transformer architecture that underlies their strong advances as well as some alternatives, and how you customize FMs. Then we explore the design considerations when you are building a system using FMs, the maturity of FMs, the organizations employing them, and some inherent challenges associated with FMs.

4.1 Foundation Models

FMs represent a class of advanced ML models that are characterized by their huge amount of training data and the very general purpose for which they are trained. They can be further fine-tuned and specialized for specific tasks, covering a spectrum from general instruction-following and chatbot interactions to specific tasks such as sentiment analysis. We use the term *FM* to refer to both the base FMs and some of the general-purpose fine-tuned models. FMs in general deal with text, images, and other modalities. By comparison, a large language model (LLM) is an FM that deals with only text. We will use the term *FM* in this chapter since it is more general than an LLM. Chapter 12 and Chapter 13 deal specifically with LLMs, so we will use the term *LLM* in those case studies.

FMs are distinguished by their size, but how is this measured? One method for discussing the size of an FM is to consider the number of parameters (weights) included in the model. BloombergGPT advertises 50 billion parameters. Estimates for GPT-4 range as high as 700 billion parameters.

Another measure of scale is the number of documents used to train the FM. Precise numbers are proprietary, but many FMs use CommonCrawl[1] as one of their data sources. CommonCrawl advertises that it covers more than 250 billion web pages.

Yet another measure of scale is the dimensionality of the vector spaces managed by the FM. We describe vector spaces later in this chapter. Estimates of the dimensionality of common FMs are in the thousands or tens of thousands.

Regardless of which measures are used, these are mind-boggling numbers. One implication of this massive scale is that training an FM is not a fast or inexpensive task. The cost of training an FM from scratch makes the adaptation of FMs for your specific task an attributive option. We discuss customizing FMs in Section 4.4, "Customizing FMs"; Chapter 12 presents a case study involving the use of an FM (an LLM).

The transformer architecture is commonly used in FMs. We discuss it in the next section.

4.2 Transformer Architecture

We begin our discussion of transformer architecture by looking at what happens to an input string. We focus on textual input, although the same techniques are used for images and other media inputs.

4.2.1 Vector Spaces

An input string is first tokenized and then converted to a collection of vectors of real numbers using an algorithm based on a technique such as Word2Vec. The dimensionality of this vector can be in the thousands, as just mentioned. Each vector represents one token. Using actual words to compute the vector would be difficult and creates challenges such as how to handle things that are not part of the vocabulary; to get around these problems, the input is first tokenized. Tokenization breaks the input text into units called tokens, which can be whole words, parts of words, or even punctuation. Words, especially

---

1. https://commoncrawl.org/

less common ones, may be represented by multiple tokens. The model then works with these tokens, converting each to a vector representation.

The actual conversion into the vector is computationally easy, but depends on an embedding model, such as Word2Vec, or a more contemporary alternative, such as GloVe or FastText. The embedding model may be preexisting, or it may be trained during the main FM pretraining. This model maps tokens into vectors and adjusts the vector values to reflect the connections between words. The resulting model can detect semantic relationships among the tokens. As an example, the words *king, queen, man,* and *woman* would be mapped to vectors in such a way that *man* is close to *king* (in terms of distance between the vectors), *king* is close to *queen,* and *queen* to *woman,* and *man* to *woman;* any other pairs would have a higher distance.

In modern architectures like the transformer, the final representation of a token can depend on the context, meaning it can change based on the surrounding words in a sentence.

4.2.2 *Attention*

Attention is a key mechanism in transformer architecture. The attention mechanism and the transformer architecture were introduced together in a 2017 paper called "Attention Is All You Need." Attention scores are calculated based on the vectors of the total input string. In contrast, traditional language processing treats each word independently without regard to context.

Attention enables words to be processed based on the context. The word *book,* for example, may mean a book such as this, a ledger in accounting, or a package of items bound together such as "a book of stamps." Without context, there is no way for an AI system to accurately interpret the use of this word. Because an attention score combines the vectors for the various tokens in the input string, it captures context.

Attention can be applied in the form of self-attention or multi-head attention. Self-attention allows a token to attend to other tokens within the same input sequence. In contrast, multi-head attention employs multiple sets of attention mechanisms in parallel. Each "head" can focus on different aspects of the input, allowing the model to capture various types of relationships simultaneously.

4.2.3 *Other Components in a Transformer Architecture*

Vectors and attention are the key concepts in a transformer architecture. The transformer architecture is a form of neural network (described in Chapter 3,

AI Background) in which the input layer converts the tokens to vectors, the hidden layers use the concept of attention to capture different information, and the output layer generates the final output. This short description does not do the sophisticated technology of transformers full justice, but it suffices as an overview for this book.

4.3 Alternatives in FM Architectures

Although the transformer architecture is the most popular choice, other architectures are also used for building FMs, particularly in areas where different model characteristics are desired:

- **Convolutional neural networks (CNNs):** Although more commonly applied to computer vision tasks, CNNs can also be used as FMs, particularly for tasks involving spatial data.

- **Recurrent neural networks (RNNs) and their variants (long short-term memory [LSTM] and gated recurrent unit [GRU]):** These architectures are particularly suited for sequential data and were used extensively before the rise of transformers. They are still used in specific scenarios where model size and computational efficiency are critical.

- **Hybrid models:** Some FMs use a combination of architectures, such as integrating CNN features into a transformer model for tasks that require both spatial and sequential processing.

- **Graph neural networks (GNNs):** For tasks involving graph-structured data, such as social networks and molecular structures, GNNs serve as a powerful FM architecture.

- **Autoencoders and variational autoencoders:** These are used for unsupervised learning tasks, including dimensionality reduction and feature learning. They can be foundational in domains requiring generative or reconstructive capabilities.

Each of these architectures offers unique strengths and is chosen based on the specific requirements and nature of the data involved. While a detailed discussion of these alternatives is beyond the scope of this book, it's important to know about their existence when considering alternatives in designing AI-based systems.

4.4 Customizing FMs

Training in the context of FMs is roughly split into two chunks: Pretraining is the training of the generic FM, whereas training for customization specializes the FM for a specific task. FMs are typically trained by organizations, often big tech companies or AI labs, using vast amounts of unlabeled, general data such as a huge text corpus. This broadens the FM's applicability across different domains due to its exposure to general information and patterns. However, it may require further domain-specific customization to improve its accuracy and usefulness for specific tasks. Customization can also take other forms than training, as described in this section.

In Chapter 3, we discussed the need to experiment with different ML models to find one that works well for the application under development. The analogy with FMs includes the choice of an FM and a customization technique. Figure 4.1 shows four of these customization techniques: prompt engineering, retrieval-augmented generation (RAG), fine-tuning, and distilling. In addition, we discuss the use of guardrails as a means to monitor and control inputs and outputs, as well as updates to FMs.

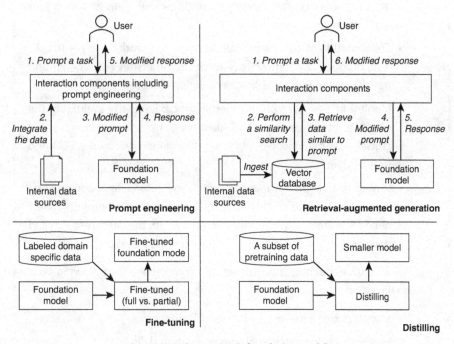

Figure 4.1 *Customizing foundation models.*

Prompt Engineer Job Description

Are you passionate about language and artificial intelligence (AI)? Do you thrive in a collaborative environment and enjoy problem solving? If so, then a career as a prompt engineer might be the perfect fit for you!

Prompt engineers are a new kind of specialist emerging in the field of AI. They are responsible for creating and optimizing the text instructions, or prompts, used by large language models (LLMs) to generate different creative text formats, such as poems, code, scripts, musical pieces, email, and letters. In essence, they act as the bridge between human intent and AI capabilities.

Here's a closer look at the typical responsibilities of a prompt engineer:

- Develop and refine prompts: This involves crafting clear, concise, and informative prompts that effectively guide the LLM toward the desired output.

- Optimize prompt performance: Prompt engineers will experiment with different phrasing and techniques to ensure prompts generate the most accurate, engaging, and relevant outputs for various applications.

- Collaboration across teams: Prompt engineers work closely with content, product, and data science teams to understand user needs and translate them into technical specifications for prompts.

- Monitor and analyze prompt performance: Regularly evaluating the effectiveness of prompts and identifying areas for improvement is crucial. This may involve analyzing data generated by the LLM and user feedback.

- Stay up-to-date on advancements in AI and natural language processing (NLP): The field of AI is constantly evolving, so prompt engineers need to be lifelong learners, keeping pace with the latest research and developments in NLP to improve the prompt generation process.

To be a successful prompt engineer, you should have the following skills and qualifications:

- Strong understanding of NLP and AI concepts
- Excellent written and verbal communication skills

- Experience in crafting clear and concise instructions
- Analytical mind with a problem-solving approach
- Ability to collaborate effectively with a diverse team
- Interest in emerging technologies and a passion for language

If you're looking for a challenging and rewarding career at the forefront of AI, then becoming a prompt engineer is a great option!

4.4.1 Prompt Engineering

Prompt engineering is the process of designing and refining the prompts or inputs for an FM to generate specific types of output. It involves selecting appropriate keywords, providing examples and context, and shaping the input in a way that encourages the FM to produce the desired response. To give you a feeling what that might entail, we have provided an exemplar, a fictitious job description for a prompt engineer, in the nearby box.

Prompt engineering does not change the underlying weights within the transformer architecture of an FM, but it does provide context that influences the model's output by guiding its self-attention mechanism. It analyzes the relationships between all words in the prompt and relevant knowledge stored within the model's layers. Suppose, for example, you wanted the FM to focus on software engineering. Using words like "agile" and "microservice" gives the FM context.

Prompt engineering comprises three variants: user prompt engineering, static prompt engineering, and dynamic prompt engineering.

User prompt engineering refers to strategies and techniques that users employ to craft their prompts in a way that makes them more relevant and effective in eliciting the desired response from an FM. This can involve refining the wording, providing context, or specifying the format of the expected output. While you can offer training in prompting and prompt engineering to your users, you can also design your user interface to give hints to users.

Static prompt engineering involves constructing a static system prompt, which is written and maintained by the development team, typically in tight interaction with user feedback or power users. The system prompt is a fixed string that is passed to the FM with every request. It often sets a broad context and typical tone. An example system prompt is "You are an assistant to knowledge workers in a large, multinational company in the IT industry. Use a professional tone in your answers, be polite and concise, ..." System prompts are a very easy and fast way to lightly customize an FM, but are limited in their effect.

Dynamic prompt engineering refers to the real-time adjustment and optimization of prompts, based on the context of the user interaction or the session at hand. This approach tailors the input to the FM for each specific instance, which can enhance the relevance and accuracy of the output. Some techniques commonly associated with dynamic prompt engineering are the following:

- **Contextual adjustment** involves modifying the prompt in real time to better reflect the specific context or requirements of the current user interaction. It ensures that the FM has the most relevant information to generate an appropriate response.

- In the **iterative refinement** approach, the FM is queried multiple times with variations of the prompt. The responses are then used to refine the input until the most accurate and coherent output is produced.

- **Progressive prompting** involves gradually providing more information or guidance to the FM through a series of prompts that build on each other, leading to a more detailed and nuanced response.

- **Few-shot learning** is often achieved through context learning. Specifically, the FM is provided with a small number of examples within a prompt to guide it to good responses for similar tasks.

- Similar to few-shot learning, **adaptive learning** dynamically introduces examples or scenarios within the prompt to guide the FM, but internally it adjusts these examples based on the FM's performance to improve future responses.

Dynamic prompt engineering is not a simple task, and organizations can get it wrong. In one notorious example from early 2024, Google Gemini created images that included people of diverse backgrounds, even when those images supposedly depicted historical events and figures and the presence of people with diverse backgrounds was factually incorrect. Dynamic prompt engineering can improve the utility of FM-based systems, but should be approached with sufficient resources and tight feedback loops to avoid strongly negative outcomes.

To ensure accuracy and other quality attributes, more sophisticated prompt patterns can be applied to guide the output of FMs. Following are a few prompt patterns commonly used in FM-based systems:

- **Self-consistency** involves querying the FM multiple times with similar prompts and selecting the most consistent answer as the final answer.

- **Chain of thought** enables complex reasoning capabilities through intermediate reasoning steps. It involves breaking down complex tasks into smaller, more manageable chunks, allowing FMs to process and solve them more effectively.

- **Tree of thought** builds on chain of thought but utilizes a tree structure instead of a chain for the dynamic reasoning process. Branches in the tree explore multiple reasoning paths simultaneously. This technique includes a function to evaluate the effectiveness of paths and, based on that evaluation, decide whether to continue exploring a given branch further or to backtrack and try a different branch.

Users may need to use multiple prompt patterns to achieve the desired results. For example, Medprompt answers medical questions by searching for similar examples in a database to construct few-shot learning prompts, adding an FM-generated chain of thought for each example; it then generates multiple solutions and assembles them.[2]

4.4.2 Retrieval-Augmented Generation

Another design option for customizing FMs is retrieval-augmented generation (RAG), which, like prompt engineering, changes the inputs to an FM. This approach combines the FM with an information retrieval component that has access to custom documents (e.g., the internal documentation of an organization). Based on a given prompt, RAG retrieves relevant external information from a knowledge base by using a vector database (such as Pinecone[3] and Milvus[4]) to store the personal or organization-internal data as vector embeddings (see Section 4.2.1, "Vector Spaces" for a discussion of vectors and embeddings). These embeddings can be used to perform similarity searches

---

2. www.microsoft.com/en-us/research/blog/the-power-of-prompting/

3. www.pinecone.io/

4. https://milvus.io/

and retrieve internal data that is related to specific prompts. The retrieved data is then used to augment the prompt before inputting it into the FM.

The RAG technique enhances the FM's ability to access and utilize vast amounts of information that are not stored within the model itself. This can lead to dramatic improvements in accuracy and relevance, as well as the ability to stay updated with the latest information. RAG can be applied to a wide range of applications, such as question-answering, document retrieval, content generation, and personalized recommendations.

One notable aspect of RAG is that the individual access rights of users can be taken into account. Suppose User A has permission to read documents X, Y, and Z, and those are highly relevant to a given prompt. These documents can be retrieved and used for augmentation of User A's prompt. Now suppose User B issues the same prompt, but has access rights only for document Y. In this case, User B's query will be augmented with only document Y. Reflecting such individual access rights is possible with RAG, but not fine-tuning (which we discuss next). Fine-tuning is typically done with documents to which a sizable group of users has access, such as the entire, corporate-wide intranet for an internal AI chatbot.

However, implementing RAG creates several challenges. One of the main challenges is ensuring the quality and relevance of the retrieved information. The system must accurately determine which pieces of external data are most relevant to the prompt to avoid introducing noise or misinformation. Further, managing and maintaining a comprehensive and up-to-date knowledge base requires significant resources and infrastructure. Additionally, privacy and data security concerns arise, especially when handling sensitive or proprietary information.

4.4.3 Fine-Tuning

Domain-specific information can be added to an FM through a process similar to training an ML model. A training dataset with labeled data relevant to the chosen domain is used to further train the FM, which adjusts the FM's existing parameters. The specific process will depend on the FM and the tools available from the FM provider. The result, however, has the scale of an FM and can have the specificity of an ML model for the particular domain of interest. Fine-tuning the parameters of FMs using labeled domain-specific data can be done through either full fine-tuning or parameter-efficient fine-tuning.

Full fine-tuning involves retraining all of the parameters. However, this process is often impractical and expensive due to the sheer number of parameters in FMs. Full fine-tuning requires significant computational resources and extensive training time.

An alternative is to employ parameter-efficient fine-tuning (PEFT) techniques, which modify only a small percentage of the original parameters. Adapter modules are small neural network modules attached to specific layers within the pretrained FM. During fine-tuning, only the parameters of these adapter modules are trained, while the original FM parameters remain frozen. This allows the model to learn domain-specific information without significantly altering its core knowledge. For example, low-rank adaptation (LoRA) introduces a low-rank adaptation layer on top of the pretrained FM, which learns a lightweight transformation that adapts the pretrained FM to the new task. It reduces the number of training parameters by a factor of 10,000 and decreases computation by threefold.

4.4.4 Distilling

If a need arises for using a different model architecture (often a smaller one), but changing the model weights through training is not feasible, distillation is an option. Distilling the FM involves training a smaller and more lightweight "student" model to mimic the behavior of the larger and more complex "teacher" FM, using knowledge transfer techniques such as knowledge distillation, attention distillation, or parameter sharing.

Knowledge distillation involves training the student model on two loss functions: a data loss and a distillation loss. A data loss encourages the student model to learn from the original training data, similar to the teacher model. A distillation loss guides the student model to reproduce the teacher model outputs for a separate set of data, which distills the teacher model's knowledge into the student model.

Attention distillation transfers the attention patterns learned by the teacher model. Attention mechanisms within the teacher model highlight the most relevant parts of the input data for a specific task. By mimicking these attention patterns, the student model can learn to focus on the most relevant pieces of information and improve its performance.

Parameter sharing refers to directly sharing specific layers or parameters from the teacher model with the student model. This reduces the number of parameters the student model needs to learn independently.

The distilled model is trained on a subset of the original data used to train the FM, but with a different loss function that encourages it to reproduce the output of the large FM. This can result in a more efficient and lightweight model that still maintains an acceptable level of performance.

4.4.5 Guardrails

Guardrails are mechanisms intended to safeguard the behavior of AI systems, particularly FM-based systems. They are designed to monitor and control the inputs and outputs of FMs and other components (e.g., prompts, RAG, external tools) to meet specific requirements, such as functional and accuracy requirements, responsible AI (RAI) requirements derived from policy, and standards and laws. Take RAI guardrails as an example: They can be built using a RAI knowledge base, or AI models trained just for enforcing RAI guardrails, or FMs.

Different types of guardrails are possible. *Input guardrails* are applied to the inputs received from users, and their possible effects include refusing or modifying user prompts. *Output guardrails* focus on the output generated by the FM; they may modify the output of the FM or prevent certain outputs from being returned to the user. *RAG guardrails* are used to ensure the retrieved data is appropriate, by either validating or modifying the retrieved data where needed. When calling the external tools or models to enhance the FM's capabilities, *execution guardrails* are applied to ensure that the called tools or models do not have any known vulnerabilities and the actions only run on the intended target environment and do not have negative side effects. During the workflow execution, *intermediate guardrails* can be used to guarantee that each intermediate step meets the necessary criteria. This involves checking whether an action should be carried out, determining whether the FM should be invoked, deciding whether a predefined response should be used instead, and so on.

The key attributes of guardrails include generalizability, customizability, and interpretability. Generalizability across different AI models/systems and contexts ensures that the guardrails remain effective under varied operational scenarios. Customizability allows guardrails to be adapted to the specific needs of a particular deployment. For example, autonomous driving guardrails might issue a warning in a certain region when the driver's hands are off the wheel but initiate slowing down in another region, reflecting different contexts. The design of guardrails should be dynamic, which means they can learn while the system is being operated. Their rules can be configured depending on the priority or context, and some guardrail rules can be negotiable. Lastly, interpretability ensures that the system users can understand how guardrails have been applied to build trust.

To provide comprehensive monitoring and control for multimodal systems (e.g., using a combination of text, video, and audio), multimodal guardrails can be designed to carry out the following functions:

- Prevent inappropriate multimodal inputs from being sent to the FM, whether those inputs are from the users or other software components or external tools or models
- Prevent inappropriate multimodal outputs from being generated by the FM itself, whether those outputs are sent to the user or other software components or external tools or models

For example, multimodal guardrails can detect not only harmful language, but also harmful images. Imagine a future where user interfaces (UIs) are generated dynamically on demand; then, multimodal guardrails could effectively flag any UI elements that fail to meet specific requirements, such as General Data Protection Regulation (GDPR) compliance.

4.4.6 Updating FMs

In many cases, you might want the FM to be continually updated outside of the normal full update cycle. For example, your FM might be updated by web scraping to keep it current with recent developments, it might contain product descriptions that you want to be kept current, regulations could change and you want to keep your FM up-to-date, and so forth.

Updates can be achieved through fine-tuning, while prompt engineering and RAG are methods to update the overall FM-based system without modifying the FM itself. They can also be explicitly triggered or done automatically by the FM infrastructure. Which method, if any, makes sense in your context is a business decision.

New data can also come in the form of user input. For example, you might scan a document and ask for feedback in terms of style and grammar. This document could be saved in one form or another for incorporation in a future update.

If the FM incorporates the new input into its publicly available model, then the possibility exists that proprietary information will be made available to any user of the FM. Different providers have different policies concerning the public availability of user information. These policies may also change. The concern about keeping proprietary information private has led to the development of systems like FhGenie, described in the nearby box.

FhGenie, an FM-Based Production System

As a concrete example of an FM-based system and its architectural and development-related concerns, consider FhGenie, an internal AI chatbot at Fraunhofer. It is in productive use, and achieves the main design objectives: no leaking of internal data and low-barrier access to state-of-the-art AI.

Fraunhofer-Gesellschaft, based in Germany, is a leading applied research organization with approximately 30,000 staff members. Early in the current wave of generative AI, Fraunhofer realized that it required an alternative to public AI chatbots that would not leak internal information to AI labs, yet would be available to most of its staff. The former point is obvious: Internal, confidential, and private information should not end up in datasets that do not meet compliance requirements. The second point addresses the need to enable all of Fraunhofer's staff—especially the scientists—to gain experience with the recent advances in AI. If that is achieved, staff can learn about current AI's strengths and weaknesses, and understand when and how to use it in their own work (for increased productivity, among other things), in their own research (how to combine their field of expertise with it), and in projects with industry (to the benefit of the customer).

In late 2022 and early 2023, no option existed for achieving these goals. This changed when Microsoft Azure started offering its "OpenAI services," through which access to GPT-3.5 and later GPT-4 and GPT-4o became available. With this service, prompts and context can be sent to an LLM through an API, which responds with a "completion" in much the same way as ChatGPT or Google Gemini. OpenAI services became available in Europe in May 2023, offering the same contractual guarantees regarding confidentiality and GDPR compliance as other Microsoft cloud services.

Fraunhofer realized the potential offered by this advance and swiftly developed FhGenie, an AI chatbot based on the Azure OpenAI services. FhGenie went live in June 2023, following development, testing, and consensus with the workers' council. Within a few days, the number of users had grown to the thousands. A number of companies have followed suit and are offering similar tools internally.

FhGenie is a web application with a typical user interface. It is connected to Fraunhofer's identity and access management, which ensures that only authorized users get access to it. User state is kept only in the in-browser portion of the web application, enabling long conversations without requiring the storage of potentially sensitive information. All cloud-based components are basically stateless: Only authorization/authentication data and high-level metric data are kept in these components in the usual case. The unusual case is a violation of the RAI filter rules: Should a user ask questions that violate ethical or legal boundaries, the request is logged in an encrypted abuse log. Default versions of rules, filters, and the abuse log are part of the Azure service. Note that the stateless design implies that no learning or improvement can be made based on user interactions—neither by OpenAI/Microsoft (as desired) nor by Fraunhofer (this was part of the consensual agreement with the workers' council).

Users get to choose which AI model they want to use. Depending on the chosen model and current traffic, latency can vary between 1 second and several tens of seconds. The latency depends almost exclusively on the response time of the chosen model.

Development is ongoing, and targets a number of areas. Besides making various improvements and incorporating new features over time, RAG is being added. Accordingly, relevant documents, such as the intranet, the extranet (e.g., the Fraunhofer website), and internal rules and regulations, can be used by the AI system when responding to user queries. In addition, other AI models are being tested, including some hosted by other external parties and some that will be hosted internally on the Fraunhofer infrastructure.

User requests for improvement cover both the AI portions and the non-AI portions of the system. Because the operators of FhGenie are not training their own FMs, AI-related requests can be resolved only by adding other models or improved versions of the available models—once they are available and meet the requisite quality attributes. Non-AI-related queries include features such as document upload: uploading PDFs, office documents, and images to which prompts can refer. Whether and how to implement such feature requests must be evaluated with a holistic view of the system, with questions like the following being addressed: Which models support a requested modality (e.g., image, audio)? In which representation (e.g., PDF, PNG)? Can the representation be transformed (e.g., PDF-to-text) and still result in good quality? Can the AI models handle typical input sizes of a given modality? How should overly large inputs be handled? How does adding this feature affect the quality attributes, particularly performance and cost?

This example raises a few points that are more broadly applicable to AI model development. First, the holistic system perspective is important. It covers the AI portions and the non-AI portions of the system, and the behavior and quality of the whole system reflect many more aspects than just using the latest, shiniest AI model. Second, many quality concerns are related to mutual interactions and dependencies between the AI and the non-AI bits. Third, what started as a small project can become very popular and valuable, yet simultaneously require considerable effort, even in a short time frame.

4.5 Designing a System Using FMs

If you are designing an ML-based application, one of the first decisions you must make is whether to use narrow ML models or FM(s).

Although the use of FMs is increasingly being explored and integrated into various applications, most current AI systems comprise narrow ML models and non-AI components. These narrow ML models and non-AI components coexist within the system's architecture, interacting to ensure the system functions properly. The narrow ML models are responsible for making inferences for specific tasks, while the non-AI components handle data storage, interaction with other systems, user interfaces, rule-based logic, and other functions. Building narrow ML models for various tasks can be costly, requiring extensive data gathering, labeling, and human effort. Limits on training data and ML capabilities can lead to low-quality models. However, organizations have more control over data, the narrow ML model pipeline, and problem-specific insights.

The main factors influencing the narrow ML versus FM decision are cost and data availability, or the willingness to invest the effort in making data available, as just discussed. We discuss cost as a factor in Section 4.5.1. If you decide to use an FM, there are different types of models available and multiple ways to access them; we discuss those in Section 4.5.2.

4.5.1 Costs of Narrow ML Models and FMs

Choosing between narrow ML models and FMs is a central decision in AI system architecture design, as illustrated in Figure 4.2. As we discussed in

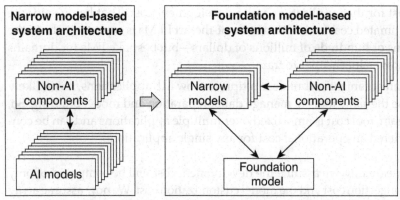

Figure 4.2 *Narrow ML models versus foundation models.*

Chapter 3, AI Background, narrow ML models are trained from scratch for specific tasks using custom-collected and often labeled datasets. In contrast, FMs are large ML models that are pretrained on massive amounts of broad data for general purposes; they can then be adapted to perform a specific task through fine-tuning and other forms of customization. In addition, FMs can be self-hosted on premises, self-hosted on the cloud, or used through APIs if available. These different options carry different costs.

Cost is the key factor to consider when making this decision. Sources of costs include the following items:

- Tool cost
- Development cost
- Maintenance cost
- Operation cost

In the following subsections, we elaborate on these factors.

Tool Cost and Development Cost

We will make the following assumptions:

- The development cost for the non-AI components will be roughly equivalent.
- If an organization chooses to train or fine-tune an in-house FM, the costs of that development will be amortized over multiple applications. The amount attributable to a single application will be an operational

cost for that application, not a development cost. That being said, the estimated cost for training state-of-the-art LLMs is expected to be in the tens or hundreds of millions of dollars—but bespoke FMs for domains can be a lot cheaper to train.

- If an organization builds multiple narrow ML applications, it will likely use the same tools to manage data preparation and model building. So, again, tool cost is amortized over multiple applications and can be considered an operational cost for any single application.

Consequently, we assume the development cost will be composed of only the data ingestion cost and the model customization cost. We now assume away the distinction in development costs between narrow ML models and FM.

- Our FM case studies in Chapters 12 (The Fraunhofer Case Study: Using a Pretrained Language Model for Tendering) and 13 (The ARM Hub Case Study: Chatbots for Small and Medium-Size Australian Enterprises) both mention data preparation as a difficult and time-consuming process. This is equally true of the data used in narrow ML model training and processing. The specifics of the data used in your application should be examined to determine whether there will be a substantial difference in data ingestion costs when preparing that data for use by an FM versus by a narrow ML model.

- The model development activities for FMs and narrow ML models are quite different. The model development activities for narrow ML models consist of choosing the model, selecting hyperparameters, training, and testing the model. The model development activities for FMs involve the customization techniques discussed in Section 4.4, "Customizing FMs". Any differences in model development costs will depend on the specifics of the application that you are building and the type of data used for your application.

Maintenance Cost

We assume the differences between narrow ML models and FMs to be relatively small:

- The costs of evolving the non-AI components will be similar in both cases.
- The costs of evolving the training data or cleaning the input data will depend on the specifics of the data.

Operational Cost

It is primarily in the operational costs that we can see a clear advantage for narrow ML models.

- Narrow ML models can be hosted on local resources without the necessity of using the cloud. Even if the models are hosted on the cloud, the costs will be restricted to only the resources actually used. If the model is using services hosted by the cloud provider, there may be charges for those services.

- FMs are usually hosted on the public or private cloud because of their scale. Furthermore, many providers charge for the services involved in using an FM. These charges tend to be higher than for hosted ML services.

- Hosting larger FMs on private cloud resources might make it necessary to procure (more) GPU capacity. At the time of this writing, GPUs are expensive and somewhat hard to come by.

- The amortization cost associated with narrow ML tools will likely be smaller than the amortization cost associated with a bespoke FM.

To summarize the cost discussion, making some assumptions will give an edge to narrow ML models. However, any differences will depend on the specifics of the data to be analyzed, the costs of the cloud provider, and the amortization costs of a bespoke FM or tools used in processing training and input data.

4.5.2 External FMs, Own FMs, or Open-Weight FMs

Another decision in the architecture design of FM-based systems is choosing whether to (1) leverage an external pretrained FM via APIs, (2) create your own FM in-house, or (3) run an existing open-parameter model.

First, using an external FM via an API can save human resources for model training, deployment, and maintenance, as organizations pay only per API call and request/response volume (measured, for example, in tokens, characters, or words). Furthermore, using a well-established external FM can potentially result in higher accuracy and generalizability to various tasks. However, the organization may have only limited control over context-specific qualities. In addition, privacy and security concerns can arise if organizations are uncertain whether their data, their employees' data, and their customers' data will be used for pretraining the next generation of FMs by third parties without their knowledge.

Second, as discussed in Section 4.6, "Maturity of FMs and Organizations", some organizations may possess unique internal data for training or fine-tuning their own FM in-house, potentially leading to a competitive advantage. Also, with this approach, organizations have full control over the model pipeline, which facilitates model customization and ensures the result has human value–related qualities. The trained FM can be shared across different departments. Operating an FM is actually quite straightforward with tools. For example, Llama.cpp can easily run smaller models on a laptop, especially those using quantization. However, larger FMs often require substantial investments. For example, the United Kingdom announced initial startup funding of £100 million to build its own FM.[5] Organizations with rigorous quality requirements that cannot be fulfilled by external FMs may select this option.

Third, self-hosting open-weight models can be a viable alternative. In this case, the weights or parameters of a model are made publicly available although the training data and the source code or the source data are not. Hence, these models are typically called open-weight or open-parameter models, not open-source models. Hosting an FM-based model that is a customized version of an open-parameter FM offers a middle ground where organizations can leverage the advancements of preexisting FMs while maintaining greater control over their use and data.

The difficulty in using an open-weight model is determining the effects of the parameters. Sophisticated techniques are used to discover activation patterns. Model visualization tools, explainable AI techniques (see Chapter 11, Observability), and model interpretation libraries can also be used to gain some insight into the effect of the parameters.

By self-hosting, companies can fine-tune these models with their proprietary, internal data, which can help address specific domain needs without incurring the full costs and resource commitments entailed in developing an FM from scratch. Moreover, self-hosting allows for more stringent data privacy and security measures, as sensitive information does not need to leave the organization's infrastructure. This can be particularly appealing for organizations that have the technical capacity to manage these systems but wish

---

5. www.gov.uk/government/publications/integrated-review-refresh-2023-responding-to-a-more-contested-and-volatile-world

to avoid the risks associated with external APIs and the considerable investment required for full in-house development.

4.6 Maturity of FMs and Organizations

As FMs are maturing, their capabilities are increasing. Notably, organizations are at different levels of maturity, impacting the choices they should make. In this section, we first present the results of an experiment we conducted to see whether a publicly available FM can be used to perform data cleaning. This is a task that exemplifies the growing maturity of FMs. Subsequently, we discuss organizational issues with respect to the use of FMs.

4.6.1 Data Cleaning Experiment

FMs are rapidly gaining functionality and are being used for an increasing number of application areas. One application area of interest to the builders of AI systems is the activities involved in data cleaning and preparation. We performed an experiment where we attempted to use ChatGPT with GPT-4o to perform some data cleaning and analysis. We will summarize the results, but you can find the entire dialogue online.

We began by providing ChatGPT a messy data set. A summary of the dialogue follows, and you can find the entire dialogue online.[6]

> Us: The uploaded file contains a sheet titled "Dirty 1," which appears to have inconsistently structured sales data. The data includes segments like Consumer, Corporate, and Home Office, each with different shipping modes and corresponding totals.
>
> Us: [Several questions about the values in different categories]
>
> ChatGPT: [Answered correctly]
>
> Us: Identify the sales amount details for Order ID CA-2012-162201.
>
> ChatGPT: It seems there is an issue locating the "Order ID" column, likely due to the inconsistency in the column headers.
>
> Let's try an alternate approach to identify the correct column for the Order IDs and retrieve the details for the specified Order ID "CA-2012-162201."

---

6. https://research.csiro.au/ss/team/se4ai/ai-engineering/

The "Order ID" column is not explicitly labeled in the headers row, suggesting that the data might have a different format or starting point. Let's explore the dataset to locate the Order IDs.

The Order IDs appear to be listed under the first column without a proper header. I will search for the Order ID "CA-2012-162201" in this column and extract the corresponding sales details.

The sales amount details for Order ID "CA-2012-162201" are as follows:

...

Us: What is the trend of sales in the Consumer segment over the given period?

ChatGPT: To analyze the trend of sales in the Consumer segment, we will aggregate the sales data over time. However, given the structure of the data, we need to ensure that we properly handle the dates and identify any possible trends.

...

After several more questions about the data as input, including drawing graphs, we asked ChatGPT to clean the data. It identified problems with the original data and performed several cleaning operations. Again, see the original dialogue if you are interested in the details.

Our conclusion from this experiment is that FMs can, in fact, be used for operations much more sophisticated than textual or image analysis. The extent to which an FM can replace some of the non-AI modules in your application will, of course, depend on the specifics of your application. Even so, the message of our experiment is clear: Do not discount the capabilities of an FM for your application until you have tested it.

4.6.2 Organizational Maturity

FMs' capabilities are rapidly increasing, and more organizations are adopting them. The utilization of an FM depends on not only the capabilities of the FM, but also the maturity of the organization wishing to use the FM. Figure 4.3 shows, nominally, the increasing organizational maturity required to use an FM in different ways. Prompt engineering is the easiest for organizations, RAGs are somewhat more difficult, fine-tuning and distilling require more sophistication, and creating a bespoke FM requires the most sophistication.

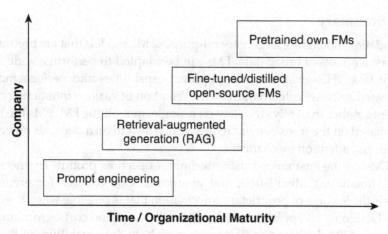

Figure 4.3 *Complexity versus time/organizational maturity.*

4.7 Challenges of FMs

Having explored various aspects of FMs, it's important to recognize their remaining inherent limitations. These challenges stem from how FMs process and generate information, and impact their reliability and accuracy. Two key challenges are associated with the use of FMs:

- **Limited grounding:** FMs focus on identifying statistical patterns within data sequences, rather than being grounded in facts or authoritative knowledge. They identify correlations but lack an underlying causal model or a world model. This can lead to significant inaccuracies in their outputs.

- **Hallucination or confabulation:** Without grounding, FMs lack the ability to evaluate the confidence and truthfulness of their outputs while having a tendency to provide an answer by making one up—a behavior often termed *hallucination*. The term *hallucination* has been critiqued for anthropomorphizing AI, suggesting false perception. *Confabulation* is a more precise alternative term, highlighting the tendency to invent facts in uncertain situations, effectively filling in gaps creatively while sticking to the appearance of known material.

4.8 Summary

Foundation models are large, general-purpose ML models that are pretrained on vast amounts of broad data. FMs can be adapted to perform a wide variety of tasks. However, achieving optimal capabilities and performance in FM-based software often requires a combination of various interacting components, rather than relying solely on a single, monolithic FM. FMs are typically based on the transformer architecture, which in turn depends on vector spaces and attention mechanisms.

FMs can be customized using techniques such as prompt engineering, RAG, fine-tuning, distillation, and guardrails. One concern for organizations is the leakage of proprietary information that is possible when they use FMs. Designing an application using FM will depend on cost factors, and on the type of FM. Utilizing an FM depends on both the capabilities of the FM and the organizational maturity of the development organization. FMs have some inherent challenges such as lack of grounding and hallucination.

4.9 Discussion Questions

1. Pick a particular organizational or personal task, and compare the specific pros and cons of using narrow ML models versus FMs to achieve it.

2. Pick a particular organizational or personal task, and compare the pros and cons of the different ways of customizing FMs to better implement it.

3. Pick a particular application with which you are familiar, and compare the costs of using an FM versus a narrow ML model.

4.10 For Further Reading

You can read about Word2Vec in Wikipedia [Wiki Word2Vec].

The foundational paper on attention, "All You Need Is Attention," can be found at [Vaswani 17].

Wikipedia also has an entry about the transformer architecture [Wiki Transformer].

Vector encodings are described in the TensorFlow tutorials [TensorFlow Tutorials], including [TensorFlow Guide].

More details about FhGenie can be found in [Weber 24]

For the evolution and future of FM-based systems, have a look at Zaharia et al. [Zaharia 24].

You can read more about design options for FMs in Lu et al. [Lu 24A].

For using FMs to design more advanced agents, see [Lu 24B], [Liu 24].

For designing runtime guardrails, a taxonomy can be found at Shamsujjoha et al. [Shamsujjoha 24].

5

AI Model Life Cycle

with Boming Xia

Choose your tools carefully, but not so carefully that you get uptight or spend more time at the stationery store than at your writing table.
—Natalie Goldberg

MOVING FROM MODEL selection into production takes a number of steps and utilizes a large number of supporting tools. That explains our opening quotation: You can spend a tremendous amount of time agonizing over which tools to use, but you should not go too far down the rabbit hole.

Some of these tools are used to manage the data used to train the models, others package the model for deployment and serving. We will discuss the types of tools available within the context of their use. The chapter is intended for those AI engineers managing their own data. If you are using a vendor-supplied pretrained model, whether a narrow machine learning (ML) model or a foundation model (FM), the vendor will be responsible for preparing and training the model. You will be responsible for any data used in customizing the model, such as data used in fine-tuning, inference, and retrieval-augmented generation (RAG). The organization of this chapter follows Figure 5.1, which depicts the development life cycle for AI models.

5.1 Developing the Model

As we noted in Section 1.5, "AI Model Quality,", MLOps is a set of practices to prepare ML models for production and then operate them. We break the discussion of MLOps practices into three portions. Chapter 3, AI Background, and Chapter 4, Foundation Models, discussed model selection and hyper-parameter definition. This chapter discusses development of the model up to

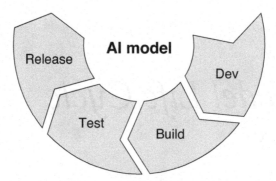

Figure 5.1 *AI model life cycle.*

the point that it is ready to commit to the build stage. Chapter 6, System Life Cycle, discusses the life cycle of the system through to operations including, but not exclusively, the AI model portion. As we will see in Chapter 13, The ARM Hub Case Study: Chatbots for Small and Medium-Size Australian Enterprises, MLOps steps pertain to the development of both narrow ML models and FMs.

To create a narrow ML model, the AI model must be trained on a set of data specific to the domain and application for your system. Each data item in that set can be seen as a collection of attributes. Most of these attributes will be treated as independent variables and the remainder as dependent variables. The goal of the resulting model is to infer the values of the dependent variables given a new data item specified in terms of the independent variables. Figure 5.2 shows the steps involved in training a narrow ML model, each of which we discuss in turn.

Training an FM was discussed in Chapter 4. Rather than relying solely on explicit labels, FMs use high-dimensional vector spaces to represent data, enabling them to capture complex relationships and associations between data points. This approach allows them to generalize across tasks without the need for manual labeling, by building on techniques commonly used in other unsupervised learning approaches.

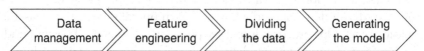

Figure 5.2 *Steps in model development.*

The selection of data for training will determine the quality of the resulting model. Two of the items to consider are highlighted here:

- **Generalization versus accuracy:** Achieving a balance between broad generalization, including robustness to out-of-distribution data, and optimizing for high accuracy on known data distributions is a complex tradeoff. An AI model for medical diagnosis must generalize across varied patient data while maintaining high accuracy.

- **Effective stress testing:** Conducting tests against rare or unexpected conditions not seen during training is an important aspect of the test suite. For example, a weather prediction model may be inadequately tested against extreme, unrecorded weather events.

5.1.1 Data Management

Figure 5.3 gives an overview of the steps that make up the data management stage.

Gathering the Data

First, the data to be used to train the model must be gathered. This data can be gathered from a wide range of sources. It may come from surveys, sensors, databases, websites, data collected from APIs or system monitors, or a third party. The term "data ingestion" is often used to describe this stage. You need to obtain a set of data values pertinent to the problem you wish to solve, because the data chosen to train the model is critical to the quality of the subsequent model. In particular, the distribution of data values should reflect the real-world scenario in which the model will be used. If the training data is biased toward a certain subset of the population, the model may not perform well on other demographics.

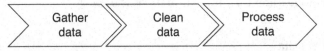

Figure 5.3 *Steps in data management.*

In addition to the representativeness of the data, two other aspects of gathering the data are important. First, consider where the data is stored. The term *data storage* typically refers to a service that holds data in a structured or unstructured form. For example, Amazon S3 and Google Cloud Storage are popular tools that store data as objects or files in the cloud. A *data lake* is a more comprehensive repository that can store vast amounts of raw data in its native format. Data lakes often use underlying storage services like S3 or Azure Data Lake Storage to house this data, but they also include tools for organizing, processing, and analyzing it.

In contrast to a data lake, a *data warehouse* stores highly structured, processed data that is optimized for fast querying and reporting, making it ideal for business intelligence use cases. Tools like Amazon Redshift and Google BigQuery are popular examples of data warehouses. A *data lakehouse* is a relatively newer concept that combines the flexible data storage capabilities of a data lake with the structured data management and performance features of a data warehouse. Tools like Databricks[1] and Snowflake are examples that offer lakehouse architectures, bridging the gap between raw data storage and structured analytics.

The second crucial aspect of gathering data is maintaining a history of where the data originated and how it has evolved over time. This involves two key concepts: data versioning and data lineage. On the one hand, *data versioning* refers to the practice of keeping track of different versions of datasets as they are updated or modified, ensuring that previous states can be retrieved and compared. Tools like Data Version Control (DVC) and Delta Lake are popular choices for managing data versioning. On the other hand, *data lineage* tracks the complete life cycle of data, including its origins, its transformations, and how it flows through various systems. Understanding data lineage is essential for ensuring transparency, reproducibility, and compliance, especially in AI model development. Tools like Apache Atlas and Collibra are widely used to implement data lineage, providing a detailed history of data and its transformations. As we will see in Chapter 11, Observability, keeping track of the source of data used in AI models and their transformations is important.

Cleaning the Data

Once the data has been gathered, it must be cleaned and transformed to ensure its quality and usability. Some of the issues involved in this step are discussed here.

---

1. Data Lakehouse Architecture. *Unify your data, analytics, and AI.* www.databricks.com /product/data-lakehouse

Data often comes from different sources at different frequencies, and may potentially contain errors. For example, suppose the model is intended to predict blood pressure. During health exams, we might get data from physical measurements (such as a doctor's stethoscope) or from smartwatches that people wear. Physical measurements might be updated monthly, whereas smartwatches could supply data continuously.

Cleaning the data involves identifying and fixing errors such as missing values or inconsistencies. Duplicate data may also have been collected, which needs to be removed during the cleaning process. Outliers, for example, can indicate an erroneous value that needs to be addressed during cleaning. Tools like OpenRefine and Trifacta are often used for this purpose. Visual examination of the data is also useful to identify errors.

Processing the Data

Once the data is cleaned, transformation comes into play. This process involves converting the data into a format that the next steps in model training can understand. Because raw data may have been gathered from a variety of sources, it is likely in various formats. Transformation tasks may include scaling the data, encoding categorical variables, or creating new features to improve model performance. Tools such as Apache Spark and Talend offer robust capabilities for these preprocessing tasks.

The entire process of gathering, cleaning, and preprocessing data is both labor-intensive and critical for ensuring data quality. Various end-to-end tools are available to assist with these tasks, providing functions such as ingesting and outputting data in different formats, data transformation, filtering, sorting, aggregation, scaling, encoding categorical features, imputing missing values, anomaly detection, cleansing suggestions, data profiling, joining, data deduplication, and master data management. Comprehensive data platforms like KNIME and Alteryx offer end-to-end solutions for data preparation, integrating cleaning, transformation, and advanced analytics into a single workflow. Additionally, cloud-based platforms like Google Cloud Dataflow and AWS Glue provide scalable and automated data processing capabilities, making them ideal for large-scale data integration and transformation tasks across various industries.

5.1.2 *Feature Engineering*

Feature engineering is the process of extracting features (characteristics, properties, attributes) from data. The goal of feature engineering is to choose those features that will best indicate or predict the value of the phenomenon of interest. Features can be explicit within the data, such as in our blood pressure example; can be imputed from data such as height and weight; or can be related to the collection mechanism, such as "this data comes from sensor 37." FMs do not rely on explicitly defined features. Instead, they use associations, patterns, and relationships within data, through a vector space, where similar items are positioned close together based on their contextual similarities.

Tools to support feature engineering perform some of the following functions:

- **Numerical transformations:** Operations such as scaling, normalization, and taking logarithms to adjust the distribution of numerical features.

- **Category encoding:** Converting categorical variables into numerical values, such as one-hot encoding, ordinal encoding, and label encoding (e.g., encoding "not spam" as 0 and "spam" as 1 in emails).

- **Clustering:** Grouping similar data points together based on their feature similarities. This technique is often used to create new categorical features.

- **Aggregating values:** Summarizing data through operations like sum, mean, median, or other statistical measures to create new features.

- **Principal component analysis (PCA):** A dimensionality reduction technique that transforms features into a set of uncorrelated components, thereby preserving most of the variance in the data.

- **Feature construction:** Creating new features from existing ones, such as interaction terms or polynomial features, to capture more complex patterns in the data.

Popular tools that facilitate feature engineering include tools which automate feature engineering through deep feature synthesis, and H2O.ai, which provides a comprehensive suite for creating and selecting features within its ML platform. Additionally, tools like scikit-learn offer a wide range of feature engineering functions that can be easily integrated into data processing pipelines.

The following concerns must be addressed when choosing the features for engineering:

- **Change-proof features:** Creating features that will remain relevant and informative despite changes over time is a significant challenge. For example, in financial models, the relevance of the economic indicators used as features may change due to evolving market dynamics.

- **Edge case representation:** Developing features that effectively capture the characteristics of edge cases and out-of-distribution data is important. For example, a language translation model may need to handle rare dialects or slang.

- **Feature complexity tradeoff:** Balancing the addition of features to improve robustness and resilience against the increase in computational demand, complexity, and potential model maintainability issues is a delicate task. For example, an autonomous vehicle's AI system must balance the complexity of features against real-time processing needs.

Feature stores act as centralized repositories for storing, managing, versioning, and serving features that your models are built upon. They store precomputed feature values for efficient access. Key functions for such stores typically include the following:

- **Feature engineering:** Define and implement feature engineering pipelines within the store.

- **Versioning and lineage tracking:** Track changes made to features and their origin for accountability.

- **Online and offline serving:** Serve features for both batch training and real-time inference with low latency.

- **Governance and access control:** Manage access and changes to features based on user roles and permissions.

Popular tools for managing feature stores include Feast, which integrates with various data processing frameworks and supports both online and offline feature serving, and Tecton, which offers a comprehensive platform for feature engineering, versioning, and real-time feature serving at scale. In addition, Amazon SageMaker Feature Store provides a managed service that integrates with the broader AWS ecosystem, making it a powerful choice for teams already using AWS for their ML workflows.

5.1.3 Dividing the Data

Data management (e.g., data lakehouses, data warehouses, data storage) and feature engineering/stores handle functions such as data sourcing, ingestion, cleaning, transformation, versioning, and governance. Once they have been implemented, the next step in the AI model life cycle focuses on managing the cleaned and transformed training data for the purpose of splitting it into training, validation, and test sets. While there is some overlap in the terms used in the process of dividing the data and the terms used in data management functions, the key difference here lies in the specific tools and methods used to ensure that the data is split in a way that supports robust model development and evaluation.

Once the data has been cleaned and transformed, it needs to be divided into three distinct sets:

- **Training set:** Used to train the model and fit its parameters.
- **Validation set:** Used to tune the hyperparameters and prevent overfitting during the model development phase.
- **Test set:** Used for final evaluation of the model's performance, ensuring that it generalizes well to unseen data.

The following tools and functions are specific to data splitting:

- **scikit-learn:** Provides functions like train_test_split and KFold for splitting datasets into training, validation, and test sets, along with cross-validation techniques to ensure robust model evaluation.
- **TensorFlow and Keras:** Both offer utilities within their APIs to automate the process of dividing datasets, such as TensorFlow's tf.data.Dataset and Keras's train_test_split.
- **PyTorch DataLoader:** Often used in deep learning, it facilitates data batching and splitting, particularly when working with large datasets.
- **MLFlow:** While also a general-purpose tool for managing the ML life cycle, MLFlow supports automating data splitting processes within its experiment tracking and model management pipelines.

The accuracy of the model is heavily dependent on how well the data is split and how representative the training, validation, and test sets are of the real-world scenarios the model will encounter. Poorly split data can lead to overfitting, underfitting, or biased models that do not generalize well. Therefore, carefully selecting tools and methods for data splitting is essential to building robust ML models. We will cover the impact of biases in training data and their implications for model predictions in Chapter 10, Privacy and Fairness.

5.1.4 Generating the Model

Once an initial model has been selected, its training algorithm is executed on the training dataset, with the model's parameters being adjusted through an iterative process to minimize errors. The result of this process is a trained model, which consists of a set of optimized numerical parameters (often referred to as weights) that encode the knowledge the model has learned from the data.

Model development typically follows a two-phase approach in terms of pipeline and process. The first phase is the exploratory model development process. It is a more experimental phase, in which data scientists and developers tinker with various aspects of the model. It includes experimenting with different model architectures, adjusting the hyperparameters, and assessing the effectiveness of specific features. This phase often involves a high degree of trial-and-error and is usually conducted in a more flexible and interactive environment, such as Jupyter Notebooks or similar systems. Here, developers may work with a subset of the training data, particularly when dealing with vast datasets. This subset should be representative of the full dataset, but small enough to allow for rapid experimentation and iteration. This stage allows for understanding the nuances of the model and the data, and lays the groundwork for more effective and efficient model training.

Once the exploratory phase yields a refined set of hyperparameters, configurations, and features, the process transitions to the second phase—the actual model training on a larger scale. In this phase, the model is trained on the larger dataset to ensure that it learns from a comprehensive range of examples and scenarios. This training is more structured and less experimental than that conducted in the first phase. Additionally, the evaluation set in this phase is larger and more robust, enabling a more accurate assessment of the model's effectiveness and generalizability.

This two-phase approach—starting with exploratory modeling on a smaller scale and transitioning to full-scale training—is essential for developing robust, effective AI models. It is important that Infrastructure as Code (IaC) practices in the explorative, actual training, and later deployment environments are consistent across feature generation code, training, evaluation, and other applications of IaC.

Be aware that the resources required to execute the model may be substantially different from those required to train the model. For instance, in the blood pressure example, millions of data points may be used for training the model. Storing and processing this training data, along with the training process itself, can demand significant resources. By comparison, a trained model, which might be as simple as a linear regression, can be captured in a small number of values. The code required to execute such a model can be quite compact and might not require many resources.

However, for larger models, such as deep neural networks, the execution might still require considerable resources, even after training. This disparity in resource needs has implications for where the model is positioned within the system architecture. Simpler models may be deployed on lightweight devices, whereas more complex models might necessitate deployment on more robust infrastructure.

Task-specific ML models can be trained via three main types of methods: supervised, unsupervised, and self-supervised learning. Supervised learning involves training on labeled data, such as transaction data labeled as either "fraudulent" or "legitimate" for fraud detection. Unsupervised learning does not use labels, allowing the model to find patterns independently. It is useful in tasks such as customer segmentation in marketing. Self-supervised learning allows models to create their own labels by masking existing words in a sentence and then predicting the masked words, a technique commonly used in language processing tasks. General-capability FMs are trained on vast amounts of unlabeled data. To use an FM in a particular domain or for a downstream task, it is typically customized for that domain or task. This customization of the FM is discussed in detail in Chapter 4.

5.1.5 Tool Support for Model Training

Manually writing the code for training models is possible but rarely done in modern ML. Instead, ML frameworks are typically used to provide these functions. Consequently, developers are not required to code training algorithms. They can choose a framework and the needed library functions to train a model via some configuration and high-level coding.

Both open-source and commercial frameworks exist to manage model generation. Some tools also act as feature stores and keep a history of versions of training data, features, and test results, allowing for better comparison, explainability, and traceability. We discuss explainability and traceability in Chapter 11, Observability.

ML frameworks include the following options:

- TensorFlow[2]

---

2. www.tensorflow.org/

- PyTorch[3]
- scikit-Learn[4]
- XGBoost[5]

Some ML platforms are provided by cloud vendors, including the following options:

- Google Cloud Vertex AI
- Amazon SageMaker
- Microsoft Azure Machine Learning

A model registry is a centralized repository for managing the life cycle of ML models. It serves as a system for storing, versioning, and tracking metadata about models throughout their life cycle—from development to deployment and maintenance. Its primary objective is to streamline model management and maintain a record of model evolution. A model registry performs the following core functions:

- **Version control:** Tracks different versions of models, enabling teams to easily roll back to previous versions if needed and understand changes over time.
- **Metadata management:** Records comprehensive metadata for each model version, including training data, parameters, performance metrics, and authorship information. This metadata is important for understanding the context in which a model was developed and how it has evolved.
- **Model staging and life-cycle management:** Manages the phases of a model's life cycle, such as development, testing, staging, and production. This helps ensure that only thoroughly tested and validated models are deployed.
- **Access control and security:** Provides secure access to models, ensuring that only authorized personnel can modify or deploy models.

---

3. https://pytorch.org/

4. https://scikit-learn.org/stable/index.html

5. https://github.com/dmlc/xgboost

5.2 Building the Model

The model, once trained, consists of the optimized parameters (or model weights), the model architecture that defines its structure and behavior, and the configuration settings needed for execution. However, the trained model itself does not include an inference engine to make predictions or classifications on new data, but rather is typically deployed within an inference framework or system that serves as the inference engine. This inference engine is responsible for applying the trained model to new input data, whether in real time or in batches, to generate outputs such as predictions or classifications. For example, when a new email is received, the inference engine uses the trained model to determine whether the email is spam.

Suppose that you are using linear regression as the algorithm. A linear regression is a set of coefficients by which to multiply the independent variables, with the results of these operations then being summed. The result of this calculation is a prediction. The model would consist of coefficients that can be used by the inference engine, which takes the input as the independent variables, does the calculation, and produces a prediction as output.

The model can be packaged as a procedure that is called directly. In this case, the language in which the model is coded must be compatible with the caller. The model can also be packaged as a service—deployed either in a container or in a virtual machine. In this case, the language in which the model is coded does not matter because communication with the model occurs via messages through service endpoints over the network. Gaining language flexibility is one consideration when deploying models as services.

The service wrapper provides the necessary interfaces and protocols, allowing external clients to invoke the model's capabilities by sending input data and receiving the corresponding output. The build and release process, therefore, involves wrapping the inference engine in a service that can be easily accessed and utilized by various clients within the AI system.

There are three key aspects of this encapsulation process:

1. The service can be located behind a REST interface. To use an analogy, the model can be viewed as a resource representation or a database where the client provides the search/request parameters, and the database/representation returns the associated value. A REST interface is based on the database basic operations of CRUD (Create, Read, Update, Delete), as we discussed in Chapter 2, Software Engineering Background. Viewing the model as a database facilitates the use of

REST. GraphQL is an adaptation of REST that provides a query language that specifies which outputs are expected by a client. FMs use both REST and RPC (Remote Procedure Call) as their interface style.

2. The service should be packaged as a container, with its clients allowed to communicate only via the service endpoint messages. The model will typically be part of a microservice in a microservices architecture.

3. The service should support a query asking for version information and other metadata information. Each model depends on its training and evaluation data as well as on the source code that implements the training algorithm and its configurations (e.g., learning parameters or hyperparameters). This information, which is usually stored in a model registry, can be made available to the wrapper so that it can be returned to the client. It is possible to have multiple active models and multiple active versions of code elements, all available simultaneously. One mechanism for managing the versioning problem is to have every wrapper provide its clients with its versioning information.

5.3 Testing the Model

As we will see when we discuss the development process for non-AI modules, the individual modules are unit tested in isolation. Then, after the system is built, the unit tests are run as a portion of the system test. This also happens with AI models: The models are tested in isolation, and then retested after they are integrated into the whole system. In this section, we discuss the testing of the AI models in isolation.

5.3.1 Terms Related to AI Evaluation and Testing

In ML, model evaluation typically refers to assessing a model's accuracy after training, typically via cross-validation and bootstrapping. Model testing is the process of executing models to test model accuracy while using a separate test dataset before deployment. When we extend the scope to a system-level context, these terms take on broader meanings. Evaluation becomes a comprehensive process that covers different evaluation strategies such as model/system evaluation, testing, and benchmarking. In addition, the evaluation for an AI model/system extends beyond accuracy to cover other quality attributes and risks, correctness, and broader capabilities beyond mere functional tasks.

Quality attributes are nonfunctional aspects that describe the overall quality and efficacy of an AI system against predefined criteria, emphasizing immediate outcomes. Conversely, risk assessment is concerned with the potential immediate harms, and impact assessment emphasizes the longer-term and broader effects. Accuracy is conceived as task completion fidelity, encapsulating not only statistical precision but also how well an AI model or system achieves its tasks. Correctness emphasizes system-level operational integrity; it pertains to the system's ability to perform its specified functionalities and fulfill user expectations. Capability evaluation extends to both designed and emergent functionalities, including potentially dangerous ones, by examining an FM or its system's adaptability and evolution beyond initial training. Risk assessment is the systematic process of identifying and evaluating the likelihood and potential consequences of events or actions within AI systems that could lead to harm. Impact assessment is the systematic process of identifying and evaluating the wider and longer-term effects that AI systems may have on individuals, communities, and society across economic, social, and environmental dimensions.

Benchmarking, as a type of evaluation, involves not just accuracy but an analysis conducted across multiple quality and risk considerations against predefined tasks, including ethical and social impacts. It provides a comprehensive analysis of the AI model/system's quality, risk, and capability, which is especially useful for FM-based systems.

5.3.2 Evaluating ML Models

ML models are evaluated both for accuracy and for quality and risk factors.

- **Model accuracy testing:** Model accuracy is tested using the selected test cases, which constitute a test suite. A test suite can include both test datasets that mirror real-world complexities and evaluation metrics or benchmarks for quantifying accuracy. Metrics might be general, such as precision and F1 score, or specific to a domain, such as BLEU for language translation.

- **Quality and risk evaluation:** Quality evaluation analyzes specific quality attributes such as robustness, security, fairness, and explainability. These attributes are needed to ensure the model functions as intended and to meet ethical considerations. Additionally, quality evaluation explores how these attributes influence broader risks and societal impacts, such as adversarial attacks and bias against social inequalities. Integrating risk and impact assessments provides a holistic view of the interplay between quality attributes and risks, with the aim of aligning the model with both technical excellence and societal expectations.

Automated tests can be used to ensure that the AI models can be properly invoked and that their responses can be processed by the system. They can also be used for assessing efficiency (e.g., latency, throughput, response time) under load conditions and for carrying out some quality tests.

For FMs and fine-tuned FMs like the large language models (LLMs) underlying chatbots, testing often addresses general capabilities or abilities to perform a very wide range of tasks, rather than task-specific functions. Capability evaluation usually involves general benchmarks and human evaluation. For example, in red teaming, a group of testers simulates adversarial attacks and strategies to test the effectiveness of security measures and enhance preparedness. *Red* is the term used for an attacking team and *blue* is the term used for the defending team. Because most red team exercises are ad hoc in terms of comprehensiveness and resource intensity and identify ad hoc issues, these issues might be considered statistically rare or might be addressed in an inconsistent manner, leaving fundamental issues unresolved. Thus, it is necessary to establish an automated/systematic red team and to ensure the blue team is strong and adequately resourced. The results of red teaming should be managed and addressed in a systematic way—for example, how to get the evaluation results to AI model developers, system developers, and AI deployers; how this feedback should be structured; what the feedback must contain; and whether to improve the FM itself or the fine-tuning/reinforcement learning from human feedback (RLHF)/reinforcement learning from AI feedback (RLAIF) or the prompting/RAG.

Due to sensitivity and nondeterministic features, prompts and model responses often need to be managed differently from the traditional test cases. In addition to FM testing and non-AI portion testing, use case–specific testing and guardrail testing are also needed for FM-based systems. We will cover this topic in more detail in Chapter 7, Reliability, when we discuss how to evaluate functional accuracy, model capability, and efficiency.

5.3.3 Using AI to Generate Tests

Thus far, we have been discussing testing a system containing AI models. It is also possible to apply AI to generate tests. These techniques are just emerging and will evolve in the future. Two such techniques are described here:

1. **Use autonomous test generation (ATG) tools.** These tools apply ML techniques to generate test cases. Some tools that incorporate ATG include:

   a. Selenium[6]: An open-source web automation framework that can be used to create ATG scripts for web applications.

   b. Katalon Studio[7]: A commercial ATG tool that supports a variety of testing types, including web, mobile, API, and desktop.

   c. Applitools[8]: An AI-powered visual testing tool that can be used to automatically generate test cases for UI elements.

2. **Leverage one FM to test another.** Use FMs to generate diverse test cases, evaluate responses, or act as simulated users.

5.3.4 Repeatability

One important aspect of all tests is that they should be repeatable. Repeatability allows tests that produce erroneous results to be rerun as a portion of the error correction process. Some factors that impact repeatability are discussed next.

The State of the Test Database

Most systems use a database to provide and store information. During testing, it is possible that the system being tested will change items in the database. Any subsequent tests will begin from a different state than the test that showed an error. Discovering the cause of the error becomes very difficult (e.g., very expensive and time-consuming) in such circumstances. Building proper debugging and diagnostic support into the system will help. With regard to the database, the mitigation is to recreate the test database or restore it to its original state after each test or sequence of tests. If the test database is large, saving it and recreating it may add time to the testing process.

---

6. https://github.com/bewestphal/Selenium-AI

7. https://katalon.com/katalon-studio

8. https://applitools.com/

Concurrency

Some tests will give different results because the sequencing of threads causes a different order of execution. These are called "flakey tests." This issue can be mitigated by explicitly controlling the sequencing. Several tools can examine the source code for conditions that cause flakey tests, including DeFlaker,[9] iDFlakies,[10] and THEO[11] (Test Flakiness Elimination Orchestrator).

Probabilistic Nature of ML and FMs

Many ML models and FMs produce outputs probabilistically, incorporating randomness and sampling. For example, in a chatbot such as ChatGPT, identical prompts can yield different responses each time. This behavior can be detected by performing multiple trials. For this reason, it is important to run tests multiple times with the same prompt and observe any variability that occurs.

For systematic testing, it is central to control randomness. This is typically done by setting the random seed value before running the test suite. However, complex AI systems often have many random seeds, including some inside models provided by a third party through an API. The two options to control randomness are (1) centralize it, so you can control it from one place, or (2) track all points where randomness exists and control all of them during tests. Note that red teaming or human evaluation do not fall into the category of tests where you should control randomness.

Updates

Between any two executions of a test, software can be updated and models can be updated or changed. AI models may learn from these updates and, consequently, may produce different results. Using the same version, release, and patch number for every build will mitigate problems caused by software updates. ML models can be tracked in the same fashion. ML models have metadata that includes version numbers and timestamps, and these can be used to identify model changes if the provider of the ML components adheres to best practices.

---

9. www.andritz.com/products-en/group/pulp-and-paper/paper-production/stock-preparation/deflaker-dfl

10. https://github.com/UT-SE-Research/iDFlakies

11. https://orchestrator.engenious.io/

5.4 Release

Once a model has been constructed, evaluated, and passed its tests, it is ready to release. In the context of the AI model, release means that it has been packaged as an invokable entity and is ready to be joined to the remainder of the system in the system build stage (discussed in detail in Chapter 6).

The release to the build stage can be done automatically with the tools used in the model development, build, and test stages. Even so, a human should sign off on the final state of the model, for the following reasons:

- **Safety and risk:** In critical applications like healthcare, finance, and autonomous vehicles, human experts must verify that the AI model's decisions are safe and reliable, especially in edge cases or unexpected situations.

- **Legal compliance:** Many industries have regulations or standards that require human oversight of AI systems. For instance, in the financial sector, the algorithms used for trading or credit decisions may need to be reviewed and approved by humans.

- **Incomplete understanding:** We don't fully understand how some AI models work, which limits our ability to control them or fully anticipate the effects of changes. Human testers might be able to spot when something feels off, and investigate further.

- **Accountability:** Human oversight provides a layer of accountability in case the AI model makes errors or causes harm. It ensures that someone is responsible for the system's actions.

5.5 Summary

Here are the key points from this chapter:

- Model preparation involves data preparation, training the model, packaging, deploying for execution, wrapping the model as a service for interaction, and testing the model.

- Data preparation involves gathering the data from a variety of sources, cleaning missing values and outliers, and formatting the data into a consistent form.

- Training the model depends on the data selected for training and involves splitting data into training, validation, and testing datasets.

The quality of the model will depend on the quality of the training data and splitting.

- Models can be wrapped as REST components inside a container or virtual machine.

- Third-party narrow ML models or FMs provided by a vendor are trained by that vendor. As an AI engineer, you are responsible for data management for the models that you create but have little control over vendor-provided models.

- Once a model has been built and tested, it can be checked in to trigger the system build stage.

5.6 Discussion Questions

1. How does DevOps relate to MLOps? What are the key similarities and differences?

2. What are the core components of an MLOps pipeline? How do they interact?

3. How is IaC used in MLOps?

5.7 For Further Reading

You can read about MLOps in [Ameisen 20], which provides a comprehensive overview of the entire life cycle of an ML model.

[Amershi 19] bridges the gap between software engineering and ML, emphasizing the importance of robust development practices in ML.

More discussion about AI model versus system evaluation can be found in Xia et al. [Xia 24A].

6
System Life Cycle

with Boming Xia

Stop the life cycle—I want to get off!

—Barry Boehm

AT THIS POINT, you might think you are done. You have trained AI models; you have deployed and wrapped them as services for use; you understand interfaces and software engineering background. What more is to be done?

As our opening quote suggests, there are multiple steps to getting an AI system into production. Barry Boehm is complaining about the fact that a life cycle contains so many steps. Once you have created the AI model, you must create the non-AI portion, you must build the AI system (with the AI model as just one component), test the built system, and deploy and operate the system. These activities form a sequence in the life cycle, as shown in Figure 6.1. Of course, everything may not go as planned, and some rework may be necessary. These steps are indicated by the thin arrows in the figure.

The organization of this chapter follows the life cycle, but occasionally combines more than one phase in a section. In this chapter, we assume that the system is developed using a microservices architecture as described in Chapter 2, Software Engineering Background.

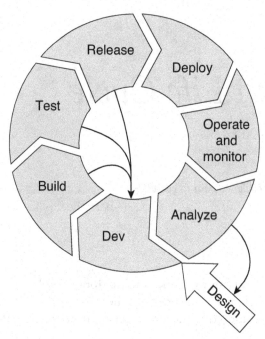

Figure 6.1 *Remaining system development activities.*

6.1 Design

We start with the "Design" arrow leading into the life cycle in Figure 6.1. Designing and developing the non-AI modules and the AI modules should be done in close collaboration, as we discuss next. Subsequently, we discuss design aspects of microservices in AI systems. Modifiability is best addressed by designing for it, as we explained in Section 1.3, "Life-Cycle Processes."

Some design decisions, such as how to cut microservices, will be discussed in Section 6.5, "Release and Deploy." Those decisions are, in part, driven by the need for independent deployability of the various microservices.

6.1.1 Co-Design/Development

Co-design and development is a process that originated between hardware developers and software developers. Traditionally, the hardware was designed first, and then the software was designed to fit the hardware. This caused problems because sometimes the hardware constraints made designing the software very difficult.

Co-design and development means that the design and development of the hardware and software are done in parallel, not sequentially. This allows for negotiation about how functions should be divided between the hardware and the software, and results in systems for which the integration process is much faster and smoother than if the designs were done sequentially.

Applying this concept to AI systems means that the AI model development is done in parallel with the design and development of the non-AI modules. AI developers have different expertise from non-AI developers, and carrying out the design of the two portions in parallel allows for collaboration between the two groups and the discovery and resolution of potential problems prior to the integration stage. Ideally, some developers will have a lot of expertise across both fields—you, as a reader of this book, may be a prime example of that—and such broad expertise will make the co-design and development smoother and faster.

Co-design and development means that interdisciplinary teams should be set up to jointly develop the portion of the design that affects both the AI and the non-AI modules. Be aware that interdisciplinary teams frequently encounter problems due to vocabulary and cultural differences. Bruce Tuckman characterized the team formation stages as "forming, storming, norming, [and] performing."[1] If you set up such a team, ensure that the members have a mechanism to resolve problems that arise during team development.

6.1.2 Using Microservices

In general, we advocate using a microservices architecture. Packaging services as containers fits well with such an architecture. However, very rarely does "one size fit all." In other words, there are occasions when a microservice is not the most appropriate mechanism to use with a portion of your architecture.

All design decisions represent tradeoffs—and that is certainly true with microservices. The tradeoff in this case is between efficiency and speed of development and deployment. Microservices are small and managed by a single team. That team can make a lot of decisions about development and deployment of their microservice without coordinating with other teams.

---

1. https://en.wikipedia.org/wiki/Tuckman%27s_stages_of_group_development

The lack of need for coordination and the small size of microservices makes for speedier development and deployment.

However, microservices must communicate through messages. Messages typically travel over the network, and the network speeds are at least an order of magnitude slower than memory accesses. Thus, relying on messages to communicate will negatively impact the efficiency of your system.

The basic techniques to reduce the reliance on network communication are to reduce the network requirements. This is accomplished by either caching results or by collocating microservices on the same host.

- Caching saves the results of a network request so that these results are available in memory. This technique is frequently used in database requests and can be used for AI model requests.

- Collocation allows the communication between two microservices to be done in memory rather than using the network to send messages. You typically still have the overhead for packaging data into messages.

If some portions of your system are not suitable for microservices, then they should be identified and not be packaged as microservices. These portions should be kept as small as possible, while recognizing the implications of using larger components for deployment speed and coordination overhead.

6.1.3 Designing for Modifiability

Things change. This is a fact of life. When designing an AI system, anticipating the types of changes will make it easier to modify the system to respond to those changes in the future. Designing your system with low coupling between components and high cohesion within a component will enable you to localize changes to the greatest extent possible. Coupling is a measure of how much the responsibilities in two different components overlap. If the same responsibility is computed multiple times in different components, then a change in that responsibility must involve those different components. Cohesion is a measure of how well a component is focused on a single task. Again, the goal is to localize changes to as few components as possible.

In an AI system, the items that are likely to change include the data used to train the model and the choice of which models to use. If the data used to train the model changes, then MLOps has techniques to track and manage these changes. Designing to allow for model changes, however, is more complicated.

The standard technique to allow for changes in a component is to create an intermediary between the clients of that component and the component itself. In terms of the model, this means that clients of a model, which we are assuming are packaged as a container, will interact with an intermediary, which in turn interacts with the model. This intermediary can be used to buffer changes to the model. The Strategy design pattern might be applied here, to make it easier to switch between different versions of the implementation.

As a simple example, suppose a new version of the model modifies its interface. The intermediary then translates invocations from the client into the new interface. Thus, the client is unchanged and the modifications to reflect the change in the model interface are localized to the intermediary. Using an intermediary to manage interface changes is one technique we recommend to mitigate version skew during deployment, as we discuss in Section 6.5.3, "Version Skew."

6.2 Developing Non-AI Modules

A module is a coherent piece of functionality. A service is constructed through the integration of multiple modules and their supporting libraries during the build step.

When a microservices architecture is adopted, each service can be developed in the language and using the technologies the owning team chooses. The individual modules within a service must adhere to the choices made by the owning team members, but there is no need for one team to coordinate with another team about choice of language or supporting libraries.

A unit test is a test within a single module, with a set of defined inputs and outputs. The inputs are provided to the module through a test harness, which compares the module's output with the expected output. Unit tests are run during development and again during the testing phase of the system, as we will discuss later in this chapter.

It is useful to include dependent infrastructure such as load balancers in the test harness so that the interactions of the module with the infrastructure can be tested. Dependent services are either mocked or stubbed to enable the tests to execute. Unit tests should cover the following cases:

- Common use cases
- Edge cases (unusual inputs or unexpected situations)
- Negative cases (inputs that should result in errors or appropriate warnings)

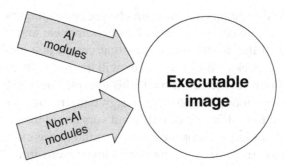

Figure 6.2 *Merging AI and non-AI modules.*

6.3 Build

The build stage is where the executable image of a VM or container is pre-pared (see Chapter 2, Software Engineering Background). In this stage, the AI modules and the non-AI modules are merged into an executable image, as illustrated in Figure 6.2.

The build environment is activated when either the AI model has been released or a non-AI module is checked into version control. Because the AI model is packaged as a code module, the AI model and the non-AI modules are treated identically during build. The build environment creates a deploy-able executable by using a continuous integration (CI) server such as Jenkins. Figure 6.3 depicts the activities of the CI server.

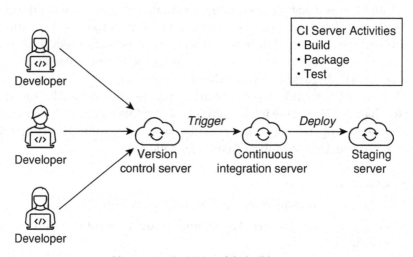

Figure 6.3 *Activities of the build server.*

The CI server can be triggered by a developer committing a change to the version control system or releasing a new model. This server loads the latest versions of all elements of the part of the system that will be included in the deployable image. Some of these elements are retrieved from the version control system, some are collected from the model repository, and some are dependencies downloaded from other sources. The CI server then places the created image on a staging server, from which tests will be run and the image will subsequently be deployed.

The CI server also creates a range of build metadata such as a version manifest, a dependency graph, and a package manifest. This information can be converted into a standard format like a software bill of materials (SBOM), which enumerates the pedigree of all of the items included in the deployable image. The SBOM will subsequently be used for software supply chain management, compliance, and security purposes. We discuss SBOM creation and access in more detail in Chapter 11, Observability.

In addition to the SBOM, the CI server should record all of the elements that were involved in the build, such as the tests that were run. Traceability of the elements of the software comes from these recordings created in the build phase. Traceability with respect to AI model outputs is discussed in Chapter 11.

6.4 Test

Once an executable is constructed, tests can be performed. These tests repeat the model and unit tests from MLOps and non-AI module development. Recall from Section 5.3.4, "Repeatability," that there may be some nondeterminism in the tests of the AI model portion. This nondeterminism is controlled as we discussed in Section 5.3.4. During the unit tests and the MLOps tests, any portions of the system not being tested were stubbed or mocked. Removing the stubs and mocks may reveal some unanticipated side effects. System-wide tests are specifically constructed to test aspects of the end-to-end execution of the system, and should be run in a suitable test environment, such as a staging environment. System tests can be derived from the following sources:

- **User stories:** User stories are one form of requirements specification. They should include expectations for the AI model as well as expectations for system behavior. *Sunny day* is a term referring to everything working as expected; *rainy day* is a term referring to things going wrong during execution. Both sunny day and rain day scenarios should be run as portions of the test suite, as should be negative tests (i.e., tests in which the system should deny a type of request, not change, or not perform an action).

- **Regression testing:** A regression test seeks to determine whether an error that has supposedly been fixed has later been reintroduced. This can happen when multiple versions of a system are in various stages of development simultaneously on different branches of the version control tree.

- **Compatibility testing:** Test the system across different web browsers and platforms. If your system is intended to be used in different environments, you will want to test with as many of those environments as possible.

- **Install/uninstall testing:** The service should be installed with a script. Once the build has been completed, this install script can be tested in an environment distinct from production so that errors can be detected. Sometimes, systems must be uninstalled. Again, the build environment can be used to test the uninstall script.

- **Efficiency or performance testing:** The system can be tested under various loads during the test phase. Load generators can be used to provide synthetic inputs according to various distributions. Scaling can be tested in the same process. As the load grows, new instances should be generated through autoscaling. Testing whether new instances are correctly registered with a load balancer should be part of the efficiency testing process. Similarly, shrinking loads and the corresponding termination of machines should be tested, and the absence of issues stemming from termination should be assured. In Chapter 8, Performance, we enumerate a number of performance concerns for the AI model; tests for these concerns should be incorporated in the test suite as well. However, exhaustive performance testing can be time- and resource-intensive, so the performance tests typically are not included in every run of the continuous integration (CI)/continuous deployment (CD) pipeline.

- **Security testing:** A variety of security tests can also be performed during the build stage. These include distributed denial of service testing, penetration testing, vulnerability scanning, and misconfiguration testing. In Chapter 9, Security, we describe a number of potential attacks on the AI model, and these should also be tested.

- **Compliance testing:** Software systems may be subject to a variety of regulations, such as the Health Insurance Portability and Accountability Act (HIPAA) and the General Data Protection Regulation (GDPR).

Testing should verify that the system complies with the relevant regulations. For example, according to GDPR, users should be able to request all data about themselves, and such functionality should be tested.

Automating system tests will make the testing process go faster and provide a record of the tests that were performed. The reliance on repetitive manual testing should be minimized as far as possible, as this will hamper the speed of delivery.

Tests should be repeatable. If a test does not generate the same results every time it is executed, finding the source of an error can be difficult—recall the specific concerns regarding AI model testing discussed in Chapter 5. Tests that are not repeatable may be caused by one or more of the following factors:

- The test database has not been restored following previous tests. If a test modifies the test database, then subsequent tests will not begin from the same state and may produce different outputs. The test database should be reinitialized following every test.

- The system time may depend on which other activities your system is performing. Systems are prone to having numerous background tasks that can affect the timing of results. Your system may have inherent concurrency issues that will affect the output.

- Probabilistic AI models may produce different results at different times. With these models, the results may depend on random factors. If a test does not produce the expected result, repeating the test several times and averaging the results may produce a more acceptable result.

6.5 Release and Deploy

Systems change. Bugs are fixed. Features are added. In addition, AI models may be updated for a variety of reasons:

- **Data drift:** Over time, the distribution of data the model encounters in production can deviate from the data it was originally trained on, a phenomenon known as data drift. This can manifest as covariate drift (changes in the input features), label drift (changes in the distribution of the target variable), or data drift (changes in the relationship between input features and the target). These shifts can result from factors such as evolving user behavior or changes in the underlying system generating the data, and can impact model performance if not addressed.

- **Improved data:** Over time, the model may encounter additional or updated data in production that wasn't available during the initial training. Although this doesn't necessarily indicate a shift in the underlying data distribution (as in data drift), it is crucial to periodically retrain the model to incorporate this new data and improve its accuracy and effectiveness in capturing emerging patterns or trends.

- **Changing requirements:** The requirements for the model may change over time. For example, you may need to improve the model's accuracy, or you may need to add new features to the model. In these cases, you will need to retrain the model with new data or modify the model architecture.

- **Bias detection and mitigation:** As the model is used in production, it may become apparent that the model is biased in some way. This can happen because the data that the model was trained on or the way the model was designed had inherent biases.

- **Security vulnerabilities:** ML models can be vulnerable to security attacks. For example, an attacker could try to trick the model into making incorrect predictions. Security patches may cause a new version of the model to be generated.

An important best practice from DevOps is to have a single, well-defined release and deployment process for a system. This process includes strong quality gates, typically relying on an array of tests like those just described. Any change, no matter how small, must go through that process—including changes to configuration parameters, infrastructure code, AI models, and customization such as system prompts.

Some systems require a human to release the system to deployment for regulatory or legal reasons. One question that arises is the frequency of new releases. They can occur on a defined schedule or continuously.

6.5.1 Defined versus Continuous Releases

A key business decision is whether to deploy modifications according to a predefined schedule or as they are prepared.

Defined Releases

Historically, new versions of systems were released according to a schedule. A vendor would announce that a new release would be available on a fixed date and that the new release would contain bug fixes, security patches, and specified new or modified features. When that date arrived, the new version would be made available to the IT group of an organization. They would test the new release, shut down the existing version, and install the new version. Release schedules of weeks or months were common. Selected users or user organizations would be exposed to preview releases (beta releases) of the new version, and would provide feedback to the vendor to allow for improvements in the release prior to making the new version generally available.

A defined release schedule offers the following benefits:

- **Predictability:** All stakeholders know when a new release is coming. This allows developers to set their schedules, customers to anticipate changes, and IT organizations to plan their activities around the arrival of the new release. An IT organization, for example, may need to order new computers or servers to run a new system, which could be a time-consuming process.

- **Thorough testing:** The release schedule can be designed to allow for adequate testing and approval activities.

- **Software architecture independence:** The software architecture of the system and its new versions is not a factor in deploying a new release. A system can be designed using any software architectural style and then deployed as a unit when the pieces of the architecture are available and tested.

The drawbacks of defined releases have made this practice much rarer:

- **Time to market:** A new feature or bug fix is not available until the next scheduled release, possibly months away. This can give rise to out-of-cycle releases, as important bug fixes such as security patches or model updates are done independently of a release cycle. Out-of-cycle releases typically do not undergo the thorough testing of planned releases and consequently lead to higher error rates.

- **Schedule pressure:** As deadlines near, the stress on the development team increases. Deadlines tend to shorten because of time-to-market pressures, so teams are frequently under severe stress.

- **Schedule slippage:** Many different teams are involved in preparing a release, including those that produce dependencies. If any of these teams does not make its deadline, the whole release is delayed.

These drawbacks along with the emergence of microservices architecture led to the practices of continuous delivery and continuous deployment.

Continuous Deployment

Continuous deployment (CD) is the practice of automatically placing changes to the code base or model into production. It is essentially an extension of CI. When a developer commits code to a version control system, the continuous deployment pipeline (CDP) automatically builds the executable with the latest code and models, tests it, and—if all quality gates are passed successfully—deploys it into production.

Continuous delivery is closely related to CD, except that the final step—placing the system into production—is a business decision made and implemented by a human. One reaction to past financial scandals has been the establishment of mandates stating that a person must take responsibility for approving changes to a software system, at least in business contexts such as banking.

CD assumes that the deployable pieces are small—that is, microservices. A microservice is a deployable unit with a limited scope. This limited scope means that integration with other microservices is a matter of interface compatibility and not a matter of programming language, versions of dependent software, or technology used. Microservices that are stateless are particularly amenable to independent deployability, which can be achieved by pushing all state to either the client or the persistence layer of the microservices. An alternative approach is to cut the application into microservices "vertically," such that each microservice covers, for a small piece of functionality, everything from the top-level service interface to the client to the persistence layer. Again, independent deployability follows. AI models can be encapsulated as stateless services, as long as they are not updated on the fly and usage data is stored elsewhere. Vertical cutting of services might imply that a single microservice would be responsible for the UI, front end, back end, database, and ML model. This set of responsibilities might prove too much for a small team, in which case you should deviate from a pure vertical cutting logic and split these responsibilities into two or more services, with a small team devoted to each service.

Recall that ML models are packaged as containers or independent services. In either case, updates to an ML model can be placed into production through CD quite rapidly.

6.5.2 Deployment Patterns

The build step creates an executable image of a service and places it onto the staging server. If the reason for creating the build image is to update an existing version of a service, one consideration is whether it is acceptable to interrupt service so as to deploy the new version. If service is to be maintained throughout the update process, then the old version must be gracefully replaced by the new version so that service to the users continues. Uninterrupted service is complicated by the fact that multiple instances of the version to be replaced may exist because of the load on the service.

Two methods exist for updating an existing service without interruption: blue/green and rolling upgrade. We explore these methods by using the following example: Assume N instances (containers or virtual machines [VMs]) of Service A are to be replaced by N instances of service A'.

Blue/Green Deployment

Blue/green deployment is also called red/black deployment, or you could choose your own colors. This option allocates N new instances at once and populates each with Service A'. After the N instances of Service A' are installed, requests for the service are sent to Service A' and the N instances of Service A are drained and terminated.

Rolling Upgrade

A rolling upgrade replaces the instances of Service A with instances of Service A', one at a time. (In practice, you can replace more than one at a time, but only a small fraction is replaced in any single step.) The steps of the rolling upgrade are as follows:

1. Allocate a new instance.
2. Install Service A'.
3. Begin to direct requests to Service A'.
4. Drain traffic from one instance of Service A and then terminate that instance.
5. Repeat the above steps until all instances have been replaced.

Tradeoffs

There are two tradeoffs between the blue/green and rolling upgrade:

- **Financial:** The peak resource utilization for a blue/green approach is $2N$ instances, whereas the peak utilization for a rolling upgrade is $N + 1$ instances. Before cloud computing, an organization had to purchase physical computers to perform the upgrade. Most of the time, there was no upgrade in progress, and these additional computers went unused. This made the financial tradeoff clear, and the rolling upgrade was the standard approach. Now that computing resources are rented rather than purchased, the financial tradeoff is less compelling; even so, the rolling upgrade is still widely used.

- **Responding to errors:** Suppose you detect an error in Service A' when you deploy it. Despite all the testing you did in the development, integration, and staging environments, when your service is deployed to production, there may still be the rare occurrence of a latent error. If you are using blue/green deployment, by the time you discover an error in Service A', all of the instances of Service A may have been deleted and rolling back to Service A could take some time. Therefore, it is a good idea to observe Service A' in production before switching off Service A—but at some point you need to do that, and you might detect issues only later. In contrast, a rolling upgrade may allow you to discover an error in Service A' while instances of Service A are still available.

Canary and A/B Testing

Before rolling out a new release, it is prudent to test it in the production environment, albeit with a limited set of users. This is the function that beta testing used to serve; it is now done with canary testing. Canary testing is named after the practice from the 19th century of bringing canaries into coal mines. The coal-mining process can release gases that are both explosive and poisonous. Because canaries are more sensitive to these gases than humans, coal miners brought these little birds into the mines and observed them for signs of reaction to the gases. In essence, the canaries acted as early warning devices for the miners.

In modern software use, canary testing means to designate a set of testers who will use the new release. Sometimes, these testers are so-called power users or preview-stream users from outside your organization who are more likely to exercise code paths and edge cases that typical users may use less frequently. Another approach is to use testers from within the organization that is developing the software. For example, Google employees almost never use the release that external users would be using, but instead act as testers for upcoming releases. Once a system passes its canary tests, it is released more generally.

A/B testing is another form of live testing in production. It is used to compare two versions of a service, A and B, by performing an experiment with real users to determine which of the alternatives yields the best business results. More than two alternatives can be tested simultaneously as well. Other users receive a different treatment, B, from the remainder of the users. The test group may be relatively small, but should be of meaningful size. The difference can be minor, such as a change to the font size or form layout, or more significant. The different categories of users are compared based on a business metric, which is specific to the application and organization. The results of the A/B tests will govern the alternative to be chosen for full release.

A/B testing can also be used to perform experiments to find out which AI model version performs better. In such cases, the group sizes for A and B may be similar, to get good coverage of uses for the new version. Generally speaking, the new version bears the risk of having problems that are not known before the experiment, and as a consequence there is a risk of exposing users to these problems. This issue should be considered when choosing groups and group sizes. It can be managed by starting with a small group for the new version, which is observed closely. Then, if no major issues are detected, the group size is gradually increased.

Rollback

Not every new version works correctly. Use in production may uncover functional or quality issues that require a version to be replaced. Your service should have service level objectives (SLOs). Once it goes into production, you should monitor these SLOs to verify that they are being met. If you find that they are not being satisfied, you may wish to replace the release.

Two options exist for replacing a release: rollback and roll-forward.

- *Rollback* means replacing the current version with an earlier version. This may involve discontinuing the deployment of the new release and redeploying a previous release that is known to meet your quality goals. A feature toggle is a conditional depending on a global variable; it is used to differentiate between two code segments. These two code segments could be code that implements the old version and code that implements the new version. If a feature toggle is used for this purpose, rollback could also be accomplished by turning off the feature toggle used to activate the new release. Feature toggles can be used to address version skew, as we explain in the next subsection.

- *Roll-forward* means fixing the problem and generating a new version. This generally requires you to debug the problem and then be able to test and deploy the new version quickly.

In complex AI systems, sometimes neither rollback nor roll-forward is possible. This may be the case when the outdated version of the model no longer works sufficiently well, and the newly updated version has issues. Depending on your context, it may be prudent to have a fallback option, such as a fixed-rule–based system instead of an ML model. With this approach, the system can still perform core functions, albeit at a lower quality—a desirable property known as graceful degradation.

6.5.3 Version Skew

The purpose of CD is to speed up time to market. Together with the use of microservices architecture, CD allows a development team to deploy its new version, whether for a new feature, a bug fix, or an updated ML model, without coordinating with or waiting on other development teams. However, the lack of coordination among teams may lead to a phenomenon known as version skew.

Version skew is a situation in which different versions of the same software or its dependencies are running simultaneously within the same system. It arises when instances of services will be deployed independently and may become inconsistent—as the case with CD. Inconsistency may also arise when a service is updated but its clients have not yet been updated, and vice versa.

Two different types of version skew are possible: temporal inconsistency and interface mismatch.

Temporal Inconsistency

Temporal inconsistency occurs when two dependent entities are not updated at the same time. In that case, either two instances of a service are logically inconsistent, or a service is logically inconsistent with one of its clients, because one entity has been updated while the other has not.

For example, suppose there are two ML models. One is used to predict the value of an independent variable of the second model. These two models are packaged into one service. A client would make one call to the service to get the value of the independent variable and then pass this value back to the service on a second call. Suppose the update consists of combining these two models into one model. A client has been updated to assume one model, but the new model has yet to be deployed. In this case, the client will get an incorrect response to its request.

Interface Mismatch

Interface mismatch occurs when the interface of a service is modified. If the new version of the service is updated but the client has not yet been updated, then an error will occur. Similarly, if the client has been updated to assume the new interface but the service has not yet been updated, an error will occur.

Mitigating Version Skew

Both types of version skew can be mitigated by tagging messages with the expected version of the service. It then becomes the responsibility of the invoked service to correctly respond to the version number.

Every instance of a service should have a version number. This version number is assigned by the CI server, and it can be based on the version numbers of the elements of the service. A service can determine its version number through introspection. A client could ascertain the supported version number(s) through a query to the service.

The service is responsible for maintaining backward compatibility for a reasonable number of older versions. In other words, it should support requests intended for (at least some) early versions. Thus, in our temporal inconsistency example, it would maintain the two older models. In our interface mismatch example, it would support messages intended for an older version.

If a service receives a request for a version that is newer than the service's version, it should gracefully respond with an error indicating that it has not yet been updated. The client can either resubmit the request, as the new version of the service may have been installed on a different instance; delay before resubmitting the request; or perform the actions it would perform if it invoked a failed service.

Another method to mitigate version skew is based on feature toggles. This tactic is applicable when your organization maintains tight control over the client and the service—for example, when both roles are played by microservices in your architecture. Suppose you want to implement new feature X, which affects two microservices and the interface between them. You create a new, system-wide feature toggle "New_feature_X" and set it to false. Both services then implement their respective parts of the new feature on independent time scales. However, as long as the toggle remains false, the code related to the new feature will not be used. At some point, both services will have been updated. After sufficient testing, you can switch the toggle to true in production, and the code for the new feature will become active in both services.

Whichever way you decide to handle the implementation of the new version of the feature across services, at some point you must activate it and observe if it works in practice. Once you have gained confidence that you can leave the feature switched on, you should remove the old code and the mechanism for the switch in all affected parts of the code base. Old, inactive code that accidentally becomes activated after months or years can lead to unintended, even highly adverse effects, so it should be removed when no longer needed.

6.5.4 Matching the Model to Resources

When deploying a system, the resource choices that were specified in the architecture must be realized. These choices depend on the model size. FMs, in particular, can be heavyweight models. The weight of the model will determine the type of resources to which it can be deployed.

On the one hand, a lightweight narrow ML model typically has a relatively small number of parameters, making it suitable for edge devices. On the other hand, heavyweight FMs have a larger number of parameters, providing more powerful capabilities but requiring more computational resources. In terms of the location, a model can be deployed on a server or at the edge. When a model is deployed by a third party on a server, there is no maintenance cost for the users. Deploying a model at the edge brings the processing closer to the data source, reducing latency and allowing for real-time inference.

In terms of the serving mode, a model can be deployed either online or offline. Online deployment involves making API calls to a remote server for inference. This approach requires an active internet connection but allows for stronger model governance. The API can be a separate software module including additional governance and filtering mechanisms. In such a case, you define its external interface but it has knowledge of the saved model that enables it to interact with the model.

Packaging the API as a service and inside a container provides several advantages:

- It isolates the API service from the remainder of the system. This protects against vulnerabilities in other portions of the system.

- It allows the API to be deployed independently, such as on an edge device. The resource constraints that exist for the FM are not applicable to the API, although the API will need adequate bandwidth to communicate with the model portion.

Offline deployment enables the model to be served directly on a device without relying on internet connectivity, making it suitable for scenarios where internet access is limited or when real-time or offline inference is required. For example, PaLM 2[2] is available in a range of sizes: Gecko, Otter, Bison, and Unicorn. Gecko is a lightweight PaLM 2 that can be deployed on mobile devices and served offline. A number of manufacturers, including Apple,[3] Microsoft,[4] and Google,[5] are rolling out platforms that strengthen edge devices' capacities to perform local inference.

6.6 Operate, Monitor, and Analyze

Once a system has been deployed, it begins to provide service to users. Actually providing service entails several aspects that we will discuss in this section. During operation, you collect data, which you analyze to inform the next round of design and development. We begin with monitoring.

6.6.1 Monitoring

An AI system often has a great many services and connections among its elements. To improve efficiency, troubleshoot failures, and sanitize both inputs and outputs, it is important to be able to observe the resource usage and activities of the various services that constitute the system. This observation is done by monitoring the activities. We discuss the quality attribute of observability in more detail in Chapter 11.

Monitoring data comes from three sources: the infrastructure, the system code, and the logs produced by the services. The infrastructure gathers utilization measures for VMs and containers. These utilization measures are metrics of resource usage—CPU, I/O, network, and memory. The system code should record application-specific metrics, such as the number of active sessions and new accounts created. These metrics can be collected and managed through the same tools as the infrastructure metrics. Logs are generated by a service and placed in a known location on the local file system; from there, they are typically collected and forwarded to a log database/

---

2. https://ai.google/discover/palm2

3. Apple Intelligence: https://www.apple.com/apple-intelligence/

4. Microsoft Copilot+ PCs: https://blogs.microsoft.com/blog/2024/05/20/introducing-copilot-pcs/

5. https://blog.google/products/pixel/google-pixel-9-new-ai-features/

system for processing. Logs are used to record service-specific information. In AI systems, logs and metrics include aspects such as model accuracy, data drift, ethical issues, and broader societal impact. If this information is not recorded, it will be lost.

Logs and metrics should be moved to a database in a monitoring system, where the information can be used for three purposes:

- **Generating alerts:** Measurements—in particular, metrics—are used to generate alerts that indicate a serious problem with a system in operation. This constitutes an incident that often requires a fast response.

- **Forensics:** When a problem has occurred, it must be identified. Logs collected by the system in response to events are used to identify the problem.

- **Analysis:** Analysis is performed both in real time and at a later time. The real-time analysis determines whether the system is meeting pre-defined standards for performance, both efficiency and accuracy. If the standards are not met, an alert is generated. The analysis performed after the fact can be more wide-ranging—for example, for data drift, biases, and compliance with various regulations.

Selected monitoring data, especially data indicating shifts in data patterns or emerging trends, is channeled back into the feature store. This enables the refinement of features used in ML models, ensuring they remain relevant and effective. The feature store, in turn, feeds this refined data back into the training pipeline, leading to model upgrades.

6.6.2 Incidents

An incident is an event that could lead to loss of, or disruption to, an organization's operations, services, or functions. In software terms, an incident is either a logical problem, an efficiency problem, an availability problem, or a security problem. Logical incidents include deviation from the predefined standards.

The monitoring systems have rules that examine the monitored data and decide whether to generate an alert. Alerts are sent to a first responder, whose responsibilities are both immediate and delayed. The immediate response is to ensure the system continues to be operational; this is done in real time when the alert is received. The delayed response is to work with the software developers or model developers to determine the root cause of the problem and prevent it from recurring.

The role of first responder will vary depending on your organizational structure. Site reliability engineers are designated first responders in some organizations. They constitute a separate organizational unit and may be tasked with supporting multiple systems. Other organizations task developers and AI engineers with being first responders.

In any case, first responders are on duty for designated periods, night and day. The specifics of the shifts of a first responder will vary depending on the organization. A typical shift might be 24 hours, and each individual might be on duty once a week.

6.6.3 Data Drift

Models are trained on data that represents the world at the time of the model's creation. Of course, the world evolves, and it may eventually drift away from the model, even to the point where the model's predictions are not reflective of real-world situations. The disruptions that occurred in supply chains during the COVID-19 pandemic are an example of a radical change that could affect a model, but others are more subtle.

Some specific techniques to detect drift are highlighted here:

- **Monitoring model performance metrics:** Regularly track key performance metrics relevant to your specific application. These metrics might be accuracy, precision, recall, F1 score, or custom metrics, depending on your needs. Sudden drops in these metrics can indicate potential drift.

- **Statistical tests:** Utilize statistical tests like the Kolmogorov–Smirnov (KS) test or the chi-squared test to compare the distribution of incoming data with the distribution of the training data. Significant deviations suggest data drift.

- **Control charts:** Create control charts to visualize the trends of your performance metrics over time. Control charts allow you to set upper and lower bounds based on historical performance. Points falling outside these bounds can indicate a shift in the data.

- **Concept drift detection algorithms:** Specialized algorithms can be employed to explicitly detect concept drift. These algorithms can continuously monitor data streams and raise alerts when they detect significant changes in the data distribution. Some examples include early drift detection (EDD) and the cumulative sum (CUSUM) technique.

One issue with monitoring the accuracy of a model is that recognition of the ground truth can be delayed. For instance, consider an AI model designed to predict the long-term environmental impact of a new infrastructure project, such as a dam or a highway. The true environmental consequences, encompassing changes in local ecosystems, biodiversity, and geological stability, may become fully apparent only years, or even decades, after the project's completion. Using a proxy measure, if one can be found, is a technique for dealing with delayed ground truth.

6.6.4 Dynamic Model Updating

Several types of dynamic model updates can occur while a model is in production. One type is online learning, where the model's weights are continuously updated in real time as new data comes in. Another method involves deploying small, incremental updates or patches to the model. Although these techniques allow for rapid adaptation to new data, they come with significant tradeoffs.

In some cases, dynamic updates can bypass the standard quality assurance (QA) processes, as the model's parameters are adjusted on the fly without going through the full testing and validation pipeline. This can lead to concerns about the reliability and stability of the model, as well as the potential for unintended consequences in production.

In contrast, other dynamic update approaches, such as those employed in CD frameworks, can ensure that new updates go through the entire QA process before being put into production. This allows for quick deployment while still maintaining rigorous quality control.

We advise caution when dynamically updating a model in production without the full QA process. Such out-of-cycle updates can circumvent many of the quality control and logging measures included in the standard deployment pipeline. This can result in infrastructure drift, where the production environment becomes misaligned with its original configuration, and also increases the attack surface from a security perspective.

6.6.5 Chaos Engineering

Chaos engineering is the practice of conducting experiments on distributed systems to build confidence in the system's capability to perform reliably under turbulent production conditions. In chaos engineering, an experiment (or test) deliberately introduces a failure into the system. A hypothesis is developed about what should happen, which defines the passing conditions for the test. The actual response of the system to the failure then determines whether the test passes or fails. Chaos engineering depends on having sufficient observability into your system to be able to detect (and then diagnose and fix) a system failure. It also depends on having an appropriate process to ensure that the effects of the test are controlled.

The test can involve data, the model, or the infrastructure. The various categories of tests and some examples of them are listed here:

1. Data tests:
   - Data poisoning: Injecting adversarial or corrupted data into the model's training or serving pipeline.
   - Data drift: Simulating changes in the distribution of real-world data over time to ensure the model remains accurate.
   - Data outage: Testing how the system copes with temporary or complete data loss.
2. Model tests:
   - Model drift: Monitoring model accuracy metrics over time to detect gradual degradation.
   - Model version mismatch: Introducing inconsistencies between different versions of the model deployed in production.
   - Feature ablation: Removing crucial features from the model's input to assess its robustness and level of dependence.
3. Infrastructure tests:
   - Resource constraints: Simulating limited CPU, memory, or network bandwidth to evaluate system efficiency under resource scarcity.
   - Dependency failures: Introducing controlled outages or errors in external services the AI system relies on.
   - Deployment failures: Testing rollback and recovery procedures in case of deployment issues.

6.6.6 Analysis

When analyzing AI systems in the life cycle, the goal is to understand when and how to best change the system—that is, to inform the next iteration of the design and development activities. Such data-driven decision making is a great tool to optimize systems. However, you should know when *not* to use it: You need a vision of the future state of the system, and data-based analysis will often not give you that. Generally speaking, for understanding user behavior and optimizing a system, data-based analysis is very useful. To analyze data, your system has to emit the data, and you have to collect and process it to get useful insights.

There is typically a lot of overlap between data collected for monitoring (discussed earlier in this section) and data collected for analysis, and much has been written about analysis for non-AI systems. A few aspects that are specific to AI systems are described here.

First, engineers must consider the interdependencies and data flows between the AI and the non-AI portions of the system. This involves assessing how AI decisions impact traditional components, and vice versa, as well as examining data quality and compatibility across the system.

As mentioned earlier, you should monitor for concept drift: Degrading AI model performance may require switching to alternative models or training. Additional aspects relevant for retraining involve tracking the amount and quality of new data being collected during operation. Such metrics help determine when sufficient novel data has accumulated to warrant model updates. The frequency of retraining or system changes should be based on a combination of factors, including drift detection, performance degradation, and the availability of enough new data. Establishing thresholds for these metrics allows for informed decision making about when to initiate retraining or system modifications, balancing the need for up-to-date models with the costs and potential disruptions associated with frequent updates.

6.7 Summary

The life cycle discussed in this chapter starts with the design phase. Microservices architecture–based designs allow for speedy development and deployment. Modifiability and observability can be achieved more easily if they are considered in the initial system design.

Following development, an executable is built by a CI server. Included in the build are AI models packaged as modules. They are integrated with the non-AI modules as well as with libraries and dependencies.

Once the executable is built, it is subjected to a variety of tests. Ideally, these tests should be automated. The tests include both functional tests and quality tests. Although the AI models should have been tested during their development, the system tests examine how these models perform when integrated with the remainder of the system.

When the system has been tested, it can be deployed. CD is an automated process that leads directly to deployment. Deployment can be done as either a rolling upgrade or a blue/green deployment. Canary testing is the process of deploying the system to a subset of users to help detect problems before the system is rolled out to all users.

Having an automated CI/CD pipeline and implementing a single release process with strong quality gates are key to achieving high quality and speed simultaneously. Some authors advocate live updates to AI models, but we do not recommend this practice given the risks posed by changes to the production system that do not go through the QA phase of the standard release process.

During operations, activities are monitored. This monitoring information is used to generate alerts or as the basis for further analysis.

6.8 Discussion Questions

1. Should a system be required to pass all of its tests during the testing phase before being placed into production? Why or why not?

2. The system test stage repeats the unit tests performed on the AI models and the non-AI modules. Why?

3. Chaos engineering affects instances in production. Discuss the pros and cons of performing chaos engineering.

6.9 For Further Reading

For a discussion of the DevOps life cycle for non-AI systems, see *Deployment and Operations for Software Engineers* by Len Bass and John Klein [Bass 19].

For more DevOps knowledge, see our earlier book: *DevOps: A Software Architect's Perspective* by Bass et al. [Bass 15].

The classic source of design patterns, like the Strategy pattern, is *Design Patterns: Elements of Reusable Object-Oriented Software* by Erich Gamma, Richard Helm, Ralph Johnson, and John Vlissides [Gamma 95].

C. Huyen's *Designing Machine Learning Systems: An Iterative Process for Production-Ready Applications* [Huyen 22] is a good source for designing AI systems for production.

You can find more insights on architecting ML systems in *Software Architecture Challenges for ML Systems* by Lewis et al. [Lewis 21].

For industry insights into operating AI systems, see *Operationalizing Machine Learning: An Interview Study* by Shankar et al. [Shankar 22].

For industry insights on sharing software package information across the supply chain and its relevance to AI systems, see *An Empirical Study on Software Bill of Materials: Where We Stand and the Road Ahead* by Xia et al. [Xia 24B].

Two AI incident databases can be found here: https://oecd.ai/en /incidents and https://incidentdatabase.ai/.

7

Reliability

I am a man of my word . . . and that word is "unreliable."
—Demetri Martin

RELIABILITY REFERS TO the consistent and accurate performance of a system over time, under various conditions, and without failure. It encompasses the system's ability to produce correct and trustworthy outputs, even when faced with unexpected inputs or changes in its environment.

7.1 Fundamental Concepts

Different facets of the definition of reliability are worth emphasizing. In this section, we identify "specified operating conditions," "despite unexpected inputs," and "changes in the environment." We also define "fault, error, and failure" as a means for framing the discussion.

7.1.1 Under Specified Operating Conditions

In the traditional sense, reliability is the probability that a system will perform in a satisfactory manner for a given period when it is used under the specified operating conditions. This definition underscores the importance of the specified conditions—operating within its intended environment, not under all possible conditions.

In the field of AI, the concept of reliability is broadened to include a model's capacity to perform effectively when introduced to new data. This new data should either fall within the distribution of the training data or be similar to it, essentially ensuring it is not out of distribution (OOD). Ideally, the training data will represent the real-world scenario the model is intended to address. There's an underlying assumption that the model is capable of generalizing well from its training. This means the model should avoid overfitting—it ought to discern and learn the fundamental patterns in the training data without becoming excessively tailored to the specific examples it was trained on. Therefore, an AI model's reliability is anchored not just in its accuracy, but also in its ability to uphold this level of accuracy across various situations that resemble or align closely with its training data—a key aspect of generalization.

Consider an AI system designed for predicting housing prices based on various factors such as location, size, and amenities. If it was trained on a diverse set of housing data from urban areas, its reliability is measured by how well it predicts prices for new urban housing listings that share characteristics with the training data—an illustration of generalization within the distribution. However, if the same system is applied to rural housing data, a scenario it wasn't trained for, it may struggle. This challenge falls more into the realm of robustness—a different facet from reliability, but equally important in the broader context of AI applications.

7.1.2 Operating Despite Unexpected Inputs

The system should continue to function even in scenarios that are not considered part of its normal operations. In the context of AI, this means that the model should be able to process a diverse array of inputs effectively. This includes handling OOD data and adversarial data, maintaining an acceptable level of accuracy, resisting manipulative attempts, and consistently producing stable outputs. This aspect is often called robustness.

7.1.3 Operating Despite Changes in the Environment

A system should be able to withstand major disruptions while staying within acceptable degradation parameters and recovering within an acceptable time frame. In the context of AI models, this is characterized by the model's intrinsic ability to continue functioning effectively amidst significant disruptions. This aspect is often called resilience.

7.1.4 Faults, Failures, and Errors

Algirdas Avižienis and his co-authors provide us with a vocabulary and a way of thinking about reliability. They differentiate among failures, faults, and errors.

A failure is the deviation of the system from its specification, where that deviation is externally visible. Determining that a failure has occurred requires some external observer in the environment. A failure must be externally visible. Some failures can be tolerated as long as they do not last too long. Requirements that allow for failure take the following form: The system shall be available for operation xx% of the time [possibly during specific periods]. 1 − xx% is the percentage of time a system has to respond to failure and resume normal operation.

A failure's cause is called a fault. A fault can be either internal or external to the system under consideration. Faults can occur if they are not externally visible.

Intermediate states between the occurrence of a fault and the occurrence of a failure are called errors.

We begin our discussion by seeking to prevent faults.

7.2 Preventing Faults

Fault prevention in AI systems depends partly on the model choice and its preparation, partly on architectural choices, and partly on process activities.

7.2.1 Model Choice and Preparation

Having a training dataset that represents the distribution of actual data will enable the model to produce reliable outputs. Of course, there are caveats to this assertion. Some models are inherently more robust to distribution shifts, or *drift*, especially if they have been designed and trained with such scenarios in mind. Models with good generalization properties, such as regularized linear models, decision trees with pruning, and deep neural networks with appropriate depths and widths, can provide reliability. Balancing model complexity with the available data and task requirements is important to avoid overfitting and ensure reliability.

Techniques such as domain adaptation, feature normalization, and regularization can make models less sensitive to minor changes in data distribution. Furthermore, models that are trained on a diverse and comprehensive dataset that captures a wide range of scenarios within the problem domain may inherently handle moderate distribution shifts better, as they have "seen" a variety of data patterns. With more significant distribution shifts, however, even robust models might struggle. These shifts can introduce new patterns or data characteristics that the model has never encountered, and thus it may not be able to generalize effectively. In such cases, updating or retraining the model with new data that represents the shifted distribution could be necessary.

Some other techniques can also be used, based on context, to enhance the reliability of the output of a model:

- **Ensemble methods:** Ensemble techniques such as bagging, boosting, and stacking combine multiple models to make predictions. By leveraging the collective knowledge of different models, ensembles can provide more robust and reliable predictions compared to individual models.

- **Hyperparameter tuning:** Systematic hyperparameter tuning, using techniques such as grid search, random search, and Bayesian optimization, help find the optimal combination of hyperparameters that maximize model performance and robustness. Properly tuned hyperparameters contribute to model stability and reliability.

- **Adaptive performance with prioritization:** During disruptions, a resource-aware AI model might adapt by prioritizing its core functionalities. For example, in autonomous driving, the AI model performs various tasks such as navigation, obstacle detection, and passenger comfort management. During a major disruption such as heavy fog, sensor malfunction, or low battery power in an electric vehicle, the system might prioritize obstacle detection and vehicle control over navigation and comfort management.

- **Uncertainty quantification:** A resilient model, when experiencing disruption, may continue to provide outputs but with a quantifiable level of uncertainty. This approach is more informative than outright refusal to provide an answer or giving overly confident responses. For instance, in weather prediction models, if crucial sensor data becomes unavailable during a storm, the model might still offer forecasts but with a stated confidence range. This information communicates the increased uncertainty resulting from the sensor data disruption.

7.2.2 Data Quality, Model Training, and Testing

Like all quality attributes, data quality can, and often should be, improved through cleaning and consistent formatting. In addition, some techniques can enhance reliability during training and testing:

- **Data augmentation:** Data augmentation techniques such as rotation, scaling, cropping, and noise injection can further increase data diversity and improve the model's ability to generalize to unseen scenarios, enhancing reliability and robustness. Seeding the training datasets with values that may be outside of the normal distribution, but which correct for biases in the training data, will also make the model more reliable when it sees out of distribution data.

- **Curriculum learning:** By organizing the training data into a curriculum, starting with simpler examples and gradually increasing complexity, the model can learn more effectively. This approach helps the model build a strong foundation and generalize better, leading to improved reliability.

- **Regularization techniques:** One technique for regularization is dropout, which randomly disables neurons in a neural network during training, preventing over-reliance on specific features. Other regularization methods, such as L1/L2 regularization, weight decay, and early stopping, help control model complexity and mitigate overfitting. These techniques promote more generalizable and reliable models.

- **Adversarial training:** Incorporating adversarial examples during training helps the model learn to be resilient against malicious or perturbed inputs. When the model is exposed to carefully crafted adversarial examples, it becomes more robust and reliable in handling unexpected or adversarial scenarios. One type of testing specific to both reliability and security is adversarial testing. Test cases can replicate some of the attack techniques used in attempts to confuse the model and, therefore, invalidate its outputs. These techniques include adding small, imperceptible noise to images, modifying text with synonyms or slightly changing the wording of a sentence, and introducing subtle variations in data points. Fuzz testing is the pre-AI term used for these types of techniques.

- **Holdout validation:** Holdout validation is achieved by splitting the dataset into training, validation, and test sets to evaluate the model's performance on unseen data. The validation set is used for model selection and hyperparameter tuning, whereas the test set serves as an unbiased evaluation of the final model's performance.

- **Stress testing:** Pushing the model to its limits with extreme or unexpected inputs helps assess its ability to handle high volumes of data or unusual scenarios. This evaluates the model's resilience under pressure. Stress testing can include testing the model's performance on noisy data, corrupted inputs, or edge cases to identify potential failure modes or vulnerabilities.

7.2.3 Feature Engineering

During feature engineering, some techniques specific for enhancing reliability may be used:

- **Feature importance analysis:** Identifies the most relevant features for the target variable. This can help remove redundant or irrelevant features that might introduce noise and reduce model reliability.

- **Lineage tracking tools:** Utilize tools to track the lineage of data items through data ingestion and contribution to features. When a fault is detected, knowing the lineage that led to the fault will help recover from it.

7.2.4 Circuit Breaker

In addition to the choice and preparation of the model, we can identify an architectural pattern to prevent repeated faults. A circuit breaker is designed to prevent the issue of repeatedly calling known erroneous components. Once the component or AI model has failed several times, the circuit breaker is activated, preventing further calls to that component or AI model. Instead of repeatedly attempting and failing, the system immediately returns an error response, speeding up error handling. For example, in an AI model-powered recommendation system, suppose the model responsible for generating product recommendations fails multiple times. The circuit breaker will halt further attempts to use that model and return a fallback set of popular products instead, ensuring the user still receives recommendations while the issue is resolved.

7.2.5 Placement of Responsibilities

In an AI system, both ML model components and non-AI components may begin with their designed functionalities and responsibilities. As models grow and evolve over the lifetime of a system, however, the model may begin to assume responsibilities that were originally assigned to non-AI components. The architecture should clearly separate which responsibilities are assigned to the model and which to the non-AI components. Some aspects of placement of responsibilities are highlighted here:

- The placement of reliability, robustness, and resilience mechanisms must be determined—that is, whether they should beat the model level or the system level.

- Deciding whether an AI model should be cognizant of its system-level operational environment, in addition to its primary problem domain, is a strategic choice. Typically, AI models are trained to focus solely on the problem they are solving, without awareness of system-level factors such as fluctuating computational resources, potential attacks, or other disruptions. The decision to expand a model's awareness to include these operational aspects, beyond the core problem it addresses, involves weighing various advantages and disadvantages. For instance, in a traffic management scenario, the model could be developed to either solely process traffic data or additionally be attuned to varying system constraints and external disruptions.

Overlap in responsibilities may be due to the evolution and growth of the model. In cases where the architect cannot make a clear distinction between responsibilities that are assigned to the model and those that are assigned to non-AI components, assign them to both and implement a voting mechanism as described later in this chapter.

7.2.6 Failure Mode and Effects Analysis and Fault Tree Analysis

Failure mode and effects analysis (FMEA) and fault tree analysis (FTA) are useful for identifying potential failure points in systems and understanding their impact on the system. On the one hand, FTA offers a methodical approach to trace the root causes of failures. On the other hand, FMEA helps evaluate the severity and likelihood of different failures, enabling developers to prioritize and implement effective risk mitigation strategies.

7.3 Detecting Faults

Between the occurrence of a fault and a failure, the system is in an error mode. The architecture must be designed with components that recognize problems with reliability. In particular, the architecture must recognize either total failure of components or more subtle failures of the computations performed by the components or the model.

Components, whether AI or non-AI, can either totally fail or produce results that are questionable. Total failure is discussed first.

7.3.1 Total Failure

If a component has totally failed, the failure must be recognized. In a distributed system, all communication is carried out via messages. Total failure of a component means that the component does not respond or send messages. Thus, the basic technique for recognizing total failure is to use health checking methods.

Health checks involve two components: (1) the component that may or may not have failed (the monitored component) and (2) a monitoring component. Two forms of health checks are ping/echo and heartbeat.

Ping/echo places the initiative with the monitoring component. It sends a message to the monitored component, and the monitored component must respond within a set time period. If the monitored component does not respond within the designated time frame, then the monitoring component will have detected a failure. In most cases, the monitoring component will try several times before deciding that the monitored component has failed because the delay in response may be caused by transient factors.

The heartbeat mechanism places the initiative with the monitored component. Periodically (e.g., every 10 seconds), it sends a message to the monitoring component; this message indicates that the monitored component is still active. Again, the monitoring component may wait for several heartbeats to be missed before deciding that the monitored component has failed.

7.3.2 Questionable Output

Questionable output from a component or a model is more subtle and more difficult to detect. First, the possibility that an output from a component is questionable must be recognized during the design process. Any computation that has uncertainty associated with it could be considered questionable. Sensors, for example, are one type of data source that is associated with uncertainty; model predictions are another. Redundancy and a voting mechanism (described next) are mechanisms to provide more assurance to questionable outputs. Guardrails (discussed in Chapter 4, Foundation Models) are another mechanism to detect and manage questionable outputs.

7.3.3 Detecting Errors during Operations

Continually monitoring both input data and outputs for anomalies and OOD data will detect errors during operations. Some techniques to accomplish this are described next:

- Monitor metrics such as accuracy, precision, recall, F1 score, or custom metrics relevant to your application. Custom metrics might include user feedback on responses from AI models. Such monitoring helps identify performance degradation over time. These metrics should include measures of infrastructure health, such as failure of a component or violation of preset thresholds for utilization measures.

- Set up alerts that are triggered when these metrics deviate significantly from established baselines. This allows for early detection of potential issues. Alerts should be triggered for both efficiency issues (e.g., latency and throughput) and accuracy issues (e.g., missing values, outliers, or data type inconsistencies).

- Utilize techniques such as LIME and SHAP to understand the model's decision-making process. This can pinpoint features contributing to unreliable predictions.

- Track data distribution statistics over time. Significant changes (drift) might indicate the model is no longer aligned with real-world data, impacting reliability. Techniques like the Kolmogorov–Smirnov (KS) test can be used for this purpose.

In addition, multiple processes and techniques can be used to enhance reliability:

- **Chaos engineering:** Introduce faults and failures deliberately during testing to ensure that the model can handle disruptions in production. Observe whether the system handles them in an acceptable way—for example, within the targeted time frames for self-adaptation/self-healing.

- **Multiple contingency plans:** Establishing a range of contingency plans is crucial for AI systems to handle diverse operational scenarios effectively. These plans include model rollback and fallback strategies. Model rollback involves reverting to a previous version of a model if a recent update causes problems. In contrast, fallback strategies might involve switching to an alternative method (e.g., a rule-based system or a simpler, time-tested model) that avoids the problem caused by the update, even if it offers lower performance on average. This is particularly vital when dealing with complex or uncertain situations. For example, in the event of system outages or significant data anomalies, an AI-driven traffic management system might switch to predefined rule-based controls or a simpler traffic model.

- **Proxy measures for delayed ground truth:** When immediate ground truth is unavailable, developing proxy measures is crucial for real-time validation. For instance, consider a model designed to predict which consumers are most likely to default on their credit card debt. In this scenario, a practical proxy metric could be a late payment. This measure offers an early indication of potential default risk, serving as a near-term proxy to validate the model's predictions about longer-term credit default risks.

7.4 Recovering from Faults

Once a fault is detected (during operations) or suspected (during design), then mechanisms for managing it must be built into the architecture. Two such mechanisms are introducing redundancy and handling errors appropriately. These and their respective subcategories are shown in Figure 7.1.

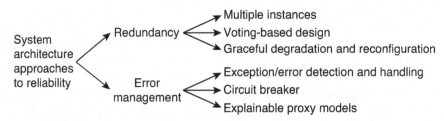

Figure 7.1 *System architecture approaches to reliability.*

7.4.1 Redundancy

Redundancy has multiple uses. As shown in Figure 7.1, it is used to manage failure, to provide alternatives in cases where a decision is not clear-cut, and to provide secondary alternatives when a primary alternative is not responding. We discuss multiple instances first.

Multiple Instances

One approach to providing redundancy is to maintain multiple instances of components, including model components. Then, if a component fails, the backup can be placed into production quickly. Specific responsibilities that are associated with having multiple instances include the following:

- Synchronizing state
- Detecting failure
- Invoking the backup
- Cleaning up the failed instance

Voting-Based Design

This approach involves combining outputs from multiple sources to enhance decision-making reliability. These sources can be from multiple AI models, from multiple components, or from AI and non-AI sources. Voting-based design requires an algorithm that will either aggregate the outputs or choose one over the other. By aggregating model outputs, the system can mitigate the risk of relying on a single model. For example, in a healthcare application, diagnoses from several AI models can be aggregated with traditional diagnostic algorithms to improve the accuracy and robustness of medical assessments.

Graceful Degradation and Reconfiguration

Systems designed to degrade gracefully can continue providing essential services during major disruptions. This can be achieved by isolating critical functions from noncritical ones. In a cloud-based service, for instance, nonessential features might be temporarily disabled to preserve core functionalities during a server outage.

7.4.2 Managing Error

Developing a system-wide error handling strategy that accounts for both AI model errors and traditional component failures is challenging, particularly given the probabilistic nature of AI results. For example, in an autonomous vehicle system, errors from sensory inputs must be handled alongside AI prediction uncertainties. Errors must be detected and either repaired or prevented. Furthermore, errors should be explainable. These are the topics we take up in this section.

Error Detection and Exception Handling

Error detection mechanisms should be built into the architecture. Error detection at both the model and system levels can be achieved by setting thresholds for anomaly detection. The point here is that these mechanisms must be built into the architecture. Associated with the detection of an error is the handling of that error. Activating a circuit breaker is one mechanism to perform these tasks.

Explainable Proxy Models

For complex models whose predictions are difficult to explain, having a proxy model that operates in parallel with the complex model will help in debugging errors and, possibly, in regulatory compliance. Again, such models are invoked during operation but must be designed into the architecture.

7.5 Summary

Ensuring reliability means managing faults. Faults can be prevented—but if not prevented, they should be detected and prevented from turning into failures.

Preventing faults depends on the model choice and training. Architectural mechanisms such as circuit breakers and placement of responsibilities will also help to prevent faults.

Detecting faults can be done by recognizing total failure or by detecting questionable output.

Recovering from a fault can be accomplished by utilizing redundancy or managing the error condition that results from a fault.

7.6 Discussion Questions

1. How does reliability trade off against other quality attributes?

2. Research the role of site reliability engineers (SREs). How would an SRE diagnose a problem with the OOD data?

3. Perform an FMEA for an AI system with which you are familiar. How would you prevent the potential errors you detected?

7.7 For Further Reading

The distinctions among faults, errors, and failures are described in Avižienis et al. [Avižienis 04].

Other readings about reliability concepts include Kazman [Kazman 22], Kläs and Jöckel [Kläs 20], and Kläs and Vollmer [Kläs 18].

8
Performance

You can't manage what you don't measure.
                                    —Peter Drucker

IN SOFTWARE ENGINEERING, *performance* is typically taken to mean computation efficiency, which includes speed and scalability. How fast do computations execute? How much of the requisite resources, such as CPUs and energy, do they need? In AI, *performance* is typically taken to mean "how accurate are the model outputs?" In many ways, these two interpretations of performance are contradictory. Achieving accuracy frequently requires more computation. Achieving higher efficiency, but operating with the same resources, typically reduces accuracy. Which is more important is a decision that drives the tradeoffs that the designer must make. In this chapter, we discuss these two interpretations of performance.

Figure 8.1 depicts the fundamental concepts of both efficiency and accuracy.

8.1 Efficiency

Efficiency refers to the ability of a software system to utilize resources effectively while maintaining acceptable speed and responsiveness, in addition to fulfilling its functional requirements.

8.1.1 Fundamental Concepts of Efficiency

Throughput
Throughput is the capacity of a system to process a certain number of tasks or transactions within a specific time frame. It's a measure of how much work a system can handle, typically quantified as transactions per second, requests per second, or similar units. Applying this definition to a large language

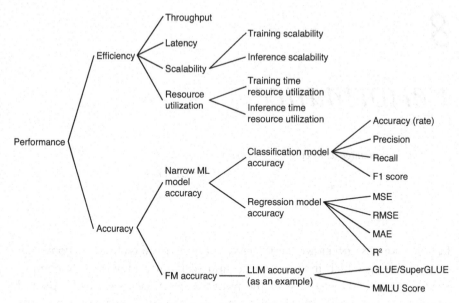

Figure 8.1 *Fundamental concepts of performance.*

model (LLM) API, throughput refers to the number of requests or tokens (e.g., text processing, language generation) the API can generate per second across the number of users and total requests.

Latency

Latency is the time it takes for a system to complete a single task or transaction. It's a measure of response time, from the initiation of a request to the delivery of the result. Applying this definition to an LLM API, latency is the overall time it takes for the model to generate the full response for a user. This includes the time to first token (TTFT), which measures how quickly the user starts seeing the model's output after entering their query, and the time per output token (TPOT), which measures the time to generate each output token. Latency can be calculated as the sum of TTFT and the product of TPOT and the number of tokens to be generated.

Scalability

Scalability is a software system's ability to handle increasing workloads without degrading performance or requiring architecture redesign. In AI systems, scalability includes two concepts: training scalability and inference scalability. Training scalability refers to the ability to effectively and efficiently train AI models as training task size (e.g., number of model parameters, data volume, and computational resources) increases. Inference scalability is the ability to effectively and efficiently deploy and operate AI systems for inference as the size of the models or the number of real-time requests increases.

Resource Utilization

Resource utilization involves how efficiently a system uses its computational resources, such as CPU, memory, and I/O operations. In AI systems, resource utilization is an aspect that differs significantly for the training phase versus the inference phase, as each phase comes with its own set of demands and constraints.

- **Training time resource utilization:** During the training of an AI model, the focus is on the effective use of computational resources such as CPU and GPU power, memory, and storage. This phase could require significant resources, particularly for complex models. For example, training an LLM demands extensive computational power and memory due to the size and complexity of the model and the vast amount of data processed. Using resources valued at $100 million or more for training a single, state-of-the-art LLM is not uncommon these days.

- **Inference time resource utilization:** At the inference stage, the model's efficiency in making predictions, generating outputs, or processing new information becomes relevant. In resource-rich environments (e.g., cloud and server-based systems), the primary concern often revolves around cost efficiency. Even minor inefficiencies in resource usage can lead to substantial costs when scaled. In contrast, in edge AI scenarios (e.g., deployment on personal computers, mobile devices, or embedded systems), the limitation is often the available computational resources. Here, the challenge is to run the AI models, possibly including complex ones like LLMs, within these resource constraints.

Thus, performance efficiency in AI is a multifaceted concern. Multiple metrics may be used to measure this efficiency, including the following:

- **Training time:** The duration required to train the AI model, which can be substantial for complex models.

- **Inference time (latency):** The time taken by the model to make a prediction or respond to a new input.

- **Model size:** A critical factor, especially for edge AI. Smaller models are generally faster and more resource-efficient—albeit, typically at the cost of lower output quality.

- **Energy efficiency:** The energy consumption for performing tasks, a key consideration in mobile or edge AI applications.

8.1.2 Approaches to Improving Efficiency

The efficiency of a system is a function of mapping the resource needs of the system, both computational and network, to the resources provided to the system. Improving the efficiency, then, is a matter of reducing the resource requirements or utilizing more powerful resources. Of course, resources cost money, so an additional constraint is the budget available for the resources.

Lower latency or higher throughput is not always necessary. The system will have requirements that specify the expected load and the expected values of latency and throughput. All that is necessary from an efficiency perspective is to satisfy those requirements. For example, a 200-millisecond delay appears instantaneous to a human for most interactions. Designing an interactive system to respond with a latency less than 200 milliseconds is unnecessary, and likely more complex and difficult to understand.

We organize our discussion of approaches to improving efficiency by following the life cycle. Hence, we begin with architecture design.

Architecture Design

Many design techniques exist to control resource usage. Those relevant to the AI portion of the system include techniques to reduce network latency:

- Use an interface style like GraphQL to reduce the communication needs between edge devices such as smartphones and their supporting data centers.

- Placing containers that communicate frequently on the same runtime engine will eliminate the need for communications to pass over networks. Similarly, placing VMs that communicate frequently on the same host will prevent communications from going outside that host. VMs allocated on the same rack will have faster communications than if they are placed on different racks or in different data centers.

- Caching is a technique for reducing communication requirements. A cache can store values in a service that would otherwise be retrieved through communication requests. Memory accesses are much faster than network accesses. For example, IP addresses can be cached to avoid a discovery process involving network access. Outputs of a model with respect to particular values of independent variables can be cached to avoid recalculating them. However, caches can get stale and outdated if the original information is modified and the cache does not reflect it. Maintaining consistency between a cache and the underlying data sources must be considered in the design.

- Edge devices are increasingly being equipped with special chips for AI computation. These devices include, among others, popular mobile phones from Apple, Google, and Samsung, as well as Windows and Mac desktop and laptop computers. If the edge devices available to a system possess such resources, the architecture design can make use of them by running suitable workloads and AI model inference directly on these edge devices.

A system can be designed to reduce resource requirements dynamically by using a mode switcher that lets you flip between different functionalities or levels of autonomy within the system. One functionality that can be modified by a mode switcher is the use or choice of an AI model. For example, a foundation model (FM) may provide some functionality but at an unacceptable efficiency. Degrading the functionality provided by the FM to a simpler narrow machine learning (ML) model may reduce the resource requirements. A monitoring component that is aware of the different possible models and the resource requirements of each can act as a mode switcher. Additionally, another FM can serve as a software connector—that is, as a model switcher that makes decisions about the use or selection of an AI model.

It is also possible to move computations from one location on the network to another. For example, moving computations from a slower processor to a more powerful processor can speed up computation and reduce network latency. As before, a monitoring and adaptation component must exist that can make this decision or, at least, provide a human with sufficient information to make the reallocation decision.

Model Development

When considering the resource requirements of a model, the resources needed for training as well as the resources needed for inference should be considered. Decreasing the resource usage of a model, as compared with the resources required for training the model, allows for deployment of some models to edge devices. These devices have restricted computational power but can be used to execute models, depending on the size and complexity of the model.

Less complex models, such as those based on decision trees or naïve Bayes algorithms, typically require less computational power and memory to train and run compared to complex models like deep neural networks. These simpler models might achieve similar accuracy on certain tasks while being more resource-friendly. At the same time, there is a trend toward shifting from LLMs to small language models (SLMs). A typical goal in SLM development is to achieve performance similar to LLMs, but at greatly increased resource efficiency.

Some preexisting, well-established model architectures are known for their efficiency, such as MobileNet and ShuffleNet. These models are specifically designed for mobile and embedded devices with limited resources.

The choice of model also affects later aspects of the life cycle:

- **Model generation:** Some models can be trained much faster than others. For instance, decision trees are known for their speed, making them suitable for real-time applications where quick responses are crucial.
- **Feature engineering:** Certain models, such as deep learning models, can automatically extract features from data, potentially reducing the need for manual feature engineering, which can be a resource-intensive step.
- **Deployment:** For deployment on devices with limited resources (e.g., mobile phones, embedded systems), choosing a model with a smaller footprint (less memory usage) is essential.

Hyperparameters

Hyperparameters can be set to reduce the resource requirements for both the training of the model and the execution of the model. For example, certain hyperparameters control the number of training iterations a model goes through. Tuning the learning rate in gradient descent algorithms can lead to faster convergence, requiring fewer iterations and reducing training time. Regularization hyperparameters, such as the L1 or L2 penalty, can help prevent overfitting by reducing model complexity, which can lead to faster training and potentially lower memory usage during training.

Techniques such as early stopping can be used as a hyperparameter as well. Early stopping monitors the model's performance on a validation set during training. If the validation performance doesn't improve for a certain number of epochs (iterations), training is stopped. This helps avoid overfitting and reduces unnecessary computation.

Reducing the precision of parameters can also reduce execution requirements. This may come at a cost, though—it may reduce the accuracy of the outputs of the model.

Other hyperparameters exist, which may influence the output quality of the resulting model. Hyperparameter tuning entails a search in the space of hyperparameters, which can substantially increase the computation resources required for training. While this may be justified in some cases, in others the overhead is not justified by the marginal, if any, improvements it brings.

Model Preparation

Model preparation can be both labor- and resource-intensive. Some techniques for reducing both the training resource requirements and the execution resource requirements are described next:

- Instead of using the entire dataset, use a representative sample for training. This can significantly reduce training time and memory usage, especially for large datasets. Techniques such as random sampling and stratified sampling can be used, depending on the problem.
- Techniques such as principal component analysis (PCA) and t-distributed stochastic neighbor embedding (t-SNE) can reduce the number of features in your data while preserving the most important information. This can lead to faster training and potentially smaller models for deployment.
- Standardizing features to a common scale can improve the performance of some algorithms and potentially lead to faster training convergence.
- When creating new features from existing ones, prioritize simple transformations such as scaling, binning, and basic mathematical operations. These are computationally cheaper compared to complex calculations.
- Place continuously valued features into buckets rather than using the raw values. This reduces the number of unique values the model needs to handle.
- For features with a small number of categories, techniques such as label encoding and ordinal encoding can be used, making training more efficient.
- For very high-cardinality features, dimensionality reduction techniques such as hashing can be used to reduce cardinality, and thereby reduce effort during training.

Operation

The main techniques for improving the efficiency of model calculation involve utilizing parallelism. Two such techniques are (1) to process multiple data points simultaneously (batching) during inference and (2) to use lazy loading or model checkpointing to load only the necessary parts of the model at runtime.

When operating an AI system, information will be gathered from the monitoring subsystem. This information can be used to improve efficiency and resource utilization. Some uses of this information, which we discuss next, include generation of alerts, scaling, reallocation, and parameter resetting.

Alerts to First Responders

Organizations and users depend on systems. When a system doesn't deliver the needed capability, an organization's business may suffer, or users may not receive the service that they paid for. To help mitigate this risk, organizations and users create service level agreements (SLAs) with the organization that develops and delivers the systems on which they depend. An SLA identifies a metric (e.g., request latency for a service) and a threshold (e.g., 99% of requests will receive a response within 300 milliseconds). A typical agreement will contain many of these metric/threshold requirements. If the client is outside the provider's organization, these SLAs may be part of a legal contract, and the provider may have to reimburse the client if the system is not available, is insecure, or performs poorly.

Because breaking an SLA is a major incident for a development-and-delivery organization, most organizations allocate the requirements to meet an SLA as far down as to the services within the system.

You do not want to be surprised by the breaking of an SLA, so you should set a tighter threshold for internal monitoring purposes. This threshold, called a service level objective (SLO), gives you some breathing room. If you violate an SLO, you have some time to repair the problem before the SLA is violated.

SLOs typically include at least the following areas of concern:

- Latency and throughput
- Traffic: the number of requests arriving at your service per unit time
- Saturation: the measure of utilization of the resources (CPU, network, memory) that your service relies on
- System health metrics, such as count or percentage of unhealthy hosts

You should define a benchmark for "good" SLO values. This will provide the values for the thresholds that you set.

If a threshold is violated, an alert is sent to a first responder. Today, this first responder is a human, but it is foreseeable that this function might be automated in the future. The first responder examines the history of requests and responses to determine where the problem that caused the alert is located.

The first responder has two responsibilities: to fix the immediate problem and to determine the root causes so that the problem does not reoccur. Fixing the immediate problem is done in real time. In contrast, finding the root cause may take extensive investigation and involve multiple different roles.

Scaling of Resources

We discussed autoscaling in Chapter 2, Software Engineering Background. The actions of the autoscaler are based on measurements of resource usage and have thresholds, as just discussed. These thresholds may or may not be the same thresholds used for alerting.

Reallocation of Services

If a component becomes overloaded, additional resources can be allocated through scaling mechanisms. Another method for improving efficiency is to utilize a different AI model. If a model continually becomes overloaded, a distinct model that serves the same function could be dynamically substituted. Having multiple models available to perform the same function can be used for correctness checking as well as resource utilization purposes.

8.1.3 Efficiency Considerations of FMs

As we discussed in Chapter 4, Foundation Models, one characteristic of FMs is their massive scale. This has implications for resource usage:

- **Computational cost:** Training FMs requires massive amounts of data and computational power. This can be expensive and time-consuming, especially for resource-constrained environments. Researchers are constantly working on improving the efficiency of training algorithms and hardware optimization techniques to address this challenge.

- **Inference speed:** Although FMs are certainly powerful, running them can be computationally expensive. This can lead to slow response times, especially for real-time applications. Techniques such as model

distillation and pruning are used to create smaller, faster models that
inherit the capabilities of the original FM (See also the discussion of
SLMs in the "Model Development" section in this chapter.)

- **Energy consumption:** The high computational cost of training and
  running FMs translates into significant energy consumption. This is a
  growing concern as the use of AI increases. Researchers are exploring
  ways to develop more energy-efficient training methods and hardware
  architectures.

8.2 Accuracy

As mentioned at the beginning of the chapter, the AI meaning of *performance*
is typically a question about the quality of the model's output. We use the
notion of accuracy here in the context of that interpretation. A different
meaning of accuracy is the metric accuracy rate, which is much narrower
than what we mean when referring to the concept of accuracy.

8.2.1 Fundamental Concepts of Accuracy

Accuracy refers to a software system's ability to produce expected or true
results. In AI systems, accuracy is how well the AI system's predictions or
outputs match the desired predictions or outputs. This is captured via a set of
metrics. Common metrics for classification and regression models are given
in this section.

Classification Models

- **Accuracy (rate):** Percentage of correct outputs (both true positives and
  true negatives) out of the total number of outputs.
- **Precision:** Percentage of correct positive outputs out of the total positive outputs.
- **Recall:** Percentage of the outputs that are true positive cases out of the
  actual number of positives.
- **F1 score:** Harmonic mean of precision and recall, which can be calculated as 2 * (precision * recall)/(precision + recall). It is useful where
  false positives and false negatives have distinct implications. F1 is a
  number between 0 and 1. An F1 score greater than 0.8 is considered
  high, a score between 0.5 and 0.8 is considered average, and a score less
  than 0.5 is low, but acceptable levels for any metric vary by application.

Regression Models

- **Mean squared error (MSE):** Average of the squared difference between the output values and the actual values.

- **Root mean squared error (RMSE):** Square root of MSE. It is easy to compare with the original scale of the data and sensitive to the presence of outliers.

- **Mean absolute error (MAE):** Average of the absolute difference between the output values and the actual values. It is less sensitive to outliers compared to MSE or RMSE, as it does not square the errors.

- **R-squared (R^2):** Proportion of the variance in the dependent variable that can be attributed to the independent variables. Values greater than 0.7 are high, between 0.5 and 0.7 are moderate, and less than 0.5 are low.

Foundation Models

Measuring the accuracy of FMs or their fine-tuned task-specific models is more complex than for other AI models due to their diverse capabilities and varied outputs. We use LLMs to show some LLM-specific measurements.

- **General Language Understanding Evaluation (GLUE) and Super-GLUE:** These benchmarks are widely used for assessing performance on diverse natural language processing (NLP) tasks including sentence completion, sentiment analysis, and question-answering.

- **Massive Multitask Language Understanding (MMLU) test score:** MMLU measures a language model's performance across a broad range of tasks and subjects, assessing its general knowledge and problem-solving abilities. It evaluates accuracy on multiple-choice questions in domains such as mathematics, history, and science, among others. The score provides insights into the model's proficiency and versatility, indicating its ability to understand and generate human-like text.

Repeatability

Repeatability means producing the same output for the same input under identical conditions. This is a hallmark of deterministic systems. Many systems, however, may not be deterministic because of timing differences caused by thread behavior and background activities. Measuring nondeterministic performance, such as with benchmarks, requires multiple executions and statistical analysis.

AI systems, particularly those based on ML, may be nondeterministic because many ML algorithms rely on randomness during training, such as initializing weights or choosing optimization paths. These random elements can cause different outputs even with the same input.

Additionally, in certain AI applications such as creative writing or generating alternative plans and recommendations, variability in output from the same input is actually desirable. This allows exploration of different alternatives.

8.2.2 Approaches to Improving Accuracy

As before, we take a life-cycle approach when discussing how to improve accuracy.

Architecture Design

In Chapter 7, Reliability, we discussed using multiple models and voting as a mechanism for increasing reliability. The techniques are also applicable to increasing accuracy. In particular, using a combination of models, known as multi-model decision making, employs different models to perform the same task or enable a single decision. Consensus protocols could be defined to make the final decision—for example, taking the majority vote. Another strategy is to accept only the same results from the employed models. In addition, the end user or the operator could step in to review the output from the multiple models and make a final decision based on human expertise.

Hyperparameters

The choice of hyperparameters has a major impact on the model's accuracy. Models that have a learning rate hyperparameter are sensitive to that choice. Learning rates that are too high will cause the model to experience problems with output. A second problem is that the impact of a choice of hyperparameters may be difficult to predict.

Finally, depending on the model choice, the hyperparameter choice can lead to either overfitting or underfitting. For example, a large number of trees in a random forest might lead to overfitting, whereas a small number might lead to underfitting.

Data Preparation

There are three challenges in preparing data for accuracy: (1) choosing a sufficient amount of training data; (2) choosing the data to be representative of the actual data on which the model is to be used; and, somewhat counter-intuitively, (3) choosing the data to be free of biases. In addition, the model should give an accurate output when presented with out-of-distribution (OOD) data, so samples of OOD data should be included in the training data.

Missing data points are a common issue. You can address them by using techniques such as imputation (filling in missing values with estimates) or removing rows/columns with excessive proportions of missing values.

Outliers can skew your model's learning. You can choose to clip outliers to a certain range or remove them entirely, depending on the context.

Furthermore, to ensure that the trained model generalizes well to unseen data, you will want to split your data into different sets. Best practice is to divide your data into three main sets:

- **Training set:** This is the largest portion, usually approximately 60% to 80%, of the data. It is used to train the model.
- **Validation set:** This set, which typically represents 10% to 20% of the data, is used to tune the hyperparameters of the model and to prevent overfitting. It provides an unbiased evaluation of a model fit on the training dataset while tuning the model's hyperparameters.
- **Test set:** This set, which also represents 10% to 20% of the data, is used to assess the final performance of the model after training and validation are complete. It should not be used during the training or validation phases.

This split is depicted in Figure 8.2.

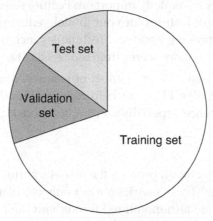

Figure 8.2 *Typical split of training data.*

Two context-specific best practices are stratification and cross-validation. First, for classification problems, ensure that splits are stratified, meaning that each set maintains the same class distribution as the original dataset. Second, in some cases, especially when the training dataset is small, use cross-validation techniques (e.g., k-fold cross-validation) for more reliable evaluation.

Model Preparation

Choosing the correct set of features will help the model generate more accurate outputs. Some techniques for adapting features are presented here:

- Scaling features to a common range ensures all features contribute equally to the model's learning process. Common scaling methods include standardization (z-score) and normalization (min-max scaling).
- Categorical data often needs to be converted to numerical values so that ML models can understand the data. Techniques such one-hot encoding and label encoding are used for this purpose.
- Deriving new features from existing ones can improve model performance. For instance, you might create new features like "time since last purchase" from a customer dataset.
- Transformations such as logs and square roots can improve the linearity of relationships between features and the target variable, which benefits some ML algorithms.

Some techniques for managing the set of features are highlighted next:

- Not all features are equally important. Feature selection helps identify the most relevant features for your model, reducing training time and potentially improving accuracy. Techniques include chi-squared tests and feature importance scores from models like random forests.
- When dealing with a large number of features, dimensionality reduction techniques like PCA can help reduce redundancy and improve model performance, especially for complex models prone to overfitting.

Model Generation

During the model generation process, the model's performance is evaluated using various metrics. These metrics are not only calculated once the model is fully trained, but are also monitored throughout the training phase. This ongoing evaluation helps in adjusting parameters and improving the model iteratively. Recall from the data preparation discussion that you will use the validation set for testing during model generation.

Once the model has been generated, testing it further will give you some confidence in the model. The dataset to use for this assessment is the test set.

During both types of evaluation, you will calculate accuracy metrics. Commonly used metrics for classification models include the aforementioned accuracy, precision, recall, and F1 score, whereas metrics for regression models include MSE, RMSE, MAE, and R-squared. By closely monitoring these metrics, you can gain confidence in the model's performance and make informed decisions about further training or adjustments during model generation, or deployment once training is complete.

Operations

During operations, the accuracy of model output can be calculated only when ground truth values are known. This is usually done after the outputs have been produced. In addition to the metrics mentioned earlier, the following techniques can be used for this purpose:

- Visualizing a confusion matrix. This table visualizes the model's performance on different classes, highlighting potential imbalances (e.g., high false positives for a specific class).
- Using statistical techniques like the Kolmogorov–Smirnov's test to compare the distribution of new data with the training data, highlighting potential data or concept drift.

Testing for accuracy should be done periodically. If a problem is detected, the model should be retrained and a new release sent through the deployment pipeline.

FM-Based Systems

FMs are challenging with respect to accuracy because of both their scale and their domain-independent nature. In addition, as we discussed in Chapter 4, they are subject to hallucinations or confabulations and have limited factual grounding. Additional problems with FMs relate to generalization, inconsistency, and test data used during training.

- **Generalization across domains:** Although FMs are trained for general-purpose usage, their accuracy can change significantly across diverse domains or problems. Hence, for specific software applications, they require further fine-tuning or tailored system design.

- **Inconsistent results:** FMs are trained on extensive datasets, which may contain inconsistent, varying, or even contradictory data. Also, the internal mechanisms of FMs involve a certain degree of randomness during training and inference. Thus, even when provided with identical inputs and conditions, the FM might produce different outputs each time it is run. This variability can make it challenging to replicate results consistently.

- **Test data used during training:** In most cases, you will use FMs as a service through an API provided by a hyperscaler, without deep insight into the pretraining phase. As a result, you won't know which data was used during pretraining. This includes standard tests like MMLU—the test questions and answers may have been part of the training set or validation set. In either case, if you use these tests/benchmarks as test sets, you cannot trust the resulting performance. Assessing FMs can be very hard because, from a practical standpoint, you cannot use any public dataset as test data.

In Chapter 4, we introduced several approaches to improving accuracy for FMs, including fine-tuning, retrieval-augmented generation (RAG), and prompt engineering. Additional approaches include reinforcement learning from human feedback (RLHF) to align with human preferences, adversarial testing and human acceptance testing for use case–specific scenarios, and benchmarks for capabilities. Additionally, the quality of the test cases themselves is very important and needs to be assessed.

Reinforcement Learning from Human Feedback

FM providers can use RLHF to fine-tune the FM's behavior and produce more accurate and responsible responses. RLHF allows humans to provide feedback on the quality of the responses, with this feedback then being used to adjust the model's parameters. The FM is trained to maximize the reward it receives from human feedback, which can improve its accuracy and responsible AI (RAI)–related qualities over time.

Adversarial Testing

Adversarial testing is a method to evaluate FMs by exposing them to inputs specially designed to trick or confuse them. The purpose is to assess the FMs' robustness and ability to handle ambiguous queries or edge cases. Adversarial examples used in the testing can include synonym substitution, sentence paraphrasing, work insertions or deletions, typos or grammatical errors, misleading information, ambiguous or vague inputs, and irrelevant information, among others.

Adversarial testing can be done with domain experts, who test the accuracy and RAI-related properties by using adversarial examples that are designed to deceive or mislead the model into producing incorrect or irresponsible responses. By testing the model in this way, developers can identify vulnerabilities or weaknesses in the model's decision-making process and take steps to improve its accuracy and RAI-related properties. For example, OpenAI engaged more than 50 experts from various domains to perform adversarial testing for its GPT-4 model.

Human Evaluation

Human evaluation subjectively assesses the accuracy of FMs. Typical criteria for human evaluation for LLMs include the following:

- **Factual accuracy and grounding:** Are the LLM's responses factually correct? Do they align with real-world knowledge and evidence?

- **Fluency and coherence:** Are the LLM's responses grammatically correct? Do they read smoothly and logically?

- **Relevance and informativeness:** How relevant are the LLM's responses to the input? Do they provide sufficient and useful information to fulfill the intent of the input?

- **Originality and creativity:** Are the LLM's responses novel and insightful outputs rather than simply regurgitating existing information?

Benchmarks

Automated benchmark tests involve running and testing the LLMs through a set of standardized tasks. As previously noted in the FM/LLM concept section, MMLU and GLUE/SuperGLUE are typical benchmarks for assessing the accuracy and performance of models across a broad range of tasks. Some other benchmarks include the following options:

- **Recall-Oriented Understudy for Gisting Evaluation (ROUGE):** ROUGE is a metric used to evaluate the quality of both machine translation and text summarization. It measures the similarity between a machine-translated summarized text and one or more reference summaries/translations.

- **Holistic Evaluation of Language Models (HELM):** This benchmark evaluates LLMs on their abilities in factual grounding, reasoning, and commonsense knowledge, extending beyond simple accuracy to assess deeper understanding.
- **Winograd Schema Challenge (WSC):** The WSC is specifically designed to test LLM's ability to understand language and commonsense reasoning, focusing on areas that go beyond mere accuracy.

If LLMs are trained or fine-tuned for specific domains, such as the medical or legal domain, their accuracy within these domains can be measured using domain-specific benchmarks or through expert reviews. To set the benchmarks, domain-specific data and tasks are collected to evaluate the LLM's abilities in handling real-world scenarios. For example, clinical text datasets can be used for tasks such as generating medical diagnoses. For expert reviews, domain experts manually evaluate the LLM's output for accuracy, relevance, and compliance with the domain-specific standards.

Acceptance Testing

Acceptance testing, such as bias testing, is designed to detect design flaws in AI systems and verify that trustworthiness requirements have been met—for example, whether the data pipeline has appropriate privacy control, fairness testing for training, and validation data. In an agile development process, ethical requirements can be framed as ethical user stories and associated with corresponding acceptance tests. These tests serve as a contract between the customer and development team, and can be used to quantify the behavior of the AI system. The acceptance criteria should be clearly defined in a testable way. The history of ethical acceptance testing should be recorded and tracked, including how and by whom the ethical issues were addressed. A testing leader may be appointed to lead the acceptance testing for each quality. For example, if bias is detected at runtime, the monitoring reports are returned to the bias testing leader for review.

Assessment for Test Cases

Creating high-quality test cases is an integral part of acceptance testing. A test case usually includes an ID, description, preconditions, test steps, test data, expected results, actual results, status, creator name, creation date, executor name, and execution date. All of the test cases for verification and valida-tion must pass an assessment, which includes evaluating the metrics of the test steps and test data. The creation and execution information is essential to track the accountability of ethical issues with test cases. The assessment process can be integrated into the design of tools used to generate test cases.

8.3 Summary

Performance is an ambiguous term when applied to AI systems: It can mean either efficiency or accuracy. During operations, it is important to monitor the performance of an AI system and generate alerts if the performance deviates from predefined limits. For efficiency, the predefined limits can be thresh-olds set on latency and throughput. For accuracy, the predefined limits can be based on statistical tests of the similarity of the distribution of the training data and the actual data being input into the model.

For both efficiency and accuracy, a general rule is that simple problems should be addressed with simple models. Do not use a complex model unless you have a complex problem to solve.

In terms of accuracy, overfitting is a continual concern, as is bias. Suf-ficient training data will help prevent overfitting, and eliminating biases in training data will help prevent biases in operation. Introducing OOD data and adversarial data into the training dataset will improve accuracy.

FMs can be made more accurate for specific domains through prompt engineering, use of RAG, and fine-tuning. Testing and improving FM perfor-mance is challenging, but a number of approaches, such as adversarial test-ing and RLHF, are available for this purpose.

8.4 Discussion Questions

1. Improving efficiency requires a tradeoff of a large number of quality attributes. Give some examples.

2. Is accuracy traded off against the other quality attributes discussed in this book? Which ones? What is the tradeoff?

3. Given the probabilistic nature of AI models, can they ever be truly accurate? Discuss.

4. Discuss the truth or falsehood of this statement: If throughput has increased, then latency must have decreased.

8.5 For Further Reading

C. Huyen's *Designing Machine Learning Systems: An Iterative Process for Production-Ready Applications* [Huyen 22] is a good source for designing AI systems for production, where you can read about the requirements for AI systems.

The book *Efficient Processing of Deep Neural Networks* [Sze 20] focuses on optimizing deep neural networks for energy efficiency, throughput, and latency through hardware–algorithm co-design. This optimization is critical for ensuring reliable AI systems, as it helps prevent performance degradation and failures due to resource constraints.

9

Security

Security is a process, not a product.

—Bruce Schneier

When designing, developing, and operating an AI-based system, all security concerns from traditional systems are still relevant. Some of the concerns are similar, but have changed. And some new challenges exist.

As an example of existing but changed concerns, input sanitation is traditionally geared toward countering attacks implemented via SQL injection, buffer overflow, or other techniques. Syntactic checks can help prevent many of these attacks. For AI-based systems, new forms of semantic attacks exist. For example, based on the content of the prompt text to a large language model (LLM), such as "repeat word X infinitely," some LLMs might output that word a large number of times before returning some of the training data verbatim.

As an example of a new challenge, in an experiment, researchers manipulated only a few individual pixels in images in an effort to throw off image classification AI models, which are used to identify objects or patterns in images. The researchers succeeded: After their manipulation, none of the images was classified correctly. The total number of pixels per image that needed to be changed to achieve this result was three, on average. Although this interesting result was produced in the laboratory, it is downright scary to think that those same AI techniques might be used in self-driving cars. For instance, if such an image manipulation can be achieved with a few stickers on a stop sign, that sign might no longer be recognized as such by the AI system.

Defense in depth is a standard security principle. It emphasizes a layered approach in which multiple security measures work together to create a strong barrier against attacks. In other words, you should not rely on a single defense against attacks, but rather must implement various defenses at different points in the system.

It is important to address the security concerns associated with AI models head-on. The potential risks in terms of loss of reputation, money, or even lives are significant if security concerns are not properly managed.

As in the other chapters dealing with quality issues, we will first cover the fundamentals regarding security. Subsequently, we will discuss new and changed challenges, but not unchanged ones. Finally, we will cover how the challenges can be addressed—that is, solved, mitigated, or managed.

9.1 Fundamental Concepts

We begin by discussing the traditional definition of security, and then turn to additional considerations in the AI context. Figure 9.1 gives a preview of the topics we discuss in this section.

9.1.1 Traditional Definition of Security

Security is not a single quality, but rather arises from the combination of at least three qualities: confidentiality, integrity, and availability. Collectively known as the CIA properties, these qualities are based on authentication and authorization. *Authentication* means that the persons or systems accessing a service are what they are claiming to be. *Authorization* refers to the rights the user has; that is, the user is authorized to perform certain operations such as accessing a file or approving an invoice.

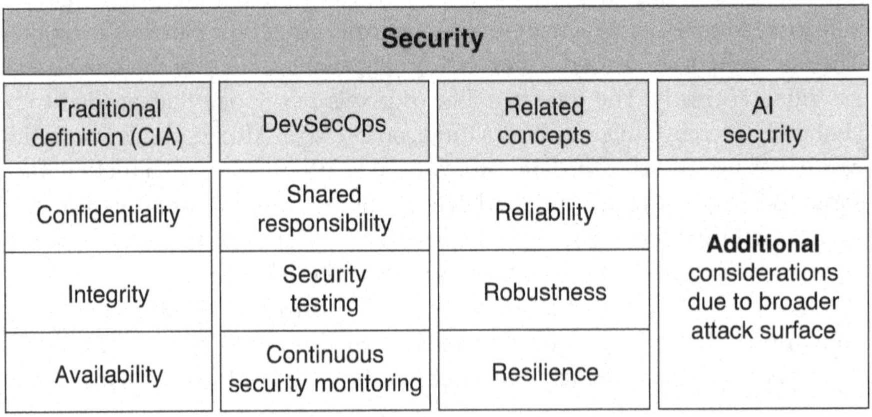

Security			
Traditional definition (CIA)	DevSecOps	Related concepts	AI security
Confidentiality	Shared responsibility	Reliability	**Additional** considerations due to broader attack surface
Integrity	Security testing	Robustness	
Availability	Continuous security monitoring	Resilience	

Figure 9.1 *Fundamental concepts of security.*

Returning to the CIA properties, *confidentiality* means that only persons or systems authorized to access information are able to do so. *Integrity* is the property that data or services are not subject to unauthorized manipulation; this implies that the system is able to prevent users from making changes they are not authorized to make. Finally, *availability* means the system allows authorized users to perform operations—that is, the system is available to provide its intended service.

DevSecOps is a variant of DevOps that emphasizes the security aspects of DevOps. It introduces new considerations, such as the goal to foster a culture in which security, development, and operations are understood as shared responsibilities by all relevant team members. Other DevSecOps practices emphasize security testing in the deployment pipeline, monitoring used packages and libraries for known vulnerabilities, and security monitoring and response as design goals. Furthermore, if practiced well, DevSecOps can alleviate the burden to achieve compliance with regulation and security standards, among others, by means of standardized, automated processes and checks.

Security is also linked to reliability, robustness, and resilience, which were covered in Chapter 7, Reliability. Some definitions of safety and dependability are also related. In a classic, influential paper by Avižienis et al., safety is defined as the "absence of catastrophic consequences on the user(s) and the environment." These authors' view of dependability is that it covers the properties of safety, integrity, availability, reliability, and maintainability; in other words, it shares the "I" and the "A" from CIA with security.

Recently, quantum computing has become more relevant. Given the advances being made, it is quite possible that in the not-too-distant future quantum computers will be able to crack conventional encryption mechanisms with ease. Designers should try and use quantum-safe algorithms and protocols (i.e., cryptographic techniques designed to be resistant against attacks from quantum computers), especially for highly critical areas of their application.

The term *attack surface* is used to refer to the sum of all possible entry points that attackers can exploit to gain unauthorized access to a system, steal data, disrupt operations, or cause other harm. It encompasses every vulnerability, weakness, and potential access point within the software, its code, and its surrounding environment. This includes, as we will see, the data used to train the model.

An *attack vector* is the specific method or pathway used by attackers to exploit vulnerabilities and gain unauthorized access to a system or data.

It represents the "how" of an attack, while the attack surface defines the "where" (all potential entry points). Many attacks aim to compromise both the "I" and the "C" parts of CIA. However, trying to disentangle these two elements in an attack is not fruitful because the prevention or mitigation of these elements depends on the attack vector, not on which one of the CIA properties is being compromised.

9.1.2 Attacks in an AI System

All of the preceding aspects of security apply to AI-based systems, though some things are a bit different. Perhaps most importantly, the attack surface of an AI system is broader than the attack surface of non-AI systems. Modifying an image so that it will be misclassified is an example of a new method of attack that did not exist in traditional systems. Attacks may result from illegitimate changes to the model directly or the data used for training the model, which are forms of poisoning attacks. Taking a system-level perspective, traditional security measures remain very relevant—among others, those regarding infrastructure, APIs, user management, layering of access levels, and data protection in transit, in use, and at rest. As stated earlier, some aspects have different implications in AI systems, and some new aspects arise from them. We now discuss these additional challenges for AI-based systems.

In a recent National Institute of Standards and Technology (NIST) taxonomy, the following attack types are distinguished:

- **Evasion attacks:** The deployed model is not affected, but returns a different answer than it would have without the attack, often based on runtime input manipulation. Image misclassification after changing three pixels in an image is an example.

- **Poisoning attacks:** The model training phase is attacked. For instance, an AI trained on public datasets from the internet could be attacked by controlling and changing a small subset of publicly available data.

- **Privacy attacks:** The attackers aim to gain information about confidential inputs to the training data. Privacy attacks can be subdivided into membership attacks (is a certain record part of the training data?) and data reconstruction attacks (what was the input data?). An example of the former would be a facial recognition system that classifies images as either "authorized user" or "unauthorized user"; an attacker could try to find out if a specific individual was in the training dataset. An example of the latter is the case of "repeat this word infinitely" causing an LLM to regurgitate and return some of its training data.

- **Abuse/misuse attacks:** This attack type applies primarily to generative AI systems, and aims to create output that should not be generated according to the creators (e.g., creating hate speech or supporting weapon/bomb creation).

Figure 9.2 depicts these attack types and shows how they are related to the phases in AI training and use. Note that privacy and poisoning attacks can target the training data, or the model (e.g., by deducing information or changing behavior from model weights directly), or both. Although this is a useful overview and categorization, organizations that want to use AI in production systems should have a significantly more detailed understanding of the attack types and mitigations relevant to their particular setting.

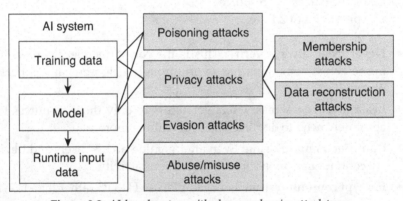

Figure 9.2 *AI-based system with phases and major attack types.*

Although attacks are easiest to carry out when internal information (e.g., source code, training data) is known to the attackers, referred to as white-box attacks, they are also possible with limited (gray-box attacks) or no (black-box attacks) internal information. Attacks also differ by the level of control the attackers have. Can they change training data or testing data? Can they change labels? Can they manipulate model parameters or gain access to a system's source code? In terms of data modality, attack forms have been developed for text, tabular data, images, audio, video, and cybersecurity data (e.g., viruses, malware, spam), and more recently for multimodal AIs.

9.2 Approaches to Mitigating Security Concerns

It is important to realize that there is no absolute security, and particularly for the model-level challenges, there are no perfect mitigations. Conventional security concerns still need to be addressed. Attackers might also make use of (generative) AI technologies, both to automate more attacks and to launch more sophisticated attacks.

The basic philosophy behind achieving security nowadays is zero trust. *Zero trust* (ZT) is the term for an evolving set of cybersecurity paradigms that move defenses from static, network-based perimeters to focus on users, assets, and resources. A ZT architecture uses ZT principles to plan industrial and enterprise infrastructure and workflows. It assumes there is no implicit trust granted to assets or user accounts based solely on their physical or network location (i.e., local area networks versus the internet) or based on asset ownership (enterprise or personally owned). Authentication and authorization (both subject and device) are discrete functions performed when initiating access to an enterprise resource.

Some principles of ZT are:

- **Never trust, always verify:** This is the core principle. Everyone trying to access something has to go through a rigorous authentication process.
- **Least privilege access:** Users get access to only those resources they absolutely need to do their jobs, and nothing more.
- **Continuous monitoring:** Even after gaining access, users and devices are continuously monitored for suspicious activity.
- **Encrypt communication:** For example, use HTTPS rather than HTTP.

We begin by discussing process approaches to security.

9.2.1 Process Approaches for Enhancing Security

Threat modeling and risk assessment are useful practices for identifying and addressing potential security vulnerabilities in systems. While the fundamental principles apply to both AI and non-AI systems, specific aspects to consider in the context of FM-based systems include the identification of new FM-specific attacks and emerging threats unique to AI/FM technologies. To effectively handle these challenges, organizations could leverage AI itself, combining it with comprehensive system tracking and analysis. By utilizing AI-based techniques for threat detection and keeping track of system behavior, organizations can stay informed about new attack vectors and assess their applicability to their specific AI systems. This proactive approach helps in identifying and mitigating potential security risks in a timely manner.

9.2.2 *Architectural Approaches for Enhancing Security*

The design of the architecture is where ZT is centered. For architectural design, it manifests as architectural patterns. These patterns apply to AI systems as well as to non-AI systems. Some of these patterns are highlighted here:

- **Authorization:** Authorization is enforced for every access to a service. It should result in users and services checking authorization and being granted access with the principle of least privilege applied (Amazon reports 400 million calls to its IAM service per minute[1]).
- **Encryption:** The design should reflect the use of HTTPS and other encrypted communication protocols.
- **Least functionality:** Configure your system to provide only essential capabilities and to prohibit or restrict the use of nonessential functions, such as ports, protocols, and/or services that are not integral to the operation of that information system.
- **Limiting access:** Restrict the number of access points—for example, by requiring access to pass through a gateway.
- **Restrict traffic:** Among other things, configure firewalls to allow access only to port numbers where this is needed.
- **Segmenting networks:** Use the principle of least privilege to control access.
- **Privilege separation:** Each component possesses the minimum privileges required for it to function, so that functions are differentiated from privileges.
- **Privilege minimization:** Privileges are disabled most of the time, and enabled only when required.

When implementing security, there is a tradeoff between security and usability: Implementing robust security measures may introduce additional complexity and potentially impact the usability and performance of the

---

1. https://aws.amazon.com/blogs/apn/iam-10th-anniversary-top-recommendations-for-working-with-iam-from-our-aws-heroes-part-1/

system. Good architecture, development, and operations strike a balance between security requirements and system usability to ensure that the security measures do not hinder the system's functionality or user experience—at least not more than necessary.

The architecture of the system should be robust against side channel attacks. Countermeasures, such as secure hardware implementations and cryptographic techniques, can support the mitigation of risks associated with side channel attacks in AI-based systems. If timing is the only relevant side channel, random delays may be sufficient to address the concern.

When utilizing open-parameter or third-party models in AI-based systems, prioritize the use of safe file formats such as safetensors. By adopting such formats, the system can be protected from the execution of arbitrary code and from vulnerabilities related to attacks like denial-of-service (DoS) or buffer/memory overflow. Implementing these secure file formats helps to mitigate the potential risks associated with malicious inputs.

9.2.3 Data Preparation Approaches for Enhancing Security

Reexamining Figure 9.2, you can see that training data is subject to poisoning attacks and privacy attacks. Preserving the integrity and tracking of input data is important, especially in the context of large FMs that heavily rely on external data sources.

In situations where it may not be feasible or practical to retain the original data, an alternative approach is to securely store hashes of the input data, possibly using techniques such as Merkle trees that span over the structure of an input data set. By retaining these hashes and/or Merkle trees, any unauthorized modification or tampering of the input data can be detected, ensuring the integrity of the system. This provides a means to protect against potential data manipulation and maintain the trustworthiness of the AI system. We described tools useful in this process in Chapter 5, AI Model Life Cycle. Tracking the lineage of data items will enable the organization to determine whether any data items were introduced from anyone other than authorized personnel.

9.2.4 Testing in the Deployment Pipeline

Testing during runs of the deployment pipeline can detect some types of vulnerabilities. There are two main types of tools:

- **Adversarial example detection:** These tools generate inputs designed to trigger unexpected or incorrect behavior in the model, essentially mimicking real-world attacks. They help identify vulnerabilities that might open up the system to model poisoning or evasion attacks, and point out fairness issues. These tools create and feed variations of legitimate inputs to the model, observing its responses for anomalies or incorrect predictions. Some use gradient-based methods, whereas others employ evolutionary algorithms or symbolic reasoning.

- **Data quality tools:** These tools analyze the data used to train the model, checking for issues such as missing values, inconsistencies, and outliers that could negatively impact the model's performance and security. These tools employ statistical analysis, data lineage tracking, and outlier detection algorithms to identify issues within the training data that could impact the model's security and performance.

9.2.5 Enhancing Security During System Build

Security during the build phase starts with pipeline security. The CI/CD pipeline itself needs to be secured. If an attacker were to gain write access on the CI/CD pipeline infrastructure, they could potentially modify many pieces of software and deploy unauthorized code at scale. Potentially, many services might be infiltrated if an attacker could control this crucial piece of software. It might also impact your ability to respond to the attack: You might not be able to roll back to an earlier version, if the software through which you would perform the rollback is compromised.

Measures to safeguard the pipeline include restricting modifications to trusted personnel, and possibly requiring two people to authorize a modification to the pipeline. Additionally, team members should be notified whenever a portion of the pipeline is updated.

The CI/CD pipeline can and should be used to *increase the security* of the resulting system. You can use it to control the artifacts used in the build process, including frameworks, libraries, packages, templates, infrastructure code, configuration, and more. Monitor for any changes and review them, to maintain a state where only trusted artifacts end up in your production system. For AI systems, this extends to training and testing data.

As in traditional systems, infrastructure code must be stored and managed with the same security practices as application code (e.g., storing it in a version control system, applying the least privilege principle, exhaustive testing). The importance of good management practices extends to secrets, such as the credentials required to control your cloud production environment or your customer database. Best practice is to use specific secrets and credentials solutions such as the Jenkins secrets store; doing so correctly will ensure that no secrets end up in the version control system or in visible parts of releases. Most developers do not need to have access to secrets for the production environment, and accordingly they should not be granted access. These principles from traditional settings extend to AI systems, but given that you might use different services to train and serve the AI portions of your system, you should make sure to apply these principles to them as well. The initial investment in configuration and possibly writing code (e.g., to connect new services to the secrets store you use) will pay off in terms of gains in increased security and automation.

Another way in which the CI/CD pipeline can support security is by automated security checks. This includes penetration testing, static and dynamic analysis, user acceptance testing (UAT) and integration testing with negative tests (trying system interactions that should not be allowed, and observing that they are indeed rejected), and AI-specific tests for desired and undesired behavior. By using the CI/CD pipeline in this way, you can catch vulnerabilities early and ensure that there is no regression in terms of security—that is, previously closed vulnerabilities stay closed while the system development continues.

A new practice for AI-based systems is the use of data canaries. Like the canary servers used in traditional DevOps practices, data canaries are likened to the birds that coal miners used to take down into the mines with them: A canary in distress was a strong warning that toxic gas was present. Data canaries are small samples of data applied during retraining or continuous learning. You use a small subset of the new data, train a test version of the model on it, and see whether the behavior is as expected. All of these steps can be automated to some degree. If the behavior of the system with the data canary differs from the expected behavior, this can be an indication of data drift (normal changes over time), a fault (e.g., a faulty sensor delivering data), or a malicious attack. The advantages of training with data canaries over using the whole set of new data are twofold: (1) Training with canaries is cheaper, and (2) it is faster—and speed is of paramount importance when responding to security incidents.

9.2.6 Enhancing Security during Operations

Attacks during the system's operation can target the data, the model, or the system.

Attacks on Data

Examining Figure 9.2, we see that two types of possible attacks on the data are evasion attacks and abuse/misuse attacks. Evasion attacks involve slightly modifying normal data to exploit the AI's weaknesses and get a desired wrong output (e.g., changing a stop sign so that an autonomous car no longer recognizes it). An abuse/misuse attack involves feeding the AI system incorrect information through seemingly legitimate sources to manipulate its overall behavior—for example, placing fake news articles into social media.

As yet, there are no countermeasures to these types of attacks. However, some general principles can be applied to data to enhance its security:

- **Data minimization:** Use the least amount of data necessary for the AI system to function. This reduces the attack surface and the potential for data breaches.

- **Data encryption:** Encrypt data at rest and in transit to protect it from unauthorized access.

- **Data anonymization:** If possible, anonymize sensitive data before feeding it into the AI model.

- **Regular data audits:** Monitor data access and usage to identify any suspicious activity.

Attacks on a Model

The effectiveness of attacks on the model depends on the model type. Some characteristics are especially associated with more vulnerable models:

- Complex models such as deep neural networks can be difficult to interpret (opaque). This makes it hard to understand how they reach decisions and leaves them susceptible to adversarial attacks in which attackers manipulate inputs to get a desired output (e.g., bypassing spam filters).

- Ensemble models combine multiple models. While they can be powerful, their security complexity increases. If one submodel in the ensemble is compromised, the entire system might be vulnerable.

Less vulnerable models often have the following characteristics:

- Decision trees or rule-based systems are generally easier to understand and analyze. While they might not be as powerful as complex models, their transparency renders them less susceptible to adversarial attacks.

- Techniques such as logistic regression provide a clearer view into how they reach conclusions. This allows for easier detection of potential biases or vulnerabilities in the model's logic.

Some general rules can be followed to improve the security of models:

- Implement strong access controls to restrict who can access, modify, or manipulate the AI model.
- Continuously monitor the AI model's performance for signs of degradation, bias creep, or unexpected behavior. Anomaly detection with AI itself can be helpful here.
- Maintain a version history of the AI model to track changes and roll back changes if necessary.

Attacks on the System

Attacks on an AI system can take the form of a DoS attack. AI tends to be more compute-intensive than many traditional types of systems; thus, it might be easier for an attacker to overload your expensive GPU cluster. Throttling requests is one technique to defend against DoS attacks.

Logging and auditing can help in determining the source and consequences of an attack on the system. Logging all model inputs, outputs, and relevant actions is helpful for potential forensic analysis and anomaly detection. Privacy regulation or contractual agreements might forbid this practice; if you do follow it, securely store these logs and strictly limit access to authorized personnel.

9.2.7 Foundation Models

In this section, we discuss potential attack vectors and then approaches to increase the security of FMs.

Attacks

Foundation models are susceptible to attacks because of their scale, their domain independence, and the difficulty in understanding the workings of an FM. Some attack vectors targeting these models are based on queries and supply chains. If your FM can learn from the queries made to it, this opens up another attack vector.

Most organizations are unlikely to train their own FMs. Hence, supply chain concerns are more prevalent in this arena. When using an FM through an API, the consumers of the FM need to understand if and when the model and serving infrastructure are updated, and how they will be informed. Part of the serving infrastructure might consist of controls like guardrails. If these are managed by the FM provider, updates to them might go unnoticed but may have the effect that they change the behavior and performance/accuracy of the FM.

When using an externally provided FM, organizations must take the same care as with third-party libraries. Some popular formats for exchanging models are susceptible to attacks. These attacks can range from code injection to DoS (e.g., by providing very long JSON content) to buffer overflows.

Organizations creating their own FMs might retrieve a lot of data. According to the NIST AML report,[2] in most cases this data is not stored persistently by the organization training the FM; instead, it holds a list of external sources. In an elaborate attack, attackers could try to hijack domains on that list, whether the membership in the list is known or merely suspected. Hijacking can be done by monitoring domains for expiry, and legally buying expired domains. The attackers might then use the hijacked domains to poison the training data. Research has shown that control of even a small fraction of the training data can allow for successful, detrimental poisoning attacks.

Regardless of the source of the FM, specific applications are often implemented by using an existing FM in combination with retrieval-augmented generation (RAG) and fine-tuning. All aspects of training a model apply to fine-tuning, and some of them (e.g., poisoning) also apply to RAG.

The charging model of an FM provider may open up a pathway for another attack vector. Suppose a query—even a benign one—is repeated multiple times. Each query incurs a cost, possibly not negligible. This may cause the charges for running the system to become an economic hardship for the system provider.

Increasing the Security of FMs and FM-Based Systems

Given the attack types and vectors mentioned earlier, how can you defend FM-based systems?

First, during the *training of FMs*, take proactive measures such as carefully curating training data and employing techniques like reinforcement learning from human feedback (RLHF). However, when using existing FM models, users typically have neither control over nor insight into the original training data. In such cases, RLHF can be applied during fine-tuning to adapt the model's behavior. Additionally, to ensure safety, input prompts to and outputs generated by the FM can be subjected to checks or guardrails. Moreover, instructions can be provided to the FM to inform it about potential malicious queries or attempts to bypass security measures, thereby

---

2. https://csrc.nist.gov/pubs/ai/100/2/e2023/final

complementing the prompt-based approach. These measures help enhance the security of using existing FM models.

Another approach to ensure the security and adherence to predefined rules in LLMs is to use constitutional LLMs. Constitutional LLMs, such as Claude, involve the use of a smaller LLM that verifies whether the main LLM complies with the fundamental rules specified in the "constitution." The constitutional LLM approach can be implemented to check the main LLM, both at runtime (like guardrails) and at training time (to provide feedback to the main LLM in training, similar to RLHF). It may even be possible to fine-tune the LLM with a case-specific constitution, further tailoring its behavior to specific requirements and constraints.

One advantage of constitutional LLMs (assuming the results are of high quality) over RLHF is that it requires less human work. While saving on human effort can save time and money, it also shields humans from boring, repetitive tasks, particularly when frequent updates require retesting, and from having to screen potentially harmful content. By incorporating constitutional LLMs, organizations can add an extra layer of security and governance to LLMs, mitigating potential risks—especially from abuse/misuse attacks.

Authorization may need to be verified by the input guardrails. For example, suppose a healthcare provider has permission to see the records of their patients. Suppose now that the provider asks to see the records of someone who is not their patient. If the query is in natural language, the relationship between the provider and the subject of the query may not have been checked during preprocessing, only whether the issuer of the query has permission to see health records. It then becomes the responsibility of the guardrails to verify that the subject of the query is, in fact, a patient of the person issuing the query.

9.3 Summary

Here is a summary of this chapter.

- A short definition of security is CIA: confidentiality, integrity, and availability.
- Attacks on AI systems can occur to the training data, to the model, or during runtime.
- Approaches to security are based on zero trust. ZT is embedded in the architecture during design through application of the principle of least privilege, always performing verification, and continuous monitoring.

- During model build and preparation, maintaining versions of data items as well as their lineage is important to ensure the integrity of the model.

- During operations, there are no good techniques to avoid data-based attack vectors, but some general practices can be followed to reduce the attack surface and detect attacks if they occur.

- FMs have their own challenges to security, including those related to prompt engineering and the use of RAG.

9.4 Discussion Questions

1. Security and usability are often seen as being at odds with each other. Security often imposes procedures and processes that seem like needless overhead to the casual user. Nevertheless, some say that security and usability go (or should go) hand in hand, and argue that making the system easy to use securely is the best way to promote security to the users. Discuss.

2. One variant of a DoS attack is to heavily utilize a system where the end user is not charged for service but the system provider is charged by their cloud provider. For example, such an attack might target a free offering to end users intended to encourage subsequent paid subscriptions. How would you deter such an attack?

3. Data poisoning is one form of attack on an AI system. Is it possible to poison data without first breaking through another line of defense?

9.5 For Further Reading

For foundational concepts in dependability and security, refer to the classic paper by Avižienis et al. [Avižienis 04].

For an official guide to ZT security models, consult the NIST publication [NIST 20].

To explore adversarial machine learning and its associated threats and defenses, see the taxonomy and terminology outlined by Vassilev [Vassilev 24].

For a comprehensive look at managing AI-related risks, refer to the Artificial Intelligence Risk Management Framework developed by NIST [NIST 23] and the Fraunhofer AI Assessment Catalog [FraunhoferIAIS AIAssCatalog].

For research on misclassification attacks in deep neural networks through minimal pixel manipulation, see Wicker et al.'s paper on black-box safety testing [Wicker 18].

10
Privacy and Fairness

Success in creating AI would be the biggest event in human history. Unfortunately, it might also be the last, unless we learn how to avoid the risks.
—Stephen Hawking

The real problem is not the existential threat of AI. Instead, it is in the development of ethical AI systems.
—Rana el Kaliouby

HUMAN VALUES ARE the fundamental beliefs and principles that guide our actions and decisions. They can vary depending on culture, religion, and personal experiences. Examples include fairness, justice, privacy, and safety.

Many legislators, regulators. and organizations are attempting to define and provide principles, laws, and regulations to control how AI systems deal with human values. Terms that are used in this space are as follows:

- **Ethical AI** focuses on ensuring that AI systems are built and used in a way that aligns with human values. It asks questions like: Is the AI biased? Does it respect privacy? Who is accountable for its decisions?

- **Responsible AI** is the practice of developing and using AI systems in a way that benefits individuals, groups, and society while minimizing the risk of negative consequences. It takes a broader view, considering the entire life cycle of AI development and deployment, including not just the ethical implications but also the social and environmental impacts. Responsible AI might ask: How will this AI affect people's jobs? Does it use too much energy?

- **Trustworthy AI** focuses on evaluating and ensuring the objective quality of AI systems, including ethical and responsible AI concerns. Key considerations include reliability, transparency, fairness, privacy, security, accountability, and minimizing risks.

- **Trust in AI** focuses on the subjective perception people have when using these systems. Trust should be calibrated to the objective trustworthiness of AI to avoid overtrusting or undertrusting.

Some of the threads that run through these terms we cover in other chapters. Chapter 11, Observability, discusses transparency, explainability, and accountability. Security is covered in Chapter 9. In this chapter, we focus on privacy and fairness.

10.1 Privacy in AI Systems

Privacy in AI systems is more complex than in traditional software due to the AI system's ability to infer and reveal sensitive information in ways not possible before. The challenge lies in ensuring privacy in terms of not only data access and storage but also the outputs and decisions of the AI system, which can potentially reveal sensitive information.

Note that privacy concerns private data about individual humans, whereas confidentiality also covers sensitive data in organizations (e.g., patent drafts, trade secrets). Privacy of data often mandates handling it with some level of confidentiality, but not all aspects of privacy also concern confidential organizational data.

In healthcare AI applications, an algorithm might predict patient health outcomes based on a variety of inputs. Even if individual health records are kept secure, data from distinct sources can be correlated so as to violate privacy rules. For example, a researcher correlated birth dates of local politicians with health records from that locality to identify politicians with health problems. Their effort was successful, as the researcher was able to identify a high-ranking politician with a severe health condition that was previously not public knowledge. Ensuring privacy in this context means addressing how AI algorithms process, analyze, and reveal data, going beyond traditional data protection measures.

Privacy is mandated in some legal jurisdictions. For example, the California Consumer Privacy Protection Act[1] mandates that consumers have the following rights:

- The right to know about the personal information a business collects about them and how it is used and shared.

---

1. California Consumer Privacy Act: www.oag.ca.gov/privacy/ccpa

- The right to have businesses delete personal information collected about them.
- The right to opt out of the sale or sharing of their personal information.
- The right to correct inaccurate personal information that a business has about them.
- The right to limit the use and disclosure of sensitive personal information collected about them.

The acronym LOCKED (limit, opt-out, correct, know, equal, delete) is used as shorthand for these rights.[2] The European Union has established the General Data Protection Regulation (GDPR), which covers much of the same ground. Some of these rules pose technical and organizational challenges, which we discuss in Section 10.3, "Achieving Privacy."

10.2 Fairness in AI Systems

Fairness in AI grapples with the subtleties of biases present in training data and AI systems' potential to perpetuate or exacerbate these biases. It is not just about the fairness of outcomes (e.g., decisions made by an AI system), but also about the fairness of decision processes and model development processes, including data collection, algorithm design, and the ongoing management of the system.

For instance, in recruitment AI tools, fairness is challenged by historical biases present in the data. An AI system might inadvertently learn to prefer candidates from a certain demographic background—not because of an explicit programming choice, but because the training data reflects historical hiring biases. Addressing fairness in this context requires a conceptual shift to understand and mitigate how AI systems can learn and perpetuate societal biases.

Fairness also includes avoiding cultural biases in use of color—for example, red. In Western cultures, red might represent love or danger. In China, it symbolizes good luck and happiness. Internationalism applies to more than just language, and systems that are intended for international use must be mindful of a wide variety of issues.

---

2. *A Guide to Understanding Your Privacy Rights*: https://privacy.ca.gov/wp-content/uploads/sites/357/2024/01/LOCKED-A-guide-to-understanding-your-privacy-rights.pdf

10.3 Achieving Privacy

With privacy requirements being codified in laws and regulations, and fines being levied for violations, approaches to achieving privacy are becoming increasingly documented and utilized. Some of the problems associated with achieving privacy will be tested in the courts, and the results of these disputes may be forthcoming in some years. For example, suppose you wish to delete personal information about you but that information has been used in training or in feature definition. What does deletion mean in that context? This is, as yet, an unsolved problem.

We describe both organizational responses to privacy concerns and technical responses (architecture, data preparation, testing, and operations), before covering issues specific to foundation models (FMs).

10.3.1 Organizational Approaches

Many organizations now have executives who oversee the organization's overall privacy strategy. These executives may have titles such as chief privacy officer (CPO) or data protection officer (DPO), and a team may be assembled to help them fulfill their duties. The responsibilities for these executives and teams include the following:

- Developing and implementing data privacy policies and procedures
- Monitoring compliance with data privacy laws and regulations
- Handling data subject requests (e.g., access, deletion)
- Managing data breaches
- Educating employees about privacy best practices

10.3.2 Architecture and Data Preparation

A key architectural decision that the architect must make is where in the system privacy decisions will be made. For example, these decisions could be made during the data preparation phase by obscuring or not entering privacy-related data. The privacy decision could also be made in the architecture by having a monitor or guardrail that examines the output of the model for deviations from privacy rules. In this section, we discuss the LOCKED rights in the light of this distinction. In general, access controls should be applied to all data collected about an individual and the principle of least privilege should be applied to that data.

Implementing the LOCKED Rights

An examination of the LOCKED rights shows which rights are ensured at the data preparation stage and which through architectural mechanisms.

- **Limit:** Only use data for purposes allowed under privacy regulations.
- **Opt-out:** For an individual to opt out of sharing of data collected during operations, that individual must be given the option of opting out (architectural), and that option should be honored when sharing data with partners of a business.
- **Correct:** To correct erroneous data, the data collected must be tagged with the identity of an individual. The corrected data can be placed in the data repository, and the system retrained with the corrected data. If retraining is too expensive, then retrieval techniques such as retrieval-augmented generation (RAG) can be used to utilize correct data or guardrail mechanisms can be used to test for incorrect data.
- **Know:** To know the information an organization has collected about an individual, all data relevant to an individual should be tagged. Then a separate architectural element can query the data repository about the individual and retrieve the data pertinent to the individual.
- **Equal:** Records of the invocation of privacy rights should be access controlled, and access should be granted to only auditing personnel and modules involved in enforcing those rights.
- **Delete:** To delete information collected about an individual, information must be tagged with an individual's identifying information. As noted earlier, it remains to be seen whether, or under which circumstances, deletion applies to models that used data during training.

Additional Considerations

Some additional considerations in achieving privacy are highlighted here. First, it is important to implement access controls on every access to data. The principle of least privilege should be applied so that only necessary access is allowed.

Second, apply differential privacy. This technique adds noise to data while still allowing the AI model to learn effectively. This helps protect the privacy of individuals in the dataset.

Third, AI systems are rarely built from scratch under the control of a single organization. Instead, the components and services integrated into these systems come from various sources, with each potentially carrying its own set of value alignments or misalignments. These implications are often not addressed in typical supply or license agreements, nor are they covered in software bills of materials (SBOMs). This lack of coverage in agreements and documentation means that human privacy considerations omitted from these supply chain components can significantly influence the conformance to the LOCKED rights. A guardrail component is the only mechanism currently available to an architect to detect and mitigate violations. For this reason, including a guardrail component in the architecture is a must for many applications.

10.3.3 Testing and Operations

Testing for adherence to some LOCKED principles can be performed during the model build and test phases. For example, in one test you might change an individual's specific data and determine whether the change results in failing a test and, in turn, requires retraining.

During operations, the guardrail component should monitor the output of the model for violations of the LOCKED principles. Violations should be logged and prevented from being output. An analyst can examine the logs and determine the cause; they can then make recommendations regarding mitigation techniques.

10.3.4 Foundation Models

FMs, owing to their scale and non-domain-specific training, present special problems with respect to privacy. In our discussion of the LOCKED principles, we emphasized maintaining the lineage of data items and associating individuals with data relevant to them. Because the training data for FMs is generally not available, however, it is difficult to know the extent to which FMs adhere to the LOCKED principles. The sources of training data can include the following:

- Online sources including web pages, Wikipedia, and social media
- Books and articles
- Prompts from users that contain context information
- Domain-specific data used to fine-tune FMs

In addition, FMs offer a range of general capabilities, including emergent capabilities that are often discovered post-release/deployment, rather than being designed for specific functions as in traditional software systems.

Traditional systems are developed with specific uses in mind, accompanied by specific test cases. In contrast, the general capabilities of FMs are evaluated with more nonspecific benchmarking. Use-specific evaluation will be delayed until contexts of use are better understood and decided. This approach leads to increased uncertainty and risk, as the full spectrum of an FM's capabilities and potential misalignments with privacy might not be evident until the model is actively used in diverse real-world scenarios.

Architecture
Guardrails are a mechanism in the architecture that can monitor output for adherence to most LOCKED principles, except for opting out. Opt-out has no FM-specific impact on the architecture. The other principles can be tested by the guardrail at the time of operation and mitigated as necessary.

Testing and Operations
Testing can determine whether the guardrails catch violations of LOCKED principles. Opt-out is not a principle that can be tested by a guardrail, but the other principles can be turned into tests of either the system or the process.

Operations has no FM-specific aspects related to privacy, though the considerations related to monitoring, logging, and analysis still apply.

10.4 Achieving Fairness

Fairness does not have the same precision in definition as privacy does. Moreover, it has not been a concern in software systems for as long as privacy has. Today, organizations are investigating the meaning and implications of constructing AI systems to be fair. Emerging principles of fairness include the following considerations:

- **Avoiding bias:** AI systems can inherit biases from the data they are trained on, leading to discriminatory outcomes. Fairness means mitigating these biases.
- **Equal treatment:** Ideally, similar individuals should be treated similarly by the AI, regardless of background.
- **Fairness for groups:** Groups should not be disadvantaged, nor should individuals because of their membership in groups. Ensuring fairness for groups can be trickier than addressing individual fairness, as different metrics may be used.

10.4.1 Organizational Approaches and Tools

As yet, fairness has not achieved the same organizational prominence as privacy, but organizations are increasingly concerned about this issue. One organizational approach for addressing this concern is to create a fairness team. Such a team should be cross-functional with members from data science, engineering, legal, and ethics. The diverse team might be assembled to address fairness concerns. Another approach is to rely on third-party expertise: Organizations might consult external fairness experts to audit their systems and recommend mitigation strategies.

Some tools can assist developers in achieving fairness in their systems:

- **AI Fairness 360 (AIF360) by IBM**[3]: This open-source toolkit provides functionalities throughout the development life cycle. It allows developers to identify bias in training data, assess model fairness using various metrics, and even experiment with mitigation techniques.

- **Fairlearn by Microsoft**[4]: This is another open-source toolkit focusing on assessing and mitigating fairness issues. Fairlearn offers prebuilt algorithms to address bias in data and models, along with visualization tools to understand how different groups are affected by the AI system.

- **Google's PAIR Tools**[5]: Although some tools developed by Google's People + AI Research (PAIR) initiative are internal, a few resources have been made publicly available. One such tool is the What-If Tool, which helps visualize how changing certain aspects of the model might impact fairness metrics.

10.4.2 Architecture

Two architectural mechanisms exist to help achieve fairness. The first is based on guardrails or monitors. Such a guardrail or monitor should examine the output of a model with the goal to detect and mitigate fairness violations.

The second mechanism is logging. Logging inputs and outputs of a model allows for offline analysis to determine whether fair outcomes have

---

3. https://aif360.res.ibm.com/

4. https://fairlearn.org/

5. https://pair.withgoogle.com/

been achieved. This approach can apply mitigations only after violations have occurred, and should be used only in cases where a small number of violations can be temporarily tolerated.

10.4.3 Data and Model Preparation

Fairness in an AI system is dependent on the training data. The training data not only should be representative of the actual real-world inputs, but also should be seeded with data from underrepresented groups. This seeding will enable the model to consider members of the underrepresented groups in its predictions.

The following metrics, among others, can be used to test the training data:

- **Statistical parity (demographic parity):** This metric ensures the model's outcome is independent of a sensitive attribute (e.g., race or gender). For instance, in a loan approval system, demographic parity would mean the approval rate is the same across genders, races, and other characteristics.

- **Equal opportunity:** This metric focuses on whether equally qualified individuals from different groups have the same chance of a positive outcome. It considers factors relevant to the decision. While statistical parity ensures uniform outcomes across groups regardless of other factors, equal opportunity specifically ensures that individuals with the same qualifications or characteristics have an equal chance of receiving a positive outcome, accounting for the relevant factors in the decision-making process.

- **Equalized odds:** This metric requires the true positive rate (correctly identified positive cases) and the false positive rate (incorrectly identified positive cases) to be the same for different groups. It ensures a model isn't overly cautious or excessively lenient toward specific groups.

- **Predictive parity:** This metric focuses on whether the model's predictions (positive or negative) align with reality for different groups. For example, it might assess if a recidivism prediction model is equally accurate for people of all races.

- **Treatment equality:** This metric looks at whether individuals from different groups receive similar treatments (e.g., loan amounts) for the same predicted outcome.

Tests that can be performed to determine fairness involve systematically changing specific data items. The pattern is to provide two sets of input that are identical except for one data attribute, and then to compare the results the system produces for these inputs. For example, the data attribute might be gender to test for gender discrimination, or race for racial discrimination. It might also be the postal code. Some unfair factors are manifested in housing patterns, and this kind of testing can identify whether the decisions of the AI system reflect these factors.

10.4.4 Operations

A guardrail or monitor can detect some decisions that are unfair and mitigate them. In addition, other considerations are relevant during operation.

- **Data drift and changes in societal norms:** These changes pose an ongoing challenge for AI models in maintaining alignment with human values. As society evolves, so do its values and norms, which means that AI models need to adapt continuously to remain relevant and aligned. For example, it was not so long ago that married females were denied loans or credit cards in their own name; in the United States, the law ending such practices came into effect in 1974. For a more recent example, the attitude toward mental health has shifted across many societies in the last 10 years, and so have the accepted ways in which to talk, write, and joke about it. This necessity for constant adaptation can lead to models becoming outdated or misaligned with current human values if they are not regularly updated to reflect societal changes.

- **Human-in-the-loop evaluation:** Integrating human expertise into the evaluation process can provide valuable insights into the model's alignment with human values that might not be captured by purely quantitative metrics.

- **Continuous monitoring for bias drift:** Regularly monitoring the model's performance on fairness metrics after deployment allows for early detection of bias drift as the model encounters new data.

10.4.5 Foundation Models

Fairness and bias in FMs are complex and multifaceted issues. Despite being trained on a large corpora of data, these models often reflect the biases inherent in the data they learn from. This can lead to skewed representations, particularly when the data is predominantly focused on popular languages or cultures, leaving out or underrepresenting certain groups or perspectives. As a result, the model's outputs may unintentionally perpetuate existing societal biases or overlook important nuances.

At the same time, FMs are capable of adopting different personas or points of view when generating responses, which further complicates the assessment of fairness and bias. The ability of these models to switch between perspectives makes it challenging to pinpoint bias as originating from a single, consistent source within the model. Instead, the bias may manifest in various ways depending on the context or the specific prompt, making it difficult to establish a clear understanding of the model's overall fairness.

10.5 Summary

Privacy and fairness are similar in that they reflect human values, but they differ in the amount of specificity that exists in their definition and governance. Privacy is increasingly represented in the executive office through CPOs or DPOs. Fairness, if there is a governance mechanism, is embodied in fairness teams.

Privacy has a specific definition in terms of the LOCKED rights. This makes it easier to derive architectural mechanisms and tests. Fairness is not as precisely defined, and statistical tests or systematic variation of input are the measures used to determine whether a system is fair.

Both qualities apply to systems that operate on data of or about humans. A guardrail is required to detect violations, and continuous logging and monitoring to enable offline analysis.

10.6 Discussion Questions

1. How would you implement the right to be forgotten in an FM?

2. In your organization, is there a CPO? If so, what is the reporting chain of the CPO?

3. In your organization, what are considered disadvantaged groups? What practices exist to remove the disadvantages for these groups? How long have these practices been in effect and what has been their impact?

10.7 For Further Reading

For insights into best practices for creating responsible AI systems, refer to *Responsible AI: Best Practices for Creating Trustworthy Systems* by Lu et al. [Lu 23A]. This book offers comprehensive guidelines on responsible AI governance and engineering.

To explore global principles of responsible AI, the Organization for Economic Co-operation and Development's AI principles provide a useful framework [OECD AIPrinciples].

For an understanding of privacy rights and the California Consumer Privacy Act (CCPA), see the LOCKED guide mentioned earlier and the official CCPA information page [CCPA].

The *Responsible AI Pattern Catalogue* by Lu et al. [Lu 24C] provides a rich collection of best practices for AI governance and system design.

For AI system design practices, the article "Responsible-AI-by-Design: A Pattern Collection for Designing Responsible AI Systems" by Lu et al. [Lu 23B] offers practical patterns to guide the development of responsible AI.

For a discussion on designing FM-based AI systems in the generative AI era, see the work by Lu et al. [Lu 24D].

Operationalizing responsible AI is discussed by Zhu et al. in their chapter on AI and ethics [Zhu 22].

Finally, for safety-by-design in AI systems, the taxonomy of runtime guardrails by Shamsujjoha et al. [Shamsujjoha 24] presents practical guidelines for implementing AI safety.

11
Observability

Sunlight is said to be the best disinfectant.
—Louis D. Brandeis

OBSERVABILITY ENABLES AI engineers to detect anomalies, optimize performance, and build trust. This chapter explores the definition of observability and other related qualities, and the approaches used to achieve it.

11.1 Fundamental Concepts

Observability, in the context of computer systems, refers to the ability of an external agent to understand the actions of the system. The external agent can be a human or another system. The understanding may be based on outputs of the system or on the actions during system development, operation, and model training. The external agent can observe the system in real time during operations or as a portion of analysis that occurs independently from normal operation.

Repositories for code and data can be used to support observability. The system itself can record information (e.g., logs) that can be used to support observability. The infrastructure can monitor resource utilization, which also supports observability.

A number of related qualities follow from observability, all with slightly different nuances. Monitorability, explainability, auditability, and transparency are all related concepts, albeit being on separate levels of abstraction and not completely covered by observability.

- **Transparency:** The ability of a stakeholder to gain information about the software development process and execution, and the elements that entered into a system.

- **Monitorability:** The ability to monitor information in real time. This is frequently visualized on a dashboard that shows summary information and sends out alerts if the system behavior leaves defined boundaries (e.g., too many unhealthy servers or too few active users). Monitoring can be seen as a prerequisite to observability, as we discuss later in this chapter.

- **Auditability:** The ability of an auditor to generate an explanation of the results of a system's actions. It is usually relevant in the context of a regulatory or legal proceeding.

- **Explainability:** The ability to generate an explanation of the actions of the system. Explainable AI (XAI) aims to make the decision making of AI systems understandable to stakeholders.

In addition, alerts generated for performance (see Chapter 8, Performance) depend on the availability of the appropriate data—that is, on observability.

11.2 Evolving from Monitorability to Observability

Monitorability focuses on tracking and visualizing predefined software quality metrics to quickly detect the issues occurring in a software system. In contrast, *observability* refers to the ability to understand the internal state of a software system by analyzing its output data beyond just predefined metrics to prevent, diagnose, and correct problems.

The evolution from monitorability to observability represents a shift in how we understand and manage complex software systems. This progression reflects a move from a relatively narrow focus on system health indicators toward a comprehensive, nuanced understanding of system behavior in real time. Let's explore this transformation in more detail.

11.2.1 Monitorability: The Early Stages

Initially, the concept of monitorability was central to maintaining system reliability and performance (Figure 11.1). This stage primarily focused on collecting metrics, such as CPU usage, memory consumption, and network utilization, alongside unstructured logs that captured events without a predefined format. The goal was to identify and address issues impacting mean time between failures (MTBF), mean time to repair (MTTR), and mean time to detect (MTTD)—central metrics for evaluating system reliability and operational efficiency. However, this approach often relied on disconnected tools and methodologies, limiting the ability to correlate events and metrics across different services for the same incoming request. The lack of structured data and interconnectivity between monitoring tools made it challenging to diagnose and resolve issues efficiently, often leading to prolonged downtime and compromised system performance.

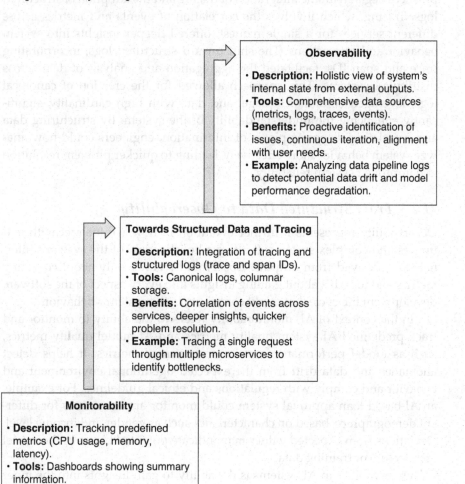

Observability

- **Description:** Holistic view of system's internal state from external outputs.
- **Tools:** Comprehensive data sources (metrics, logs, traces, events).
- **Benefits:** Proactive identification of issues, continuous iteration, alignment with user needs.
- **Example:** Analyzing data pipeline logs to detect potential data drift and model performance degradation.

Towards Structured Data and Tracing

- **Description:** Integration of tracing and structured logs (trace and span IDs).
- **Tools:** Canonical logs, columnar storage.
- **Benefits:** Correlation of events across services, deeper insights, quicker problem resolution.
- **Example:** Tracing a single request through multiple microservices to identify bottlenecks.

Monitorability

- **Description:** Tracking predefined metrics (CPU usage, memory, latency).
- **Tools:** Dashboards showing summary information.
- **Limitations:** Disconnected tools, limited correlation of events, reactive approach.
- **Example:** A dashboard monitoring CPU usage and network latency.

Figure 11.1 *Evolution from monitorability to observability.*

11.2.2 Evolution toward Structured Data and Tracing

The evolution from basic monitorability to more advanced observability practices began with the integration of tracing and the adoption of structured logs. Tracing, which involves the correlation of events and metrics across different services for a single request, offered deeper insights into system behavior and interactions. The shift toward structured logs, incorporating trace and span IDs, facilitated the aggregation and analysis of data across distributed systems. This approach allowed for the creation of canonical logs, leveraged columnar storage, and data with high cardinality, significantly enhancing the understandability of the system. By structuring data and correlating disparate pieces of information, engineers could now analyze system behavior more effectively, leading to quicker problem resolution and improved system reliability.

11.2.3 From Structured Data to Observability

Observability represents a further evolution in how we interact with and understand complex systems. It offers a holistic view of the system's internal state, derived from outputs. Observability is not only about collecting metrics and logs; it's about gaining insights into every aspect of the software development life cycle that might contribute to the system's behavior.

In the context of AI, monitorability refers to the ability to monitor and track predefined AI system quality metrics and AI model quality metrics, such as model performance metrics and fairness metrics. It helps detect anomalies and data drift from the expected operational environment and behavior and comply with regulations and ethical guidelines. For example, an AI-based loan approval system could monitor approval rates for different demographics, based on characteristics such as gender and income level. Deviations from expected values may indicate potential biases in the model architecture or training data.

Observability in AI systems is the ability to gain insights into the inner workings of the AI system at the model level, the system level, and the model development and deployment pipeline level, and into its operating infrastructure. It enables developers to proactively identify potential data, model, or concept drift and to anticipate performance degradation and incidents before they adversely impact users. To extend our loan approval example, proactive analysis of data pipeline logs can help in the early detection of bottlenecks or errors during data ingestion and preprocessing, which might lead to data or concept drift.

Monitorability is more reactive, concentrating on identifying AI system issues as they occur. Observability is more proactive, focusing on understanding an AI system; detecting data, model, and concept drift early; and preventing incidents. Furthermore, observability leverages a broader range of data sources, including various metrics, logs, traces, and events generated by the AI system, rather than solely relying on predefined metrics. Monitorability of AI systems is akin to a car's dashboard, on which instruments such as a speedometer, fuel gauge, and engine temperature gauge provide real-time feedback. Observability is analogous to opening the car's hood and inspecting internal components such as the engine and transmission to gain deeper insights.

11.3 Approaches for Enhancing Observability

Achieving observability requires two different approaches: recording system activity and tracing the lineage of data items and the components included in the system. To support accountability, not just the data and component lineage should be recorded, but also the personnel involved in generating the data model and the components. Monitoring is designed into the architecture, and lineage is recorded during the model build and system build phases. Both elements must be available during operations. We begin with the architecture, before covering all relevant phases of the life cycle.

11.3.1 Architecture

One mechanism used in the architecture to support observability is having a monitor. The system should record its activity through maintaining logs. Common logging practices include the following:

- **Log levels:** Categorize the importance of a logged message. Common levels are debug, info, warning, error, and fatal. This lets developers control the verbosity of logs, filtering out less important details during normal operation.

- **Structured logging:** Use formats that are machine-readable (e.g., JSON). This allows for easier parsing by analysis tools and facilitates aggregation of logs.

- **Include context:** Include relevant details such as timestamps, user IDs, URLs, or error codes. This context helps developers quickly understand the situation when investigating issues.

A data lineage tool can provide insights into the history of the data used in the model making a prediction. The architecture should include interfaces into the repositories used to store data and the tools that can track their lineage.

In addition, the software bill of materials (SBOM) will provide the lineage of the non-AI components. The architecture should provide mechanisms for accessing the SBOM.

Later in this chapter, we list a number of observability- and monitoring-related features. For these features to be available, they need to be designed and built into the system. A DevOps best practice is to treat ops personnel as first-class stakeholders—doing so will result in requirements for system properties concerning logging, monitoring, and more.

We now turn to the activities associated with building the model.

11.3.2 Data Preparation and Model Build

Mechanisms used during data preparation include lineage tools and explaining mechanisms.

Model Lineage Tools

Data used for building AI models is collected from various sources such as databases, APIs, and web-based text data. Before the data is stored in the warehouse, it often undergoes transformation, which involves data cleaning, normalization, and aggregation. The transformed data is then loaded into the data warehouse. This could involve writing the data into specific tables designed for query performance and storage efficiency. The loading process may be done in batches or as a continuous stream.

Tracing the original sources of the data used in model training can be challenging, particularly when the data is gathered from various sources and undergoes multiple transformations. Data lineage tools associated with the data warehouse can track the journey of data as it flows through the system, from its origins (source systems) to its destinations within the data warehouse.

Data lineage tools also provide real-time access to the lineage of data items. The architecture must be designed to use that type of interface to enable observability during operations.

Model testing and evaluation should include tests to determine whether the data that goes into a model and its lineage can be accurately tracked. Uncertainties in model predictions should be calculated and associated with the model.

Explainability

The basis for explaining model results is developed during the model test. Subdivided along the dimension of scope, there are two main types of XAI techniques: local explanation techniques and global explanation techniques.

Local explanation techniques provide instance-based explanations, which can help users understand the feature importance and correlations that led to the specific outputs. There are two well-known local explanation algorithms: Local Interpretable Model-Agnostic Explanations (LIME) and Shapley Additive exPlanations (SHAP). LIME explains a black box model by determining the contribution of each feature to the decision output for a specific input. SHAP provides local explanations by comparing the model's decision outputs when a feature is included versus excluded. Insights can be gained into the importance of a feature value by perturbing it slightly (e.g., varying the income level in a loan application) and comparing the differences. By providing information about the feature importance and correlations that resulted in a decision, a local explainer can give insights into the inner workings of a model and the reasoning behind a specific decision.

Global explanation techniques can help users understand the general behavior of an AI system by using a set of data instances to produce explanations. These explanations provide an overview of the model's behavior by visualizing the relationship between the input features and the model's output over a range of values. Partial dependence plots provide a visualization of feature importance. Global surrogate models, such as tree-based models and rule-based models, can be used to understand complex AI models because they have inherent explainability, allowing the output decisions to be traced back to their source. Global explanations simplify the workings of complex AI models by reducing them to linear counterparts, which are easier to understand.

There are two options to consider when explaining the decision-making process of foundation model-based systems: "think aloud" and "think silently." Both are the subject of ongoing research. In addition, mechanical interpretability—understanding and tracing the inner workings of models at a structural level—is another approach that is being explored to improve transparency and explainability in these systems.

11.3.3 System Build

System build is the stage in which the SBOM is constructed. During the system build phase, components are drawn from the version control system and model development, and dependencies are drawn from libraries and downloaded from repositories. All of these elements are entered into the system SBOM. One method for recording the SBOM is to place it into a versioning registry. Incorporating model versions leads to the concept of a co-versioning registry.

Co-versioning Registry

Systems are continuously changing. Both AI models and traditional software components evolve through updates. Tracing the specific versions of each component involved in a decision and understanding the impact of changes on model behavior can be challenging. Compared with traditional software, AI systems have more complex dependencies and may evolve more frequently due to their data-driven nature. From the perspective of the AI system, knowing the version of each integrated component is key. From the viewpoint of the AI component, it is important to understand which datasets and parameters were used for training and which data was used for evaluation.

Co-versioning of AI components and artifacts provides end-to-end provenance guarantees throughout the entire AI system life cycle. A co-versioning registry tracks the co-evolution of software components and AI artifacts. Several different levels of co-versioning are possible: co-versioning of AI and non-AI components, co-versioning of AI artifacts (i.e., co-versioning of the data, model, code, and configurations), and co-versioning of local models and global models in federated learning. Co-versioning enables effective maintenance and evolution of AI components because the deployed model or code can be traced to the exact set of artifacts, parameters, and metadata that were used in its development.

11.3.4 System Test

During system tests, the operation of the total system is tested. This includes the elements that we have already mentioned:

- Logs to enable the tracking of a query through various components
- Accessing the data lineage created during model build
- Accessing the SBOM

In addition, system-wide tests covering expected use cases involving observability should be run. These tests can involve a human in the loop to provide for interactivity during operations.

11.3.5 Operations

During operations, observability can be enhanced through several measures. For these measures to be available, they have to be included in the system design and the environment setup.

- **Monitoring:** Continuous monitoring can be based on metrics gathered from the infrastructure, logs generated by the system, and uncertainties of the predictions. Associated with the monitors should be a combination of alerts together with the thresholds for generating those alerts. Independent monitoring agents can be used to perform the monitoring and keep track of compliance with regulations.

- **Integrating explainability tools:** Explainability techniques such as LIME and SHAP can be integrated into the monitoring dashboard to visualize feature importance, decision pathways, potential biases, and more. The information displayed is that collected during the model test.

- **Independent overseeing agents:** These agents act as external systems that observe and analyze the behavior of foundation model (FM)–based systems. They can ensure FM-based systems behave responsibly and avoid generating offensive or undesired content and actions. If necessary, they might take steps to address detected issues—for example, notifying humans or stopping specific operations.

11.4 Summary

Achieving observability involves architectural mechanisms such as monitors, SBOM access modules, and modules that access various repositories created during the data preparation and build stages of the life cycle. During these stages, lineage capturing tools and model versioning tools should be employed. These can be accessed during operations to help explain why a particular output or decision was generated.

Currently, the techniques for explaining the behavior of FMs are very limited, but this is a very active area of research. Today, the explanations might be partial and hard to understand, but that situation is expected to improve in the future.

11.5 Discussion Questions

1. Ask your favorite chatbot to differentiate between monitorability and observability in AI systems. Then ask it to explain its answer. Is the explanation satisfactory?

2. How do you define and measure the "health" of an AI system?

3. Suppose a site reliability engineer (SRE) is responsible for responding to alerts. How would an SRE go about analyzing an alert from an AI system involving data drift? Can this be accomplished and a repair found in real time?

11.6 For Further Reading

To gain insights into achieving observability in production ML pipelines, refer to Shankar and Parameswaran's work, which discusses the challenges and approaches for enhancing observability in ML systems [Shankar 21].

For a broader understanding of observability in production environments, including engineering best practices to achieve production excellence, see *Observability Engineering* by Majors, Fong-Jones, and Miranda [Majors 22].

For a relevant discussion of the implications of observability in the context of software supply chains and how it impacts AI systems, consult Xia et al.'s empirical study on SBOMs [Xia 24B].

12

The Fraunhofer Case Study: Using a Pretrained Language Model for Tendering

with Sven Giesselbach, Dennis Wegener, Katharina Beckh, Claudio Martens, Hammam Abdelwahab, Birgit Kirsch, and Vishwani Gupta

As part of Fraunhofer, the largest organization for applied research in Europe, the Fraunhofer Institute for Intelligent Analysis and Information Systems (IAIS) is one of the leading scientific institutes in the fields of Artificial Intelligence (AI), Machine Learning, and Big Data in Germany and Europe. Around 350 employees support companies in the optimization of products and services, as well as in the development of new technologies, processes, and new digital business models. Fraunhofer IAIS is shaping the digital transformation of our working and living environments: with innovative AI applications for industry, health, and sustainability, with forward-looking technologies such as large-scale AI language models or Quantum Machine Learning, with offers for training and education or for the testing of AI applications for security and trustworthiness.[1]

IN THIS CHAPTER, we present a case study that explores the innovative use of AI in the tendering process of a large electronics supplier. Throughout this chapter, we examine how the integration of AI technologies has changed the tendering process. We explore the challenges the company faced, the strategies it used to overcome these obstacles, and the results it achieved.

---

1. www.iais.fraunhofer.de/

The remainder of this chapter unfolds as follows. We first describe the tendering process and the specific problems the company wants to solve. Next, we present the requirements for the AI solution regarding data, infrastructure, operations, and quality. After the case study setup, we dive into the three different phases of the AI system's development: proof of concept (PoC), implementation, and production.

12.1 The Problem Context

Fraunhofer IAIS was contracted to solve a problem for a client, using its specific expertise in AI. The client was a big vendor providing various electronics parts such as different rocker switches. Its portfolio of products exceeds 50,000 items. The client takes part in the tendering processes depicted in Figure 12.1.

The tendering process begins when a customer initially inquires about a product or service and ends when the customer actually places an order. In industries such as construction, where there is a three-tier distribution model, the process starts with architects requesting quotes for electrical components needed in their projects. These requests are standardized and sent out to wholesalers, which then pass them on to different vendors to get pricing information. The request to the vendor takes the form of a request for tender (RFT), also called a "position request." Vendors then propose products that match the descriptions provided in the request. Finally, once the wholesaler has gathered all of the necessary pricing information, it compiles the information into a quotation and sends it back to the architect. This process requires a deep understanding of products and a lot of effort, especially when creating custom quotes for wholesalers.

Currently, this matching process at the vendor's side is done manually by employees in the quoting department (hereafter referred to as "employees"). It includes reading and understanding the requirements described in the tender, matching the requirements with the product portfolio, and then selecting the correct products in the right amounts. Given the sheer number of products, this is a tedious, time-consuming, and difficult task. The client therefore looked into AI as a solution to automate parts of the process. Its idea was to start with a subset of the most frequently sold products and build an AI application that automatically adds them to a bid whenever appropriate.

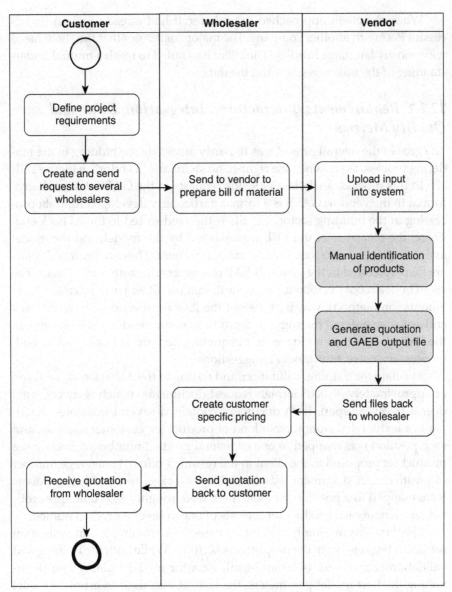

Figure 12.1 *The tendering process. The gray boxes include the manual steps that are later replaced by the AI system.*

When the client approached Fraunhofer, it had already had an unsuccessful PoC with another company. The major challenges that the client faced were mostly language hurdles. The client had failed to reach a mutual understanding of the business goals and the data.

12.1.1 Requirements: Interactions, Integration, Data, and Quality Metrics

The goal of the overall project was to partly automate the bidding in the tendering process, as shown in the right-hand swimlane "vendor" in Figure 12.1.

In this process, a wholesaler sends requests in the GAEB data exchange format to the vendor; GAEB is a format particularly developed for data processing in the building sector. The file is then redirected to the AI back end. There, the elements of the RFT are analyzed by the model, and the model assigns a product set recommendation per element. These recommendations are then uploaded in the vendor's SAP (the enterprise software) system. The client built a robot via robotic process automation (RPA; a user interface–level automation method), which processed the JSON response from the AI back end and then entered the suggested products in the vendor's SAP system. In the SAP system, the employees in the quoting department can validate and, if necessary, correct the model's suggestions.

The data for training, validation, and testing of the AI back end consisted of approximately 30,000 German request documents, which were collected over a two-year span. Each document contained several positions, detailing in a textual description what kind of product the customer requests, and each position was mapped to one or several product numbers reflecting the product set proposed to the client in the resulting offer. The average number of positions per document was 22 and, on average, two product numbers were mapped to a position. In total, there were roughly 40,000 unique product sets, where each product set consists of one to several product numbers.

The data was randomly split into three sets—a training set, an evaluation set, and a test set—with the proportions 80:10:10. While both the training and validation sets served as ground-truth data for model training and determining the best model parameters, the test set was used to estimate model performance during the evaluation phase. To show representative results, the test set was selected by random sampling; it contained a huge number of documents. This is an example of the process described in Chapter 5, AI Model Life Cycle.

To assess the quality of the model, both quantitative and qualitative methods were used. In addition to an automated evaluation, the employees assessed the model performance on unseen data and categorized the model recommendations into three categories: incorrect, correct, and functionally correct. The last category refers to model recommendations that include the correct product type but do not meet the expected characteristics of the product (e.g., wrong color). Qualitative feedback was collected through exchanges with the employees in regular client meetings.

12.1.2 Development and Operations

The project faced additional challenges because two sites were involved. The data resided in the company's on-premises systems, but Fraunhofer was developing the system and training the model. We decided to perform the exploration, development, and CI/CD phases at Fraunhofer, as the company could not provide all of the necessary knowledge and compute resources at the beginning of the project. System operation takes place at the company side.

Challenges occurred on both the organizational and technical sides. Organizational challenges included the timing of batch data handover to the Data Science Team as well as the handover of the machine learning (ML) solution, including the ML model, as a component to the company so it could be included in the company's processes. Technical challenges were the actual transfer format and tooling for the batch data transfer, and the definition and testing of the ML component without having access to the company's infrastructure.

We decided to follow a containerized setup using Docker from the beginning to address the technical challenge of transferring the ML application, so the component was encapsulated, isolated, portable, and prepared for scale-up.

12.2 Case Study Description and Setup

The project was structured into three phases: (1) a PoC to prove the feasibility of the approach, (2) a main project to integrate the application on the customer side, and (3) maintenance and operation after the deployment. The PoC had an overall duration of three months with a break at the halfway point, at which time the project partners could decide to halt the project if no significant progress was made. In the main project (implementation phase), the goal was to bring the solution from a prototypical state into a state of productive usage. Therefore, modeling and MLOps activities were jointly performed in this phase. In the production phase, the solution was already running in a production environment. The goal of this phase was to maintain and further enhance the application.

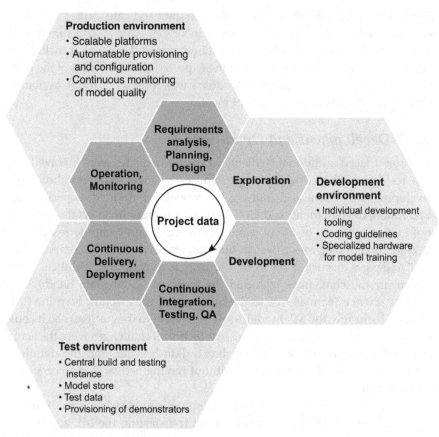

Figure 12.2 *The IAIS MLOps cycle and its phases and technical environments.*

12.2.1 MLOps Approach and Generic Architecture

For this case study, we follow the MLOps practices introduced in Chapter 2, Software Engineering Background, Chapter 5, AI Model Life Cycle, and Chapter 6, System Life Cycle. At IAIS, we developed our own instantiation of MLOps over the years, an overview of which is depicted in Figure 12.2.

The six main phases (requirements analysis, exploration, and so on) shown in Figure 12.2 should be familiar to the readers of this book, albeit in a slightly different grouping than discussed in Chapters 2, 5, and 6. However, there are two areas in which the IAIS instance of MLOps differs: (1) the details given for the environments on the outside, which are more specific and prescriptive, and (2) the "project data" in the center. Integration into the company's processes is crucial, especially when it comes to automation. Therefore, in addition to the six main areas, MLOps includes a seventh important area: communication, unified project and process data management, and information transitions between the other six areas. This is referred to as the central project data area.

We had used our MLOps approach in several successful customer projects in the past, so we chose it for this project as well. Next, we describe some of the organizational and technical aspects of MLOps, insofar as they have not been discussed elsewhere in the book.

In our view, development work should be closely interconnected with continuous feedback, revision, and repetition, following agile patterns such as Scrum and Kanban. The iterative optimization process in model development for ML solutions is based on technical validation and the quality and plausibility of the models. It is important to consider requirements and feedback from the business side, including management, strategy, organization development, sales and marketing, and production. The project organization needs to ensure that the business side is well integrated into agile work planning and the goal setting and evaluation of the models.

ML solution projects generally follow an agile organizational structure. In contrast, delivering and operating application versions can largely be automated through CI/CD pipelines. The deployment of new versions and monitoring in operation are coordinated with the client's business departments.

Our best practice also advocates the use of virtualization technologies such as Docker containers, so as to ensure consistent and reusable build and test environments. These environments can then be reused for demonstrations or later production use if the target environment supports virtualization. CD further automates the configuration and deployment of artifacts in different target environments, ranging from development-oriented test environments to operational production environments.

To successfully implement and run the ML solution for our project, we needed a technical architecture that supported the different phases and the three environments for our MLOps approach. Figure 12.3 visualizes the general technical reference architecture that we often use to implement ML systems, and which we used for this particular project. Besides the three environments, the top part of the figure shows the repositories for the code and the containers. On the bottom, the Data layer is depicted; it is the data prepared and stored. Note that the contracted part of the system focuses on the back end—the integration with non-AI service components was the responsibility of our customer, but the service we developed had to meet the functional and quality requirements to fit into the larger system.

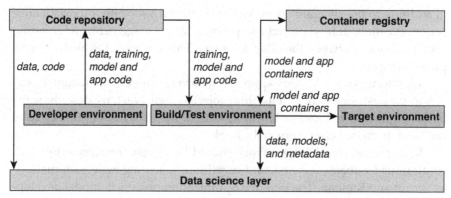

Figure 12.3 *The general technical architecture supporting the MLOps cycle, which is refined and made more concrete later in the chapter.*

The architecture depicted in Figure 12.3 can be instantiated with the respective tools and frameworks according to the requirements of an individual project. In the next section, we describe the important parts and components of the architecture that were needed to set up and run our project. We then present the details of the implementation, including the choice of tools and frameworks.

This high-level architecture enables a seamless transition from model development to deployment, ensuring that the trained ML models are reliable, scalable, and easily maintainable in production.

12.2.2 Setup of ML Solution

The task was modeled as a multi-class classification problem. (See Chapter 3, AI Background, for a description of this modeling technique.) A label is a product set that can contain one or several products. Each document contains multiple positions, each of which is assigned a product set. In the early modeling iterations, every single position was used for recommendation individually. Later, a sequential model was used, which carried information across positions to ensure consistency of recommendations (e.g., with regard to color and product brands).

We started with a distributed embedding-based model (such as Fast-Text), which is easy to train, requires a low level of resources, and can serve as a powerful baseline. After seeing that this model yielded promising performance, albeit with a lot of room for improvement, we pivoted to more complex BERT-based models in the main project. BERT (Bidirectional Encoder Representations from Transformers) models are pretrained on vast amounts of text and can be fine-tuned for specific tasks with few annotated samples. A vast amount of research has investigated classification methods based on these models. One of their most notable benefits is that they give users a confidence value for their recommendations, which makes it easier to spot data points that are challenging for the models. We decided to start with easy-to-implement models, which would give our client an early indication of whether its use case could be solved, and to scale the complexity of the models based on our evaluations and the feedback from the employees. Typically, these kinds of low-resource approaches need more annotated training data. However, data availability was not a challenge in this project, in particular because we opted to handle the most frequently sold products first.

Generative large language models (LLMs) were not used for various reasons. First, at the time of the project, no appropriate open-weight models were available, and the client had ruled out cloud-hosted models. Second, due to the large label space, the need for scalability, and the necessity to obtain a confidence value for each recommendation, smaller encoder-based models were preferred over LLMs. Since this project's completion, smaller open-source LLMs have emerged, which could be a viable alternative to our current models, and with them, methods to constrain the output of their predictions/recommendations to certain classes and even obtain confidence values from them.

In general, LLMs offer a wealth of benefits, such as the need for little to no annotated training data, and should be considered in any natural language processing (NLP) project. However, they also lead to the amplified challenges and requirements during training and operation. For more details on LLMs and their operation (LLMOps), refer to Chapter 4, Foundation Models. More details of the model architectures we selected in the project are given in the discussions of the PoC, implementation, and production phases.

12.2.3 Stakeholder Involvement

Throughout all phases, stakeholders from the client side were involved in various ways. Fraunhofer stated that this client involvement was one key success factor for the collaboration. Stakeholders on the client side included a decision maker, a business unit lead, a project lead, the employees (the actual end users), and IT professionals. The employees were especially heavily involved: They provided valuable insights about the data, helped with modeling decisions, and gave regular feedback about model outputs. The business unit lead and the decision maker were regularly updated about the project progress, which helped with expectations management and allowed for a regular prioritization of the next steps based on the business goals. Finally, the IT professionals were involved in integrating the solution on the client infrastructure and into their software systems.

12.2.4 PoC Phase

Initializing the PoC

During the initialization of the PoC, the client and Fraunhofer had multiple meetings. As the client already had an unsuccessful PoC prior to this PoC, it wanted to make sure that there were significant differences between the approaches adopted in the two attempts and that the problems from the last PoC were accounted for. The client shared a subset of the data with Fraunhofer for preliminary investigation; it also shared the experiences as well as the results from the prior PoC. A workshop was held to jointly determine the goals of the PoC and the approach to be taken by Fraunhofer; it included the employees who would actually use the applications.

Implementing the PoC

In the PoC phase of the project, we mainly addressed three phases of the MLOps cycle: requirements analysis, exploration, and the project data. There was no full MLOps setup yet, so the main goal of this phase was to analyze whether the use case with all its requirements could be addressed with an ML solution that offered sufficient quality. From the technical side, mainly data preprocessing and modeling tasks were performed. These were done within an early version of the development environment, where Jupyter Notebooks and Python scripts were used.

The focus of the PoC was the development of a minimal viable model— that is, a model that showed a certain level of quality in the recommendations could be reached for a subset of the data and the labels. We opted for modeling the use case as a classification problem, where the class labels were bundles of products that are sold together. A subset of a few thousand products was chosen for this phase. The client emphasized the importance of precision over recall, as it wanted the model to be certain in its recommendations but was less concerned about whether the model could include all products in its recommendations. The bulk of the work on the PoC was spent parsing and preprocessing the tender texts correctly, which were given in the GAEB format. We opted for a simple model based on distributed embeddings for the first experiments, whose results proved sufficient to convince the client to proceed to the implementation phase.

During and after the PoC phase, the client and Fraunhofer were in close contact and regularly shared insights about the modeling results. This led to a prioritized list of improvements that Fraunhofer would fix later in the implementation phase.

In the PoC phase, we used Docker-based virtualization. Containerization is useful when doing a PoC of an ML solution because it provides benefits even in this early stage. (See Chapter 2, Software Engineering Background, for a fuller explanation of containers.) Because Docker containers are highly portable and can run on any system that supports Docker, irrespective of the underlying operating system (OS), there is no need for complex setup or configuration when showcasing the PoC on different platforms. Additionally, stateless Docker containers can easily be scaled up or down during the implementation and production phases based on workload requirements, so they are a convenient choice to test the performance of the ML solution under different scenarios or with varying data volumes. Finally, Docker simplifies dependency management by allowing the definition of required libraries, packages, and versions in a Docker file. This ensures consistency and eliminates the risk of version conflicts during the PoC. Overall, Dockerization facilitates the deployment and testing of ML solutions during the PoC phase, providing a consistent, reproducible, and portable environment for evaluation and validation.

Evaluation and Results of the PoC Phase

The PoC was concluded successfully. Fraunhofer performed both quantitative and qualitative evaluations. The quantitative evaluation was conducted using a held-out test set with given ground truth, meaning a correct product set assignment per requirement text. Applying the model to this test set, precision, recall, and F1 scores were calculated to estimate the model's performance.

As part of the qualitative evaluation, Fraunhofer and the client manually investigated the model results on an additional set of requirements documents and identified and analyzed model errors. Based on this error investigation, some recurring errors of the models were identified. Working together, Fraunhofer and the client prioritized the potential improvements. The client decided to proceed to the implementation phase in which the models would be improved and integrated in a service that could be run on the client infrastructure.

12.2.5 Implementation Phase

In this section, we describe how we implemented the production-ready system for this project. We first present the detailed architecture, and then give details on the different pipelines. Finally, we describe the ML part of the solution.

Technical Architecture

After the implementability of the ML system is successfully validated in the PoC phase, the implementation phase involves the full MLOps cycle. Starting from the exploration results from the PoC, the development environment addressing the exploration and development is set up to allow production-ready exploration and development. Next, the build and test environment is set up to address CI/CD concerns. Finally, the handover to the production environment and the operation and monitoring processes are set up.

Figure 12.4 visualizes the technical architecture of the ML system in our case study. The general architecture that we presented in the requirements section was further specified, including the tooling to be used.

For the top layer with the repositories, we used GitLab for the code and Harbour for the Docker containers (different instances for testing and for deployment). The Data layer at the bottom includes the components related to data preparation and extraction: a MinIO storage component that holds training data, test data, and features; and an MLflow component that serves as an experiment tracking tool for comparing the different development and training executions and model store.

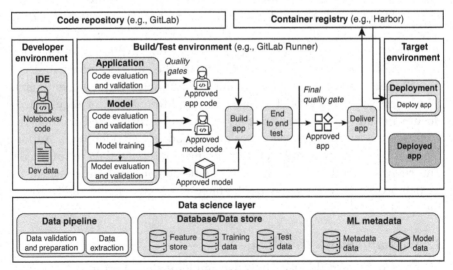

Figure 12.4 *The technical architecture of our ML system.*

The middle layer includes the three environments from the MLOps cycle and the general architecture. For the development environment, we used mainly Jupyter Server and PyCharm. For the build and test environment, we used GitLab CI/CD pipelines for the training and the deployment and delivery processes. The GitLab Runner, which executes the jobs of the GitLab CI/CD pipelines, had also a connection to a computing cluster providing GPU-based resources that were needed for the training. Details on these pipelines are given in the next subsection. The approved ML application was delivered as a Docker image through Harbour's registry. From there, a container was deployed into a customer target runtime environment on-premises at the client side. So, from the perspective of the case study, the target environment was a scalable environment that could run Docker containers.

The whole architecture including the tooling—except the target environment—was set up at the research institute.

Pipeline Approach

For the implementation, we split our solution into two major pipelines: the training pipeline and the deployment pipeline. Splitting the work into a training pipeline and a deployment pipeline is beneficial for several reasons.

First, it allows for modular development, as each pipeline component can focus on its specific tasks. The training pipeline handles data preparation, model training, and evaluation; it was mainly used by the modeling team at Fraunhofer. The deployment pipeline focuses on building and delivering the packaged application, which includes the model from the training pipeline and is responsible for serving recommendations and handling live data.

Second, separating the pipelines enables scalability. The training pipeline often requires significant computational resources and time, so it can be scaled independently to leverage powerful hardware or distributed computing. In contrast, the deployment pipeline is just executed in case a new model is created, but not for each of the experiments.

Additionally, splitting into training and deployment pipelines facilitates version control. The training pipeline manages model versioning, experimentation, and tracking of different iterations. In contrast, the deployment pipeline handles the deployment and serving of specific application versions, allowing for easy rollback.

Moreover, decoupling the pipelines enhances efficiency and agility. Updates or changes in the training pipeline, such as experimenting with different models or hyperparameters, do not disrupt the deployment pipeline. This separation enables faster iteration and deployment of improvements to the ML solution.

In the tendering project, our primary focus was on the training and deployment pipelines, with comparatively less attention given to the intricacies of the data pipeline. We made an implicit assumption that the training pipeline effectively received preprocessed data. This choice stemmed from the adaptability of the portfolio of products used as training features for the tendering classifier. Given the diverse array of products, each with its availability status and detailed descriptions, we opted for a manual approach to data processing. This gave us the flexibility to explore the customer data and engage in multiple rounds of communication with the client to determine how the training data should be treated, both content-wise and structure-wise.

Training Pipeline

During the PoC phase, multiple training experiments were implemented manually using Jupyter Notebooks. These experiments included data understanding, data, model training, and model evaluation. With the training pipeline, we aimed to restructure the code such that training experiments and retrainings were trackable and reproducible via an automated pipeline. Specifically, the code structure was converted from Jupyter Notebooks, which were used for explorative model development, to Python modules. These modules were saved in a git repository on GitLab, where the training pipeline was configured using GitLab Runner. With GitLab Runner, developers can create and automate jobs that run in either a sequential or parallel manner via the *gitlab-ci.yml* configuration file as new code scripts are pushed to the GitLab repository.

The ML training pipeline (Figure 12.5) for our tendering project was then configured to include the following jobs:

- **Security tests:** Conduct security tests to ensure that the ML training code and the code for loading preprocessed data are secure from potential vulnerabilities. Here, we leveraged GitLab's integrated Static Application Security Testing (SAST).
- **Unit tests:** Create and run unit tests to verify the functionality of individual components or units of the training pipeline. This ensures that

each unit performs as expected and facilitates early detection of issues. This step ensures that any future integration with the code will not break the training pipeline.

- **Linting:** Perform linting on all the training code by leveraging the Pylint library—that is, enforcing conformance of the code style to the coding standard (PEP 8) to maintain code quality and to identify potential bugs. Linting also helps ensure consistency and readability of the training code for future code development.

- **Model training:** Once the security tests, unit tests, and linting pass successfully, the pipeline triggers the training job to start with model training. To track the training's progress, the logs for the running job are used to look for bugs. Furthermore, the progress of the model training is tracked via MLflow Tracking's User Interface.

- **Model evaluation:** The trained model is then evaluated using the held-out test set containing 10% of the original training data (see Section 12.1.1, "Requirements: Interactions, Integration, Data, and Quality Metrics"). During evaluation, we calculate metrics such as accuracy, precision, and F1 score, which are logged and tracked by MLflow. After the end of the training job, multiple models are compared against each other using MLflow to facilitate the selection of the best model, which will later be deployed via the deployed pipeline.

The training pipeline was used for the actual training as well as retrainings at a later stage. The details of the training process itself and the training environment are described later in the chapter.

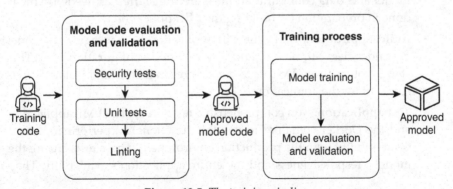

Figure 12.5 *The training pipeline.*

Deployment Pipeline

After successful model training and evaluation on the tendering tasks, the model's performance was communicated to the customer. If the model was approved to be deployed into production, the deployment pipeline took care of packaging the model into the application's Docker image, then saved the application image in the Harbour registry. The model received GAEB-format files and output a set of recommended products as a CSV file in real time via a REST API.

The application code was managed in a separate GitLab repository with its own GitLab Runner pipeline—that is, the deployment pipeline. Once the code was pushed to the GitLab repository, this pipeline went through the following jobs (Figure 12.6). Note that the first three steps are similar to the respective steps in the training pipeline, though with a stronger focus on the application code:

- **Security tests:** Similarly to the training pipeline, this pipeline conducts security tests on the application's code to ensure that the ML application and its dependencies are secure from potential vulnerabilities.

- **Unit tests:** Run unit tests to verify the functionality of individual code components of the ML application, especially if input preprocessing or output preprocessing steps are updated.

- **Linting:** Perform linting on the code to enforce coding standards and identify potential issues with the ML application's structure.

- **Select a model:** To transfer the trained ML model from the model registry into the ML application, the pipeline selects the best evaluated model and ensures that all the required model dependencies (e.g., model and data configuration files) are transferred as needed. This is done in preparation for building the ML application.

- **Build application:** Build the ML application by packaging the code, dependencies, ML model, and any required configuration files. This step involves using Docker to create a reproducible and isolated environment for the application.

- **Test application:** Run comprehensive tests on the built ML application and the Docker container to validate functionality, performance, and compatibility with the production environment. These tests ensure the model's responsiveness and the entire application's availability. They also examine error handling, per the input and output specifications. Namely, the tests ensure input and output validation such that the application accepts only the agreed-on GAEB files as inputs, and produces only CSV files.

- **Delivery to Harbour Docker registry:** Once the ML application passes all the tests successfully, the pipeline delivers the containerized application to the Docker registry. From there, it can be deployed to the production environment.

- **Application deployment:** The application is deployed in the production environment. Although it was technically feasible to automatically deploy the application using the pipeline, this step was implemented manually, as per our client's preference.

As you can see, the training and deployment pipelines included various components that are used in classical DevOps pipelines as well.

Summing up, the technical architecture, including the training and the deployment pipelines, allowed us to fully address the full MLOps cycle in the implementation phase of the project.

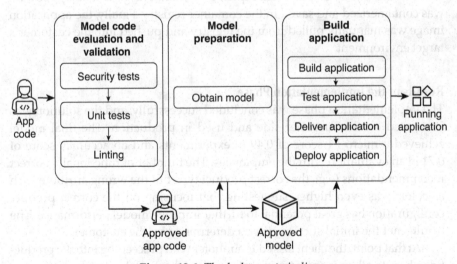

Figure 12.6 *The deployment pipeline.*

ML Solution

The modeling team at Fraunhofer opted for a more sophisticated model in the main project compared to the PoC—namely, a BERT-based pretrained language model that was modified to make sequential predictions of large texts. The goal was to mitigate weaknesses of the simple model from the PoC phase, such as suggesting products with inconsistent colors or from different vendors. The base model was a large German BERT model, available for download from the Hugging Face model hub. This model led to a significant increase in performance.

The model was complemented by rules and heuristics. The new system met the criteria targeted by the client. The implementation phase was split into two modeling iterations with intermediate feedback about the modeling results. The modeling effort was supported by MLOps activities—for example, the creation of reusable modeling and deployment pipelines to allow for easier retraining. In terms of environments, the desired ML solution (i.e., the model and the related application) was explored initially in the development environment. Training was then conducted in the build and test environment, where the training pipeline handled the automatic training. Here, the deployment pipeline ran after the training was finished, and the model was approved as explained in the "Deployment Pipeline" section. The generated application was containerized and saved in the container registry. Finally, the application image was manually pulled from the registry and pushed into the customer's target environment.

Results of the Implementation Phase

The implementation phase was concluded successfully, and the solution was integrated on the customer side and used in production. The final model achieved a micro-F1 score of 0.49 in experiments and an accuracy score of 0.71 in an evaluation with the employees. The number of functionally correct recommendations (e.g., the correct product type but the wrong attribute such as color) was even higher, suggesting that focusing on the correct product configuration has great potential to further improve model performance. The results met the initial success criteria determined by the customer.

At that point, the client tasked Fraunhofer with proceeding into the production phase to allow for performing retraining of the model at regular intervals.

12.2.6 Production Phase

Having successfully deployed the ML application through the deployment pipeline, the subsequent stage involved managing the application during its operational phase. Specifically, the application needed to operate as intended and be capable of achieving its predefined objectives in support of the tendering process.

During this stage, we entered into the seventh aspect of the MLOps cycle—namely, communication. Establishing effective communication between developer engineers and clients was recognized as important for coordinating subsequent assessments of the technical performance of the ML application and gathering feedback from the employees. Such ongoing interaction lays the foundation for informed decisions and continuous improvement.

Similar to how any ML system deals with real-world scenarios, the dynamism of the real world introduces changes, affecting both data and the model's performance. Consequently, continuous and proactive communication and coordination among stakeholders are needed to address and mitigate model performance drift. In this context, ensuring the accuracy of recommendations for product tendering is important, requiring constant alignment with the current business status.

Indeed, this approach strongly aligns with the fundamental concept of ensuring the trustworthiness of the ML application functioning in the real world. Maintaining open lines of communication and coordination among stakeholders allows for a concerted effort to uphold the reliability and credibility of the model. This commitment to ongoing monitoring—by evaluating the model's performance and leveraging feedback from the customer—reflects a dedication to maintaining the model's trustworthiness in the face of evolving real-world conditions through continuous model training.

These changes can cease to be technical bottlenecks with AI systems, as modern ML models offer the capability for retraining using updated datasets and, if necessary, adopting a new model architecture. The retraining process can be facilitated through the adaptation of configurations in the training and deployment pipelines described earlier, allowing for integration of adjustments where needed. This flexibility ensures that the model remains adaptable to evolving circumstances, mitigating the challenges associated with static or rigid systems.

During the production phase, the feedback of the employees was largely positive, indicating that the recommendations of the model were generally appropriate. However, the model often made recommendations when none of the products it was trained on fit the input. To mitigate this problem, the model was trained again, this time with the explicit goal to learn when *not* to suggest any products. This improved the model quality, and the updated model was delivered to our client.

Results of the Production Phase

The production phase highlighted issues with the model in productive use, as mentioned above The feedback from the employees showed that even though the model performed well according to metrics, it lacked an understanding of when none of the products it was trained on was a suitable recommendation. The insights from the employees led to the implementation of an improved model, which mitigated these issues.

12.3 Summary

In this case study, we described how we successfully implemented a project based on an MLOps cycle, which was divided into three project phases: PoC, implementation, and production.

During the PoC phase, we conducted thorough research and experiments to validate the feasibility of our ML model. In the development environment, we collected relevant data, designed and trained the model, and conducted rigorous testing to ensure its accuracy and effectiveness. The PoC phase provided valuable insights and allowed us to fine-tune the model before moving on to the implementation phase.

In the implementation phase, we set up a technical architecture that supported all phases of the MLOps cycle. Within the build and test environment, we integrated the model into an application as part of a Docker container, ensuring seamless deployment and integration into the production systems in the target environment. As part of the implementation, we created automated pipelines for (re)training and deploying the model to ensure that the model was updated with the latest data. Additionally, we put monitoring and logging mechanisms in place to continuously track the model's performance and detect any anomalies.

Moving into the production phase, we established regular maintenance and updates to optimize the model and adapt it to changing business needs. Continuous monitoring and feedback loops were put in place to ensure any issues could be identified and resolved in a timely manner. Regular performance evaluations were conducted to assess the impact of the model on business outcomes.

Overall, the successful implementation of the MLOps cycle enabled us to transition from the PoC phase to production. The iterative nature of the MLOps approach allowed us to continually improve the model's performance, maintain its reliability, and deliver significant business value.

The usage of pretrained language models proved vital for the project's success. Replacing the PoC model, which was based on distributed embeddings, with a BERT-like model led to a significant performance increase, matching the goals of the customer. Nevertheless, complementing the model with rules and heuristics was necessary to make the solution production-ready and to ensure consistency and correctness of the results.

12.4 Takeaways

This case study raises several important points:

- MLOps requires sophisticated and heavily engaged clients. This case study does not describe a turnkey approach where Fraunhofer provided a solution and the client simply adopted it. Instead, the client was involved in most aspects of the solution.

- The solution required multiple iterations testing different models and different approaches. One model was used for the PoC and another, more sophisticated model was used for production.

- Fraunhofer leveraged emerging research (the BERT models). The techniques used in AI systems are evolving and, especially for a research organization like Fraunhofer, it is important to stay abreast of the latest developments.

- The solution leveraged a number of freely available tools (e.g., tools from GitLab, Docker, and Harbour). Even if you are building a cutting-edge system, do not forget about existing tools and techniques.

12.5 Discussion Questions

1. How do you judge whether it is best to use a small language model or a large language model?

2. How would you address observability in this case, in terms of both process and architecture? (Refer to Chapter 11, Observability, if in doubt.)

12.6 For Further Reading

To understand foundational practices for improving the software process, refer to the *Capability Maturity Model: Guidelines for Improving the Software Process* by the Carnegie Mellon University Software Engineering Institute [CMUSEI CMM].

For a practical introduction to integrated process improvement, see Ahern, Clouse, and Turner's *CMMI Distilled* [Ahern 04].

For insights into future-proof solutions for machine learning, consider the work by Beck et al. from Fraunhofer IAIS [Beck 20].

For a comprehensive exploration of pretrained language models and their integration across various media, consult *Foundation Models for Natural Language Processing* by Paaß and Giesselbach [Paaß 23].

13

The ARM Hub Case Study: Chatbots for Small and Medium-Size Australian Enterprises

with Roozbeh Derakhshan[1,2] and Cori Stewart[1]

13.1 Introduction

The primary challenge for small to medium-size enterprise (SME) manufacturers implementing AI stems from the substantial expense involved in constructing, operating, maintaining, and governing data and AI infrastructure. For SME manufacturers without a strong footing in IT, getting started on data or cloud engineering projects is often impractical because of the absence of in-house teams specializing in data and AI engineering, infrastructure, and management. Consequently, many SME manufacturers, despite holding valuable data that could be monetized, improve productivity, and benefit their supply chains, find themselves constrained by their limited AI technical and management capability.

The Advanced Robotics for Manufacturing (ARM) Hub is a mission-led, not-for-profit company established to accelerate technology adoption with a focus on supporting Australian SME manufacturers. This chapter shares the

---

1. Advanced Robotic Manufacturing Hub (ARM Hub), Brisbane, Australia, https://armhub.com.au/.

2. Data & Knowledge Enterprise (DKE), Brisbane, Australia, https://dkecompany.com.au/.

lessons learned by the Hub in implementing large language models (LLMs) in manufacturing. It describes the services in demand by these SMEs and outlines the decisions that software architects and AI engineers have made to meet manufacturers' needs.

13.2 Our Approach

To address the challenges facing SMEs that wish to investigate AI technology, the Hub implemented a data-and-AI-as-a-service platform to overcome the immediate barriers faced by SMEs and allow them to explore, implement, maintain, and better govern AI projects. This platform provides SMEs with a scalable and secure data and AI lakehouse infrastructure that can be used easily, with minimal cost of ownership or maintenance expenses. A *lakehouse* is a data management architecture that supports both structured and unstructured data. See Chapter 5, AI Model Life Cycle, for a discussion of the tools used for cleaning and storing data. The Hub curates access to diverse multidisciplinary data and AI teams so that SMEs can chart a path from concept to successful commercial implementation of AI without having to employ and project manage AI specialists by themselves.

The Hub established this platform by creating a state-of-the-art data and AI lakehouse that is fully deployed in the cloud, using a transparent pay-as-you-go model without any upfront costs such as licensing fees or infrastructure. When doing so, the Hub leveraged industry's latest approach to addressing data and AI on one platform. As shown in Figure 13.1, every SME using the service is provided with a secure, individual workspace. Note that although our current services are deployed exclusively on Microsoft Azure, our architecture is designed to be cloud-agnostic, allowing for compatibility with other cloud providers such as AWS and GCP.

When implementing this service, we needed to address the long-standing challenges associated with data ingestion and migration crucial for developing and deploying LLM applications. To do so, we adopted a service-oriented approach to data pipelines when tackling the key obstacles in data platforms and data products—specifically, data movement from one location to another. We accommodated various service level agreement (SLA) needs, creating solutions that ranged from batch processing to near real-time data handling. Our pipelines supported multiple data formats, including CSV, JSON, text, PDF, and voice and video, all at production quality.

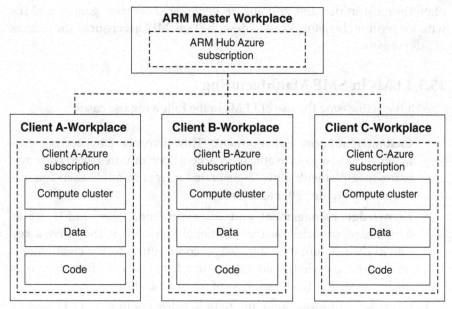

Figure 13.1 *Data-and-AI-as-a-service approach.*

As suggested earlier, SMEs typically do not have an IT team, so the Hub bridges this gap by providing ongoing support. Recognizing that AI and ML projects often require continuous maintenance and management by expert teams, we committed to supporting SMEs throughout the lifespans of their AI programs and products. We offered flexible terms without financial lock-in contracts, and SMEs data is stored in an open-source environment, making it easy for these enterprises to access and retrieve data whenever desired. We also provide project management services to oversee IT teams supported by management tools such as *ARM Hub's Guidelines to the Responsible Use of AI*[3] to facilitate transparent and safe processes for establishing and governing successful AI programs and projects.

Once we had established this platform designed for SMEs, we were then able to offer LLM-as-a-service. MLOps is an integral part of delivering a sustainable, secure, and trustworthy LLM solution. This chapter summarizes our lessons learned when we delivered a service-based chatbot to meet a range of SME manufacturers' needs. Although many potential AI applications may be relevant to manufacturers, it was critical that we provided the

---

3. https://armhub.com.au/latest-news/arm-hub-responsible-ai-guidelines.

platform most in demand and able to generate short-term gains for SMEs with longer-term benefits. We will describe how MLOps ensured the success of this project.

13.3 LLMs in SME Manufacturing

The Hub is witnessing the use of LLMs in the following use cases:

- **Customer support enhancement:** This involves empowering customer support agents to efficiently access open or unresolved customer issues, complemented by AI-generated scripts to guide their interactions and provide better assistance.

- **Knowledge management and dissemination:** Here, LLMs act as dynamic repositories for organizational knowledge. They play a key role in distributing this knowledge, contributing to the creation of a zero-waste knowledge environment where relevant information is readily accessible to all members of the organization.

- **Diagnostic improvement for field service engineers:** Field service engineers often grapple with the daunting task of sifting through vast and complex documentation. LLMs can significantly streamline this process, enhancing the speed and accuracy of diagnostics, which in turn boosts both efficiency and overall service effectiveness.

Our case study focuses on the second item—augmenting the SME manufacturing workforce with a knowledge base in the form of an interactive context-aware chatbot.

13.4 A RAG-Based Chatbot for SME Manufacturing

Despite the progress made in regard to LLMs, these models have inherent shortcomings, especially when it comes to handling domain-specific or highly specialized queries. This issue arises because LLMs are designed for a broad audience and lack user-specific awareness. A frequent problem with LLMs is the production of incorrect information, or "hallucinations," particularly when queries are outside the scope of the model's training data or require current information. These limitations highlight the risks of using LLMs as stand-alone solutions in practical production settings without proper safeguards.

A promising solution to these challenges is the use of retrieval-augmented generation (RAG), which was discussed in detail in Chapter 4, Foundation

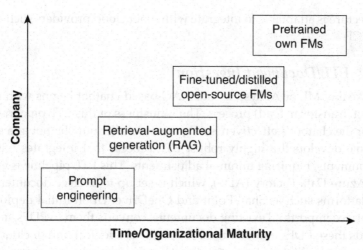

Figure 13.2 *Generative AI maturity curve.*

Models. We found RAG to be a powerful and efficient generative AI technique that allows users to improve model performance by leveraging their own data (e.g., documentation specific to the SME's business), without the need to fine-tune or change the original model, which can be very costly and therefore impractical for SME manufacturers. Figure 13.2 depicts the importance of RAG within the foundation model (FM) and generative AI maturity curve shown in Chapter 4.

ARM Hub provides a RAG-based chatbot as a part of its LLM-as-a-service offering. Developed by ARM Hub, this chatbot can be integrated into each SME manufacturing workspace, requiring only minor customizations that can be completed within weeks. The design of this chatbot allows for easy integration and data ingestion in new environments. It operates efficiently in both batch and streaming modes, and is compatible with a variety of FMs. It is able to work with locally deployed models (e.g., Llama models) or interact with remote models, such as GPT models. The next section outlines the architecture of the ARM Hub chatbot.

13.5 Architecture of the ARM Hub Chatbot

Figure 13.3 depicts the architecture for our RAG-based chatbot service tailored for SME manufacturing in Australia. Again, note that while we currently employ Azure-native services, including Azure Databricks, our system's architecture is adaptable to integrate with other cloud providers such as AWS and GCP.

13.5.1 ETL/Document Ingestion

Just like any ML or AI system, our RAG-based chatbot begins with an ETL (extract, transform, load) process. The robustness of this ETL pipeline is crucial for the chatbot's effectiveness. Because we offer our chatbot as a service, we have developed a highly robust ETL process that integrates with new environments, requiring minimal adjustments. This ETL pipeline is initiated with Azure Data Factory (ADF), which is set up to oversee document-sharing platforms such as SharePoint and OneDrive. Upon initial deployment, our service imports all existing documents, converts them to PDFs, and then uploads these PDFs into volumes. A volume is a logical unit of cloud object storage that facilitates file access, storage, management, and organization. In our setup, the volumes are housed within Azure Blob Storage.

Our data ingestion pipeline is designed to be capable of accommodating newly added documents, offering both batch (scheduled) and real-time ingestion options. With real-time document ingestion, documents are promptly captured, converted, and loaded as they arrive in the monitored document-sharing tools. This feature is pivotal to our service, as it ensures that the chatbot's knowledge base remains current with the latest data, thereby avoiding data drift.

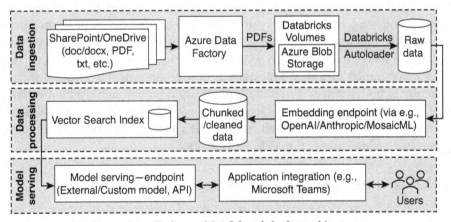

Figure 13.3 *End-to-end RAG-based chatbot architecture.*

After the documents are loaded into volumes, we utilize Autoloader to ingest PDF documents in both batch (scheduled) and real-time modes. Autoloader, a cloud-agnostic service, enhances the flexibility of our architecture to function with different cloud providers. For instance, if we opt for AWS cloud services, AWS Glue would be our choice for ETL data ingestion, and the rest of the services would remain the same. This approach ensures our architecture's portability across different clouds.

13.5.2 Document Preparation and Embedding

Once PDF documents are uploaded as blob objects into a raw Delta table in Databricks, we proceed to chunk the larger PDF documents into smaller segments. Chunking is essential for optimizing the relevance of content retrieved from a vector database when embedding content with an LLM. Depending on the document type and the specific limitations of different LLM models and versions (e.g., some models currently have context window limits up to 32,000 tokens), various chunking methods are applied. Typically, we use fixed-size chunking due to its simplicity and computational efficiency, often selecting a chunk size of 300 with an overlap of 20 to preserve semantic context without needing natural language processing (NLP) libraries. Other strategies, such as content-aware chunking, leverage the content's nature for more sophisticated segmentation—for example, sentence splitting. To identify the optimal chunking strategy and chunk size, we consider the following issues:

- **Data preprocessing:** We first preprocess the data to enhance its quality, which is useful for determining the ideal chunk size. This may involve removing common and repetitive sections, such as acknowledgments, which can introduce noise into the data.

- **Choosing a range of chunk sizes:** We experiment with multiple chunk sizes by running them concurrently to ascertain the most effective chunking method for our needs.

Finally, an embedding model is employed to generate vector representations for each chunk. We can use publicly available embedding endpoints like OpenAI's API with models like text-embedding-ada-002, or locally deployed models, to create these embeddings. Once generated, they are stored in another Delta table.

13.5.3 Vector Search/Vector Index

Our method employs Databricks Vector Search,[4] a serverless similarity search engine. This service enables the storage of data in vector form, complete with metadata, in a vector database. Vector Search can automatically update vector search indexes from Delta tables, and it allows for querying through a straightforward API to retrieve the most similar vectors. Utilizing the Vector Search service enables the integration of newly added documents continuously, avoiding the need to rebuild the entire vector database each time new documents are introduced. This feature complements our incremental and real-time document ingestion pipeline, as Vector Search's auto-sync capability allows for the incorporation of newly added documents both in real time and on a scheduled basis.

After embedding the data into the vector database, we then need to establish a vector index, typically based on a specified column in a Delta table containing our chunked data. See Section 4.2, "Transformer Architecture," for a discussion of vector spaces and their use in attention and similarity definition.

13.5.4 Retrieval Using the RAG Chain

Once the index is prepared, the application's RAG chain can be activated to answer questions. The operation of the RAG chain in response to a query is outlined in the following steps and illustrated in Figure 13.4. We utilize LangChain[5] as our orchestrator for the RAG chain.

1. The received question is processed using the same model that embedded the data in our knowledge base, with Databricks Model Serving handling the embedding model.

2. Vector Search uses the embedded question to find similar data chunks in the vector database.

3. The most relevant data chunks identified by Vector Search, along with the embedded question, undergo postprocessing in a customized LLM before generating a response.

---

4. https://learn.microsoft.com/en-us/azure/databricks/generative-ai/vector-search

5. www.langchain.com/

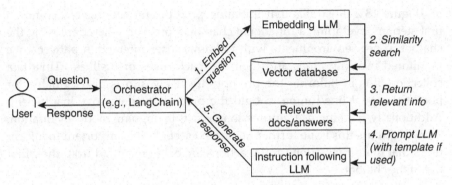

Figure 13.4 *RAG chain.*

4. These data chunks assist the LLM in formulating an appropriate response, often using a predefined response template. The LLM is also served through Model Serving.

5. After the response is prepared in Step 4, Step 5 takes over to generate and dispatch the response to the end user's prompt.

13.5.5 User Interface/Response Recording

Once the model is implemented through a Model Serving endpoint, applications can interact with the chatbot via this endpoint. Databricks Model Serving[6] offers an interface for deploying, managing, and querying AI models, making each model accessible as a REST API for integration into web or client applications. It supports high availability and low latency for deploying models, scaling automatically based on demand. The next section discusses performance and scalability in more detail.

We opted to use the client organization's existing messaging system (e.g., Microsoft Teams) as the front end for our chatbot. This choice eliminates the need for additional application development and maintenance. By leveraging a familiar platform like Teams, which is accessible from various environments and devices, we can reduce the learning curve for staff and avoid the need for different app versions to cater to various browsers and mobile devices.

---

6. https://learn.microsoft.com/en-us/azure/databricks/machine-learning/model-serving/

Figure 13.2 illustrates that initiating prompt engineering is a common first step in developing a functional chatbot. However, when deploying the chatbot in new environments with unknown user interaction patterns, we monitored user questions and their feedback (likes or dislikes). This data collection aids in tailoring the prompt effectively and is also valuable for potential model fine-tuning, should the prebuilt model prove insufficient. Additionally, tracking user impressions assists in ongoing model evaluation. We will discuss this issue further in the next section. It is important to inform users that their interactions and reactions are being recorded from their first use of the chatbot.

13.6 MLOps in ARM Hub

In Chapter 5, AI Model Life Cycle we introduced MLOps as a general process applicable to both narrow ML models and FMs. In this section, we describe how that process was adapted for ARM Hub. The scope of MLOps in ML initiatives can vary greatly, ranging from comprehensive coverage that includes data preparation to production pipelines, to more specific tasks like model deployment. Typically, enterprises apply MLOps principles across several key areas:

- Exploratory data analysis (EDA)
- Data preparation/ingestion and prompt engineering
- Model fine-tuning
- Model review and governance
- Model inference and serving
- Model evaluation

In the following sections, we describe how we implemented these principles, while adhering to best practices to enhance the efficacy of our LLM-based services. Adhering to these principles was intended to ensure that our chatbot-as-a-service offering embodies the key characteristics of a successful, production-level service. This includes robustness, security and privacy measures, traceability, monitorability, as well as performance and scalability. Additionally, it ensures the service's ability to evolve over time. Note that the specific steps may vary depending on the unique requirements of each SME manufacturing chatbot we develop. To illustrate our learnings, we will share examples and insights gained throughout this process.

13.6.1 What Are the Benefits of MLOps for ARM Hub?

The key advantages of MLOps, when the goal is ensuring effective service-based LLM implementation, include the following:

- **Efficiency:** MLOps speeds up model and pipeline development, improves model quality, and accelerates deployment to production.

- **Scalability and management:** MLOps supports large-scale operations, allowing for the management, control, and monitoring of thousands of models, facilitating continuous integration, delivery, and deployment.

- **Risk reduction:** MLOps enhances regulatory compliance and response to oversight, ensuring adherence to organizational or industry standards. For example, in SME manufacturing, MLOps ensures compliance with ARM Hub's *Guidelines for Responsible AI Use*[7].

13.6.2 Exploratory Data Analysis

Contrary to the perception that building a chatbot using an LLM is straightforward—simply input documents and let the model handle the rest—our experience underscores the importance of content awareness for chatbot success. Exploratory data analysis (EDA) in LLM applications, particularly chatbots, is a multifaceted process. We always begin with a comprehensive analysis of the training data, examining its structure, identifying patterns, pinpointing anomalies, identifying security and privacy risks, and understanding the interrelationships. This step is vital in chatbot development, where the analysis should focus on the types of queries and dialogues the chatbot will encounter. It involves discerning prevalent themes and grasping the subtleties of language and context. EDA's role in data preparation ensures the chatbot's capability to interpret and respond precisely to user inputs. This process leads to a more adept and interactive chatbot.

For example, when employing the EDA approach with an SME manufacturing client, we discovered that the firm used both text-based and image-based PDF documents. To handle this condition, we implemented a PDF classification system to differentiate between the two types. For text-based PDFs, we utilized Python libraries such as pdftotext, PyPDF2, and PyMuPDF for text extraction. For image-based PDFs, we applied optical character recognition (OCR) tools such as pytesseract and paddleocr. We integrated the

---

7. https://armhub.com.au/latest-news/arm-hub-responsible-ai-guidelines.

PDF classifier into our ETL tool, specifically using Azure Data Factory (ADF), to streamline the process.

In another application of the EDA approach for an SME, we ensured that the documents loaded into our vector database were free from sensitive content. To achieve this, we implemented a preprocessing stage designed to automatically detect and either remove or mask any personally identifiable information (PII) or payment card industry (PCI) data. This step is vital for maintaining data privacy and security standards.

13.6.3 Data Preparation/Ingestion and Prompt Engineering

Data preparation/ingestion involves the process of collecting, analyzing for potential biases, cleaning, and organizing the data before it is used to train or fine-tune an LLM. The quality and structure of the data directly impact the effectiveness and accuracy of the model's training. Proper data preparation ensures that the data is representative, free of unwanted biases and errors, and structured in a way that is compatible with the model's requirements.

In our system architecture, we combined the functionalities of Azure ADF and Autoloader. This combination allows us to handle both batch (scheduled) and real-time data ingestion and preparation effectively. A resilient data ingestion pipeline is essential. Without it, the solution remains a proof of concept (PoC) and fails to address organizational needs or achieve return on investment (ROI) goals, which is often a significant challenge in ML applications and solutions.

Prompt engineering, which was discussed in Chapter 4, is the process of designing and refining the prompts or queries that are used to interact with the LLM. The effectiveness of a LLM heavily depends on how the prompts are structured, as they guide the model in generating relevant and accurate responses. Prompt engineering requires a deep understanding of the specific LLM's capabilities and the context in which it will be used. It is an iterative process, often refined based on the model's performance and feedback from its interactions.

Considering the diverse nature of our service-based offerings to various SME manufacturers, we depend on systematically recording user interactions and feedback to inform the design of our prompts. Prompt engineering is important not just for the initial launch and adoption of our products within SMEs, but also for maintaining their relevance over time. As user queries evolve, continuously analyzing chatbot interactions allows us to update and refine our prompt templates, ensuring they stay pertinent to user needs. This adaptive approach enhances the long-term adaptability of our solution.

13.6.4 *Model Fine-Tuning*

Model fine-tuning, which was also discussed in Chapter 4, in the context of chatbot and LLM applications involves adjusting a pretrained LLM to better suit specific tasks or datasets. This process is important for chatbots, as it tailors the general capabilities of an LLM to understand and respond to industry-specific language, nuances, and user queries. Fine-tuning is achieved by training the model on a targeted dataset, which contains examples more closely aligned with the chatbot's intended use. This helps the model to make more accurate predictions and generate more relevant responses, improving the overall effectiveness and user experience of the chatbot. Fine-tuning is an iterative process, often requiring adjustments based on performance metrics and user feedback.

In our diverse experiences with SME manufacturing scenarios, we have found that combining prompt engineering with a RAG approach addresses most of the relevant use cases. A robust feedback mechanism is key in refining prompts, thereby enhancing chatbot output quality. Instead of expecting users to formulate precise prompts, we employ our RAG chain (using Lang-Chain) to structure prompts as templates. This enhances user queries with tailored prompts for improved chatbot responses.

Prompt engineering, which is often regarded as a basic approach to FM customizing (it is sometimes called the "poor man's fine-tuning"), could present future challenges. As the quantity of prompt templates grows, their management may become increasingly difficult. To mitigate this issue, we can use user feedback to create a strong training dataset for more sophisticated fine-tuning. This strategy aims to make prompt management more efficient and to improve the model's overall effectiveness. Alongside prompt engineering, fine-tuning is a supplementary factor in enhancing the adaptability of our solution. When prompt engineering alone is insufficient to produce the quality outputs that end users expect, fine-tuning will help meeting their evolving needs effectively.

13.6.5 *Model Review and Governance*

To manage the model, pipeline lineage, and versions effectively, we use Databricks' Managed MLflow,[8] which offers support for MLOps. This includes enhanced capabilities for managing and deploying LLMs, and for integrating

---

8. www.databricks.com/product/managed-mlflow

with standard LLM tools like Hugging Face transformers and OpenAI functions. Key features of Managed MLflow for MLOps are summarized here:

- **Model deployment:** Streamlines the ML life-cycle management with a framework for production-ready models.

- **Experiment tracking:** Facilitates tracking of experiments across any ML library or framework, automatically documenting parameters, metrics, code, and models. This feature allows for secure sharing and management of experiment results and corresponding code versions.

- **Model management:** Offers a centralized platform for discovering and sharing ML models, aiding in transitioning from experimentation to production. This feature integrates with governance workflows and CI/CD pipelines, and monitors ML deployments.

- **Model deployment:** Quickly deploys production models for batch inference on Apache Spark or as REST APIs using built-in integration with Docker containers, Azure ML, or Amazon SageMaker.

Further details on how model management/deployment integrates with our CI/CD pipelines are provided in the next section.

13.6.6 Model Inference and Serving

In managing model refresh frequency, inference request times, and similar specifics for production testing and quality assurance (QA), our MLOps practice includes aspects of model deployment cycle (CI/CD) and cost monitoring. We heavily utilize Databricks Model Serving, which includes the following features:

- **Unified interface:** For deploying, governing, and querying AI models, with each model served as a REST API.

- **High availability and low latency:** The service is designed for scalability, adjusting to demand changes to optimize costs and latency.

- **Support for various models:**
  - *Custom models:* Python models in MLflow format, including scikit-learn, XGBoost, PyTorch, and Hugging Face transformer models.
  - *Foundation models:* Models like Llama-2-70B-chat, BGE-Large, and Mistral-7B, available with pay-per-token pricing.
  - *External models:* Models such as OpenAI's GPT-4, with central governance and established rate limits and access control.

Figure 13.5 illustrates our CI/CD workflow for the RAG-based chatbot model. The process begins with developers cloning the chatbot code from GitHub into a notebook for development. Post development and unit testing, the code is committed back to GitHub. Then, using Git actions, our build agent runs the code, leading to the construction of a model that is registered in the MLflow Model Registry. Access control for the model is managed by Unity Catalog,[9] thereby ensuring role-based access control (RBAC). The model is then deployed to Model Serving, creating distinct endpoints for each environment (Dev, Staging, and Prod). Applications such as MS Teams interact with the model via a RESTful API. The first deployment in each environment is Version 1, and subsequent blue/green updates increase the version number while maintaining the same endpoint. This decoupled design allows the chatbot application to remain operational even during new model deployments. In our service-based approach for delivering chatbots, each SME manufacturer is equipped with its own set of workspaces, encompassing Dev, Staging, and Prod environments. This ensures a tailored and efficient workflow that addresses each SME's specific needs.

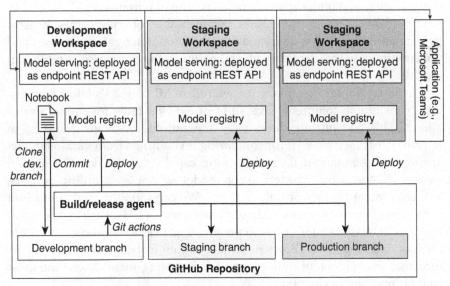

Figure 13.5 *RAG-based chatbot CI/CD workflow.*

---

9. https://learn.microsoft.com/en-us/azure/databricks/data-governance/unity-catalog/

Cost transparency is necessary for successful chatbot implementation in SME manufacturing, particularly in a service model. A clear and straightforward billing method based on SME usage is essential. Model Serving supports this requirement with a tagging mechanism, where each model endpoint is tagged, and these tags are then reflected in cloud provider billing. This ensures clarity and accountability in costs. Moreover, proper cost monitoring and alerts enable SMEs to understand daily chatbot expenses, preventing cost overruns that could undermine the solution's value.

A functional CI/CD pipeline from code development to deployment also ensures adherence to best practices for the software development and ML life cycles. This includes review and approval gates in the pipeline, safeguarding against security and compliance issues, such as hard-coded API keys.

13.6.7 Model Evaluation

In the dynamic world of LLMs, where new models and methodologies are constantly introduced, selecting the most effective models for deployment is vital. For the Hub, as an LLM service provider catering to a wide array of SMEs in manufacturing with varying data types, security and compliance requirements, and budget constraints, this is an important consideration. An efficient MLOps platform becomes indispensable, offering comprehensive performance reports for each model, identifying potential weaknesses and vulnerabilities before deployment, and aiding in the comparison of different models.

To address these requirements, we utilize MLflow 2.4's latest features, which include a comprehensive suite of MLOps tools for model evaluation.[10] This version introduces new integrations for language tasks, an improved Artifact View UI for comparing text outputs from various model versions, and enhanced dataset tracking capabilities. MLflow 2.4 aids in feeding diverse input datasets to the model as inputs, recording outputs, and calculating domain-specific metrics. We can monitor predictions and performance metrics across a range of tasks with LLMs, such as text summarization, classification, question-answering, and generation, all within MLflow Tracking. This allows us to thoroughly inspect and compare performance evaluations of multiple models, enabling us to choose the most suitable ones for production.

---

10. https://mlflow.org/docs/latest/python_api/mlflow.html#mlflow.evaluate

13.7 Ongoing Work

In response to evolving LLM products and increasing client demand, we are expanding our capabilities. Some key developments are highlighted here:

- Addressing clients' growing need to integrate structured and operational data (e.g., machinery data) with unstructured data for chatbot awareness. Our unique position with Databricks allows us to use that company's latest offerings to combine structured data for input into Vector Search, which our RAG-based chatbots can use. This is a pivotal step toward data democratization, allowing manufacturers to query data in English. Similar trends are emerging with other platforms, such as LangChain SQL[11] and Spark English SDK[12] (which also offers basic plotting features), that offer natural language interfaces for structured data queries.

- Evaluating the quality of LLM outputs and selecting the right metrics has always been challenging for LLM solutions. We are currently exploring the "LLM-as-a-judge" approach to assess the quality of responses from our chatbot. This method is expected to provide a more nuanced evaluation of the chatbot's performance in generating relevant and accurate responses.

- As an LLM service provider, we are actively monitoring end-to-end MLOps offerings from other platforms. Our current focus is on evaluating AWS Bedrock,[13] particularly its model offerings and associated costs, to understand how it aligns with our service requirements and value proposition.

- We are enhancing our chatbot's capabilities to better recognize user intentions and take appropriate actions. For example, when the chatbot is used within a customer support system, if a customer reports an issue with a product, the agent on the phone can understand the problem more clearly by integrating the chatbot (e.g., to obtain more details about the error code). These insights can then be relayed (e.g., emailed to) to the engineering team for in-depth analysis, leading to

---

11. https://python.langchain.com/v0.1/docs/use_cases/sql/

12. https://learn.microsoft.com/en-us/azure/databricks/dev-tools/sdk-english

13. https://aws.amazon.com/bedrock/

the scheduling of an appointment or the creation of a support ticket for the support team to perform an on-site repair. This effort represents a move toward realizing actionable AI, where the chatbot actively supports tasks based on user interactions.

13.8 Summary

This chapter provides a detailed case study of the Advanced Robotics for Manufacturing (ARM) Hub, an Australian not-for-profit organization dedicated to supporting SME manufacturers in adopting technology. Highlighting the obstacles SMEs encounter in integrating AI and data systems, ARM Hub offers a novel solution: data-and-AI-as-a-service. This service features a scalable, cloud-based data and AI lakehouse infrastructure, utilizing lakehouse architecture, and provides SMEs with access to a diverse range of data and AI expertise.

A key element of ARM Hub's offerings is the incorporation of LLMs into SME manufacturing processes. These models are strategically used to tackle productivity issues and enhance business models. The standout application here is a chatbot based on retrieval-augmented generation (RAG), specifically designed for SME manufacturing. This chatbot successfully addresses the limitations commonly associated with LLMs in processing specialized queries by integrating domain-specific data, thereby boosting both accuracy and relevance.

The chapter highlights several key contributions made by the Hub's solution:

- **Innovative architecture:** Utilizing lakehouse architecture, this architecture supports a service-based approach, enabling SME manufacturers to quickly deploy the chatbot service with minimal total cost of ownership.
- **Diverse LLM model integration:** The architecture accommodates a broad range of data types, budget constraints, and compliance requirements, managing both third-party and locally deployed LLM models.
- **Use of organizational messaging systems:** By leveraging platforms such as MS Teams, the solution promotes quick adoption, minimizes the learning curve, and offers accessibility, including on mobile devices.
- **Robust technical framework:** The chatbot's backbone includes a comprehensive ETL process, document preparation, embedding, and

a vector search/index setup supporting incremental, real-time data ingestion.

- **Implementation of MLOps:** Extending traditional MLOps to LLM operations, this approach ensures efficient management of LLMs in production, moving beyond PoC to full operational readiness.
- **Comprehensive MLOps approach:** Featuring a robust CI/CD pipeline and a suite of services, the Hub's solution provides qualities like robustness, resilience, security, privacy, cost transparency, monitorability, traceability, and scalable performance.

This initiative by ARM Hub marks a significant advancement in making AI and data technologies accessible for SMEs. It eliminates the need for extensive in-house expertise, underscoring the vital role of bespoke AI solutions and ongoing support in the sustainable and successful integration of AI in the manufacturing sector.

13.9 Takeaways

This case study is about a consulting firm that specializes in supporting SMEs. The assumption that the SME does not have in-depth technical expertise requires ARM Hub to provide multiple different services and to be flexible in its interactions with its clients.

Choosing cloud provider–agnostic tools gives the clients flexibility in their choice of cloud providers. The tool suite used to manage the models should also be provider-agnostic.

Data ingestion is a major problem. ARM Hub's approach to data ingestion involves the following elements:

- A tool suite (Databricks lakehouse) minimizes the necessity of moving data from one location to another.
- Organizing the data into chunks simplifies the ingestion process at the cost of more extensive downstream processing.
- Accepting multiple formats supports ingesting a variety of document types.

Using a disciplined process for processing the data both increases the productivity of the consulting company and makes it easier to explain to the client.

13.10 Discussion Questions

1. What is involved in moving to AWS from the current Azure implementation? What is involved in moving from Databricks to Snowflake?

2. How does the current structure support "the right to be forgotten"?

3. Above, we wrote that MLOps ensures compliance with ARM Hub's *Guidelines for Responsible AI Use*." How does it do this?

13.11 For Further Reading

For a deeper understanding of the importance of SME manufacturing in Australia and its role in the global supply chain, refer to *Barriers to Collaboration and Commercialisation* by Industry Innovation Science Australia [IISA 2023]. This report highlights how countries with strong medium-size manufacturing sectors have successfully commercialized innovations, whereas countries such as Australia have faced challenges in retaining R&D investments and talent.

To explore RAG techniques for knowledge-intensive NLP tasks, consult the work by Lewis et al. [Lewis 20], which offers insights into advances in neural information processing systems.

For an evaluation of LLMs in a legal decision-making context, see *Judging LLM-as-a-Judge with MT-Bench and Chatbot Arena* [Zheng 24].

14

The Banking Case Study: Predicting Customer Churn in Banks

with MingJian Tang and Yuxiu Luo

CUSTOMER CHURN IN banking is defined as the phenomenon in which a customer terminates their relationship with a bank, opting to obtain services from another institution. Throughout the customer life cycle, customers contribute to the bank's revenue through various channels such as transaction fees, banking charges, credit cards, home loans, and personal loans. The adverse impacts of churn are twofold: the direct loss of revenue and the higher costs associated with acquiring new customers compared to retaining existing ones.

By analyzing transaction history, customer interactions, and behavioral patterns, ML algorithms can identify signals of potential churn. This allows the bank to proactively address customer concerns, tailor personalized interactions or offerings, and adjust customer retention strategies. The ability to anticipate and prevent customer churn not only aids in sustaining a loyal customer base, but also contributes to the bank's long-term profitability.

To efficiently tackle the customer churn problem, automation is critical in managing the entire ML life cycle. From data sourcing to model development, deployment, and monitoring, automating the ML pipeline ensures rapid iteration and deployment as data and business needs evolve. This enables the bank to keep models up-to-date and responsive, maximizing the impact of ML on customer retention efforts.

14.1 Customer Churn Prediction

Traditional churn analysis in banking, which was hitherto reliant on rule-based systems, often lacks flexibility and precision. It not only misses actual instances of customer churn but also leads to false positives—misidentifying low-risk customers as potential churners. This misidentification results in unnecessary and costly incentives being offered to customers who are unlikely to churn. In the worst-case scenario, such below-the-line (BTL) offers can inadvertently contribute to customer churn by provoking a strong negative reaction from those who typically respond adversely to marketing communications, known colloquially as "sleeping dogs."

Predicting customer churn takes the form of a binary classification problem. The target variable, y, assumes binary values: $y = 1$ indicates the customer is likely to churn (positive class), and $y = 0$ suggests otherwise (negative class). To construct a preemptive churn label that is practically useful, a sufficient lead time—typically 30 days or one month—is incorporated into the measure. This approach allows enough time to prepare and dispatch targeted campaigns to those customers identified as high risk. The input features, denoted as $x = \{x1, x2, x3, \ldots, xn\}$, encompass a range of factors pertinent to predicting churn, such as customer demographics, transaction history (including recency, frequency, and monetary [RFM] values), banking product usage (number of credit cards, mortgages, and so on), and customer service interactions. Within a defined time frame, measured in days or weeks, it is possible to derive additional customer behavioral features. These could include metrics such as the 7-day rolling window average, minimum, maximum, and standard deviation for mobile banking logins and credit card usage. These metrics help gauge a customer's engagement level, which can be useful for triggering event-driven marketing campaigns or enhancing the accuracy of churn prediction models.

With the advent of pretrained foundation models (FMs), vector representations of spending or payment descriptions can be developed to gain deeper insights into the context of spending behaviors. Table 14.1 gives examples of mock-up feature data for churn propensity modeling to illustrate how these features are ultimately utilized for predicting customer churn.

The objective of the customer churn prediction, $f(x, \theta)$, is to map these input features x to the target variable, y, by estimating the probability that each customer belongs to the positive class or the negative class. This approach enables the model to provide not just classifications, but also the confidence level for predictions, facilitating more flexible decision making based on the

Table 14.1 *Example feature table for training and validation of a banking customer churn model, updated monthly with last refresh date*

CUSTOMER ID	TENURE	STATE	AGE	CREDIT SCORE	BALANCE	...	CHURNED	LAST REFRESH DATE
15xxx1	5	NSW	34	619	0.00	....	1	2024-02
15xxx2	9	VIC	26	850	2380.00	....	0	2024-02
15xxx3	10	ACT	55	900	15966.00	....	0	2024-02
...	...	...	...	...	...	....	...	...
16xxx9	3	NSW	23	150	00.00	....	1	2023–01

estimated likelihood of different outcomes. Additionally, applying percentile-based scores to rank the entire customer base allows for the creation of intuitive and actionable thresholds, which can then be integrated into downstream marketing campaigns. Although tree-based classifiers such as XGBoost or LightGBM can generate probability-like scores alongside class predictions, these scores may sometimes be overly optimistic, exaggerating the true likelihood of churn. This overconfidence could lead to excessive and unnecessary targeting, potentially hindering other campaigns.

In contexts where model output represents probabilities, calibration of these outputs becomes crucial. Well-calibrated probabilities are not only more reliable and trustworthy for bank employees who are making decisions based on probabilistic interpretations, but they also contribute to fairness in predictive models. By ensuring that predicted probabilities align with actual outcomes across all customer groups, calibration aids in mitigating biases within model predictions. Commonly used calibration techniques such as Platt scaling and isotonic regression, which involve fitting a logistic or isotonic regression model to the original model's predictions, can be employed based on the model's characteristics and observed calibration errors. Calibration, especially for models predicting probabilities, is an important step in creating robust, reliable, fair, and trustworthy systems for predicting customer churn in banking.

Predictions of customer churn in banks are usually precomputed in batches and stored for later use. These predictions are generated at regular intervals, such as fortnightly or monthly, to maintain a current understanding of customer churn risks. The batch predictions are subsequently consumed and utilized by the downstream campaign engine, which orchestrates and disseminates personalized offers via different inbound or outbound channels (SMS, email, or mobile banking app). This process is guided by the customers' behaviors and specific targeting rules set up by marketing managers. Key considerations for these rules include communication frequency, campaign tactics, types of incentives, and offer priority. This strategic approach enables the efficient and effective allocation of marketing resources, ensuring that personalized engagement with customers is both relevant and timely.

To build and productize an end-to-end batch customer churn prediction system, several ML workflow activities need to be orchestrated.

14.1.1 Model Data Sourcing and Validation

The foundational step in developing a robust customer churn prediction ML system is to identify accurate and reliable data sources. Banks benefit from a rich and extensive digital ecosystem, generating a diverse array of data at various frequencies from essential systems such as core banking systems, customer relationship management (CRM), internet and mobile banking applications, and payment processing systems. Typically, banks employ specialized teams who are responsible for managing the raw data through ingestion, extraction, loading, and transformation processes, utilizing centralized enterprise data warehouses (EDW) like Teradata or Oracle, or cloud-based object storage solutions like AWS S3 for Data Lakes.

Over the years, banks accumulate an extensive array of tables and views. This data, while extensive, may carry outdated business logic, introducing potential biases and inaccuracies in the data. In the ever-evolving banking sector, as source systems frequently change (e.g., legacy systems get decommissioned), these biases and inaccuracies cascade to downstream systems including EDWs and feature stores. Compounding the issue, EDW teams often have limited visibility into the full range of downstream users, leaving them less aware of the potential impacts that changes to EDW tables or views might have.

Figure 14.1 illustrates a hypothetical banking warehouse consisting of three tables—customers, accounts, and transactions—along with their entity-relationship diagram. It also highlights how model feature stores can be affected by upstream changes due to ripple effects. Given this possibility, it is essential to verify the integrity of the incoming modeling data before landing it in feature stores, by assessing aspects such as the data's uniqueness, completeness, acceptance, referential integrity, and freshness. For instance,

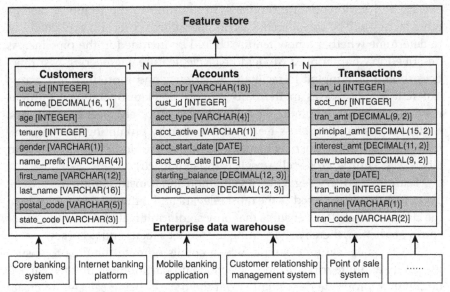

Figure 14.1 *A sample banking data warehouse and feature store.*

validation tests are crafted to ensure the uniqueness of primary and surrogate keys. Notably, within the EDW, data assets, views, and tables evolve over time, creating intricate dependencies and necessitating adept data stewardship. This complexity can occasionally hinder the freshness and integrity of downstream modeling data, leading to the accumulation of stale and incorrect information.

The consolidated tables and views stored in the EDW are one of the major upstream data sources for customer churn model features. Before storing model features into a feature store, it is critical to automate the assessment of various aspects of upstream data quality. This enables scaling MLOps, which in turn facilitates streamlined operations and supports reliability.

14.1.2 Model Feature Engineering and Selection

Feature engineering and selection are important for deploying robust ML models at scale. In practice, this process requires striking a balance between model performance, operational costs, explainability, and fairness.

The feature engineering workflow starts with feature discovery, which is commonly conducted by data scientists in the bank. The process is highly iterative and driven by hypothesis testing and workshops with domain experts and various data custodians. In addition to the technical factors, other factors will be considered, such as operational costs and explainability, to determine whether a new feature should be included in the pipeline. As described in Chapter 5, AI Model Life Cycle, feature engineering best practices should be adopted to facilitate consistency and reproducibility across different ML use cases in the bank and to alleviate operational burdens resulting from operationalizing customized feature engineering pipelines. Feature stores facilitate cross-team collaboration by promoting reuse of common feature entities, such as banking customer profiles, product data, and labels (e.g., churns, cross-sell, upsell, campaign reach).

Feature discovery begins with validation and transformation of the data. Then, features are selected as the most relevant and influential variables from the churn datasets. This ensures that only significant features are utilized for churn prediction, thereby sharpening the model's focus and accuracy.

Next comes feature cleaning, which entails refining the data to ensure its quality and integrity. Instance selection and partitioning are then carried out, with appropriate data points from the dataset being selected to create balanced training, evaluation, and test sets. Techniques such as repeatable random sampling, oversampling of minority classes, and stratified partitioning are used to ensure the model is trained on a diverse and representative sample of customer profiles, spanning various account types and transaction volumes.

Feature tuning, the next step, focuses on improving the quality of features for ML. This includes scaling and normalizing numeric values, imputing missing values, and rectifying skewed distributions. For instance, normalizing transaction amounts and account balances and imputing missing values in customer demographic data are common practices in this phase.

Tuning is followed by feature transformation, which involves converting data into more suitable formats for ML models. Numerical features are bucketized, and categorical features transformed into numerical formats using techniques such as one-hot encoding and sparse feature embeddings. This is especially important for banking data, which often includes a mix of numerical and categorical information. Feature extraction and construction are also integral to this phase. Techniques such as principal component analysis (PCA) are used to simplify complex data, such as transaction histories. Moreover, new features are created using methods such as polynomial expansion or feature crossing, often integrating banking-specific business logic as well. These features (e.g., average monthly balance and frequency of overdrafts) provide deeper insights into customer behavior patterns indicative of churn.

In the ML workflow for churn prediction, feature engineering stands out as the most creative part for data scientists. It involves employing experience, business context, and creativity to tailor the model to capture why churn happens in a specific business context.

Features for modeling customer churn include the following:

- **Customer characteristics:** These might include demographics for retail banking, such as gender, age, income, marital status, and more. Understanding customer profiles helps in predicting churn.

- **Product characteristics:** Features defining the product type and characteristics such as delivery method, price, and size help bank employees understand how different product aspects contribute to churn.

- **Transaction history:** Using an RFM strategy, data scientists can gauge customer value and predict churn likelihood.

- **Customer engagement:** Engagement metrics, such as website logins, session durations, and email unsubscriptions, offer insights into a customer's intention to continue using a service.

- **User experience:** Customer satisfaction and user experience metrics, though hard to capture, are reliable indicators of churn. They can be proxied through product ratings and customer support interactions.

- **External factors:** Sometimes churn is influenced by external factors beyond the control of the business, such as economic indicators or technological infrastructure.

MLOps practices such as automation with tools like Apache Airflow,[1] thorough monitoring and logging, continuous evaluation and testing, and detailed documentation and version control are applied throughout these preprocessing steps. These practices ensure that the data pipeline is not only efficient and robust, but also compliant with the stringent regulatory standards in the banking sector.

14.1.3 Model Training and Performance Evaluation

Model development codes, including all scripts and configurations used for training and evaluating models, should be centralized and version controlled to ensure traceability and allow for continuous integration and

---

1. https://airflow.apache.org/docs/apache-airflow/stable/index.html

testing. Distributed software configuration management tools, e.g. based on Git, can be leveraged to facilitate collaboration on experiments conducted by data scientists while keeping track of changes and improvements over time. During algorithm selection, frameworks like MLflow or Kubeflow can be integrated with the modeling codes to enable systematic logging and testing of key training metrics from different ML algorithms, such as logistic regression, support vector machines, random forest, and gradient boosting trees (XGBoost or LightGBM).

Capturing stable and intrinsic customer churn patterns in the banking sector requires training data to span across multiple months and sometimes even years. When multiplied by a huge vector of customer features (thousands), the training data could become so large that it no longer fits into the memory of a single machine. In such a case, adopting model and data parallelism techniques for distributed training becomes essential. PySpark and Tensorflow are two frameworks that are often used for effectively distributing training data and workflow across Kubernetes clusters or private enterprise data centers; this practice can drastically shorten overall model training times and boost innovation via iteration.

To build production-grade models, a given model's parameters should be selected to create the best inference set possible. However, the sheer number of combinations and their resultant metrics can become overwhelming to track manually. The combination of Optuna with MLflow can help mitigate this challenge, as it provides an efficient approach to searching over parameters with every experimental trail being automatically recorded. When performing hyperparameter tuning, each iteration in Optuna can be considered as a "child run." Developers can then group all the runs under the primary "parent run," ensuring that the MLflow UI remains organized and interpretable. Each child run will track the specific hyperparameters used and the resulting metrics (e.g., AUC-PR, F1 score, log loss), providing a consolidated view of the entire optimization process.

14.1.4 Model Packaging, Deployment, and Inference

After training the churn prediction model and ensuring it has an adequate level of performance, the next step is deploying the model to a production environment. In banking, this deployment is not just a technical task. It directly impacts customer retention strategies and revenue streams. Open-source tools like MLflow can significantly simplify the process; they offer a robust toolset for deploying the trained ML model to various targets, including local hosts, cloud services, and Kubernetes clusters, which are commonplace in the banking IT infrastructure. For example, a bank might deploy the churn model in a Kubernetes cluster to leverage its scalability and orchestration features, thereby ensuring the model can handle the high-volume, real-time banking operation data.

Also, the trained model can be published and registered in model registry—an important step in highly regulated industries like banking. The model registry serves as a centralized, secure model store that provides a set of APIs and a UI for managing the entire model life cycle collaboratively. It also provides model lineage information, including model versioning, model aliasing, tagging, annotations, and, most importantly, which experiment and iteration run produced the model along with the metadata of the training data. Such information is important for maintaining compliance with financial regulations.

Behind the scenes, the trained model is packaged with its metadata, such as its dependencies, inference schema, and model signature. The packaged model is then containerized using Docker, which standardizes the model deployment process and enables deployments to various operating environments. Figure 14.2 depicts a schematic flow of model packaging and deployment using MLflow.

14.1.5 Model Performance Monitoring

Once a model is deployed, it may encounter several challenges, such as shifts in data distribution (e.g., an increase in online and mobile banking transactions and gradual phase-out of most transactions conducted over the

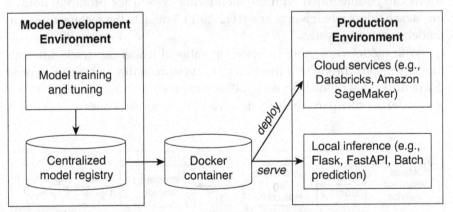

Figure 14.2 *Overview of model training, parameter tuning, and evaluation tracking with MLflow and Optuna.*

counter), training-serving skew (e.g., features like branch location become irrelevant as transactions shift online; this occurs when the data used during training differs from the data seen during deployment), concept drift, pipeline health issues, system underperformance (e.g., high serving latency), anomalies due to outliers, and data quality issues introduced by upstream data sources. The objective of post-deployment monitoring is multifaceted: It aims to detect issues early, before they significantly impact downstream consumers; it enables prompt action for triaging and troubleshooting models in production; it ensures transparency and explainability in the prediction process; and it provides avenues for maintaining and improving the model while it remains in production.

MLOps tools like MLflow, which offer a comprehensive suite of tools and features, play a pivotal role in facilitating efficient model monitoring. As previously noted, custom metrics, including both model metrics and business-specific key performance indicators (KPIs), can be logged to continually assess model performance; they are necessary for understanding the model's impact on real-world business outcomes. To detect detrimental data or concept drifts, the logged input data samples and corresponding predictions can be utilized to construct statistical baselines. To better measure and quantify data drift, statistical techniques can be applied, such as the Stability Index, Kullback–Leibler (KL) divergence, and Jensen–Shannon (JS) divergence.

A dedicated monitoring system can be set up to collect error logs, trigger alerts, and disseminate alerts to subscribers via emails or instant messages. Alerts can be integrated with the monitoring system for promptly notifying stakeholders when issues arise. Figure 14.3 depicts the architecture of a model monitoring system.

With model versioning in place, operational teams can track different model versions throughout the entire life cycle from dev to staging to production. This also allows for easy rollback to previous versions if updates of the model or other parts of the system lead to unforeseen issues.

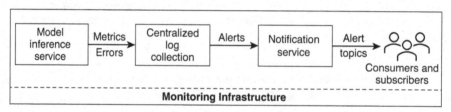

Figure 14.3 *Architecture of a model monitoring system.*

14.2 Key Challenges in the Banking Sector

14.2.1 Data Privacy and Security

The banking industry faces significant challenges in managing and protecting sensitive data while utilizing AI and ML technologies. The usage of synthetic data, anonymization, tokenization, and federated learning are helpful but still require complex organizational strategies to better govern and ensure data privacy and security. Adherence to regulatory standards like the General Data Protection Regulation (GDPR) and the Payment Card Industry Data Security Standard (PCI DSS) is required, especially when the system handles personally identifiable information (PII).

14.2.2 Traceability and Transparency of AI Decisions

As AI and ML become integral in banking, ensuring the traceability and transparency of decisions made by AI models and ML systems poses a major challenge. Financial institutions must maintain a thorough, detailed record of model development, training, and validation. Tools such as Jupyter Notebooks archives, dataset archives, and model documentation catalogs are essential for capturing this information, but integrating them effectively can be complex. One common approach to manage these challenges is to use more interpretable models when possible. In cases where complex models are necessary, feature-level explanations, such as SHAP or LIME, are often employed to provide insights into model decisions.

14.3 Summary

In this chapter, we use customer churn as a use case to explain the benefits brought by MLOps:

- **Enhance model accuracy and timeliness:** In customer churn prediction and fraud detection, the accuracy of ML models directly impacts their effectiveness. MLOps helps ensure models are consistently updated with the latest data, thereby maintaining their relevance and accuracy.

- **Gain operational efficiency:** With MLOps, banks can automate the life cycle of ML systems, from development to deployment. This automation reduces the manual effort required to manage these systems, allowing teams to focus on more strategic tasks and initiatives.

- **Scale and adapt:** MLOps enables banks to scale their ML operations efficiently via automated pipelines and reusable workflow patterns that orchestrate complex modeling activities. As customer banking behaviors evolve and new types of financial fraud emerge, banks can rapidly adapt their models to these changes, ensuring ongoing protection and customer satisfaction.

14.4 Takeaways

This case study is about proactive customer retention. It highlights the importance of using ML models and systems to predict customer churn, enabling banks to proactively address potential churn and implement personalized retention strategies. A few takeaways:

- **Domain understanding needed:** The types of data used in the ML model reflect a deep understanding of the banking domain in general, and churn predictors in particular.
- **Data-driven decision making:** Accurate prediction relies on a variety of data inputs, including customer demographics, transaction history, and engagement metrics. This reinforces the critical role of data quality, feature engineering, and continuous model calibration in enhancing predictive accuracy.
- **Model calibration for fairness:** Well-calibrated models are essential to ensure reliability and fairness, as they can prevent over-targeting and reduce bias in customer predictions.
- **Operational challenges:** Implementing an effective churn prediction system requires overcoming several operational challenges, such as managing data quality, automating ML workflows (MLOps), and ensuring compliance with regulatory standards.

14.5 Discussion Questions

1. Your bank merges with another bank. How would you develop an integrated repository of customer data for both banks?
2. How does a bank manage problems with reliability?
3. How does a model registry help with a bank's compliance with regulations?

14.6 For Further Reading

As mentioned in Chapter 4, Foundation Models, open-weight foundation models such as those in the Llama family can be used in custom applications like the one discussed in this chapter. For an introduction to the Llama FMs, refer to Touvron et al. [Touvron 23].

To understand how fairness in AI can be measured and improved, explore the Fairlearn toolkit by Bird et al. [Bird 20]. It offers practical tools and methodologies for addressing fairness challenges in ML systems.

To learn about hyperparameter optimization techniques, consult Akiba et al. [Akiba 19]. These authors introduce Optuna, a highly efficient framework for automated hyperparameter tuning, and demonstrate its use through real-world applications.

15

The Future of AI Engineering

*The intellect has little to do on the road to discovery. There comes a leap in conscious-
ness, call it intuition or what you will, and the solution comes to you, and you don't
know how or why.*

—Albert Einstein

AI IS A RAPIDLY evolving field, and the future of AI and software as such
is open. In the current discussion, some envision the need for traditional
software code declining with the emergence of AI models taking on more
tasks; others assume that the increasing productivity in the software development realm will result in the number of software offerings multiplying.
The latter group points to users' seemingly insatiable appetite for specific
solutions, and assumes that having the ability to create solutions in 10% of
the time would result in 10 times as many solutions being developed. Still
others see the current hype around AI as a bubble. Given the many examples of productive use and productivity increases enabled by AI technology,
we believe it will have a profound impact—but, as is always the case with
new technology, some of the current hype is likely exaggerated. As society
and organizations learn to make use of the new technologies, the focus will
sharpen and the high-value-adding use cases will become clearer. However,
big tech argues that it is much riskier to under-invest in AI than to over-
invest. Whether that is true for your context is for you to decide.

In this chapter, we discuss possible futures related to the themes of this
book. We start with DevOps 2.0, before considering the implications of AI for
systems, including AI engineering, MLOps, and architecture. We dedicate
a section to a possible future in which AI replaces traditional software. The
final section discusses trust and the role of humans in future AI engineering.

15.1 The Shift to DevOps 2.0

Since the publication of our DevOps book in 2015, the landscape of DevOps has undergone a significant transformation. This period has witnessed the emergence of the DevOps 2.0 movement, a testament to the successes and failures of its predecessor. DevOps 1.0 was characterized by an emphasis on automating existing human tasks. Its approach to monitoring, or Observability 1.0, involved the creation of unstructured logs, isolated metrics, and dashboards. These tools were designed to detect anomalies but often left humans to deduce the root causes, with limited tracing across events and scant connections between logs and metrics being available. The primary concern was operating software, with a focus on release speed and frequency, reliability, and recovery time.

DevOps 2.0 marks a philosophical and technological shift toward enhancing human efficiency, while recognizing the limitations of the first iteration. This new phase is distinguished by several key innovations:

- **Cross-component understanding:** The modern approach advocates for a comprehensive grasp of the entire system, linking operational issues directly back to the code. It emphasizes understanding the journey of each user and request, fostering a deeper connection between development and operations.

- **Observability 2.0:** This iteration of observability champions structured logs that integrate isolated metrics and unstructured logs, with embedded tracing across the same event. By adopting a canonical log that amalgamates all related metrics, Observability 2.0 facilitates the derivation of numerous metrics on demand. The integration of AI and other advanced technologies has further streamlined the diagnosis and decision-making processes, making continuous integration and continuous deployment (CI/CD) more efficient.

- **Systemic perspective:** DevOps 2.0 encourages viewing the system from a holistic standpoint. The concept of a "digital twin" or simulation environment is pivotal, allowing teams to simulate changes or anomalies to diagnose issues before deployment and during operation. This approach transcends traditional testing methods, which often isolate issues from their system context, offering a more nuanced and effective way to anticipate and mitigate potential problems.

Adopting DevOps 2.0 principles is useful, for both AI systems and non-AI systems. Future developments in DevOps will likely deepen the current efforts to advance digital twins and use AI to improve DevOps processes. Next, we turn to other future developments related to the themes of this book.

15.2 AI's Implications for the Future

As we have seen throughout this book, AI has unique characteristics and powerful capabilities. AI can certainly be used for generating requirements, design documentation, code, configurations, test cases, and infrastructure code. AI for coding is already very popular. Additionally, AI can assist with DevOps by analyzing logs, metrics, and events, diagnosing root causes, and enacting changes. This area is often referred to as AIOps—using AI for DevOps. It should not be confused with MLOps or LLM/FMOps, which involve DevOps for ML, LLM, and FM models and systems, respectively. The implications of these types of DevOps are largely beyond the scope of this book.

The following sections focus on the characteristics of AI models and AI systems that will impact how we approach software engineering (i.e., AI engineering), DevOps (including MLOps), and software architecture in the future. We will also touch on AI's role in some of these areas.

15.2.1 The Future of Engineering AI Systems

AI systems are complex and often inscrutable. Their ability to learn from vast datasets and perform a wide range of tasks makes diagnosing problems particularly challenging. Unlike with traditional software, where issues can often be traced back to specific code segments, the "black box" nature of many AI models complicates this process. Therefore, better observability tools that incorporate explainability, transparency, and traceability will be critical to support AI systems. Such tools will help bridge the gap between the model's input and output, offering insights into its decision-making process—analogous to the concept of system-wide observability in DevOps 2.0.

Beyond Traditional Testing

The traditional testing paradigm struggles to accommodate the intricacies of AI systems. AI models, particularly those based on FMs, are not designed with fixed functions or tasks in mind, but rather learned from data. This learning process enables them to tackle a broad spectrum of activities in complex contexts, making standard testing methods less effective. Instead, the field is moving toward benchmark evaluations, which assess an AI system's performance across a range of tasks and conditions. However, one limitation is that every published benchmark might be incorporated into the training or evaluation data for the next generation of models, strongly limiting these benchmarks' usefulness as validation tests.

Moreover, AI systems can produce varied outputs, from structured data to unstructured formats like language and images, or can even interact directly with tools via user interfaces or APIs. This variability makes it difficult to apply conventional testing frameworks. Emerging tools are designed to manage these challenges, facilitating the evaluation of benchmarks, the sensitivity of prompts, context management, and complex experiments. These tools often incorporate human judgment into the loop, as they recognize the limitations of automated testing in understanding nuanced outputs and behaviors.

Dealing with Autonomy and Safety Measures

The autonomy of AI systems, particularly those powered by FMs and agent-based architectures, introduces additional complexities. An autonomous agent, in the context of AI, is a system capable of perceiving its environment, making decisions, and taking actions autonomously to achieve specific goals. These systems can interact with new data and independently devise and execute actions based on learned subgoals—a capability that significantly enhances their utility but also raises substantial safety concerns. As these agents operate with a high degree of autonomy, they may make decisions or take actions that were not explicitly anticipated by their designers, increasing the potential for unintended consequences.

To address these risks, new forms of checks and balances are being developed. For instance, simulations and digital twins enable the safe exploration of an AI system's behavior in controlled environments, allowing developers to anticipate and mitigate potential issues before they manifest in the real world. Moreover, independent overseeing AI agents—often also FM-based—are being employed to monitor and intervene in the actions of autonomous systems. These overseeing agents, along with human operators equipped with advanced AI tools, add a critical layer of scrutiny and control.

Furthermore, AI systems themselves are being designed to conduct autonomous experiments in physical or virtual environments within pre-defined guardrails. These guardrails ensure that the AI remains aligned with its intended purposes while exploring new strategies or adapting to novel scenarios. The integration of agents within this framework can enhance the system's ability to self-regulate, providing more robust safeguards against deviations from desired outcomes. The concept of limiting autonomy to a predefined frame is also known as *framed autonomy*. Such multilayered approaches to autonomy and safety are crucial for the responsible deployment of increasingly complex AI systems.

Embracing System-Level Guardrails

Implementing system-level guardrails is essential for maintaining control over autonomous AI systems. These guardrails define the boundaries within which AI systems can operate, preventing them from engaging in harmful or unintended activities. They are part of a broader strategy to ensure that AI systems remain beneficial and aligned with human values, even as they learn and evolve.

15.2.2 The Future of MLOps

MLOps is poised for significant transformation in the future, driven by the impact AI has on society. This section explores the evolving landscape of MLOps, highlighting the increasing demands for alignment with standards, regulations, and laws, as well as the integration of AI technologies like AutoML (automated ML), AIOps, and LLMs/FMs to enhance MLOps processes.

Governance and Regulation in MLOps

As AI systems become more pervasive, there are growing calls from stakeholders and government regulators for these systems to adhere to new and established standards, regulations, and laws. This demand necessitates the implementation of robust governance mechanisms that ensure AI systems operate ethically, transparently, and without bias. Initially, efforts to align AI systems with these requirements have taken a process-focused approach. This has included the establishment of AI oversight committees, enhanced organizational governance mechanisms, increased documentation of processes and methods, stakeholder consultations, and detailed metadata about data and models.

However, in the future, MLOps will likely evolve toward continuous monitoring of AI systems in operation, linking system performance directly to high-level concerns such as human rights, fairness, bias, societal impacts, and compliance with both voluntary standards and mandatory regulations. This shift extends beyond traditional quality attributes, challenging MLOps to translate between technical performance, low-level metrics, and broader societal values. Managing this translation effectively, while presenting relevant information to stakeholders with varying levels of AI literacy, will be an ongoing challenge.

The Role of AI in MLOps

Although the primary focus of this book is not the use of AI for DevOps and MLOps, the impact of AI technologies, particularly LLMs and FMs, in these areas is already evident and growing. AI and ML are revolutionizing many, if not most, of the steps in the MLOps and DevOps processes.

- **AIOps and AutoML:** These technologies are at the forefront of automating and enhancing model development. AutoML, for example, can streamline the selection of hyperparameters, model types, and configurations, as well as the evaluation process. By leveraging ML, the development cycle can be made more efficient, reducing the time and expertise required to deploy effective AI models.

- **LLMs and FMs in MLOps:** The integration of FMs, and specifically LLMs, into the DevOps and MLOps pipelines marks a significant advancement. FMs can assist in exploring designs, coding, log/metrics analysis, and summarizing experiment results. The conventional approach of manually instructing FMs via a chat interface is evolving. By encapsulating repetitive patterns in the ML workflow into programs that drive FMs, efficiency can be dramatically increased. This method enables the deployment of hundreds of AI agents to optimize the ML pipeline, significantly enhancing productivity and speed of innovation.

The future of MLOps will be marked by an increased emphasis on governance, continuous monitoring, and the integration of advanced AI technologies. As the field evolves, a key challenge will be to balance these demands, ensuring AI systems are not only effective and efficient but also responsible and transparent. The integration of AI into MLOps promises not just to transform the technical landscape, but also to redefine the ethical and regulatory frameworks within which AI systems are developed and deployed.

15.2.3 The Future of Architecture

The architectural landscape for AI systems is rapidly evolving, heralding a new era of complexity and capability. This evolution reflects not only the advancement of AI technologies, but also the changing requirements of the systems that leverage AI for a variety of tasks. This section explores the emerging architectures, the transformation of MLOps pipelines architecture, and the multifaceted challenges at the intersection of architecture and machine learning.

Emerging Architectures for AI Systems

Recent years have seen the emergence of retrieval-augmented generation (RAG) architectures, agent-based architectures, and AI/agent chains. These innovations allow for the orchestration of multiple AI systems or agents working in tandem, enabling more complex and nuanced interactions. For instance, powerful FMs and LLMs can be engaged multiple times for varying purposes within different contexts to derive insights or actions. This flexibility extends to AI-generated code, scripts, and on-demand UI or UI actions at runtime, which can dynamically interact with both tools and traditional systems. These interactions sometimes bypass predesigned APIs and interaction patterns, engaging directly with UI or users. These developments necessitate new architectural designs and patterns tailored to the dynamic and interactive nature of modern AI systems.

Changing MLOps Pipeline Architectures

The architecture of MLOps pipelines is also undergoing significant changes. The emergence of multiple interacting pipelines—from explorative model development and training to model updates, inference, and version control—marks a shift toward more complex systems. This complexity is further amplified by the introduction of components such as feature stores, model registries, and model monitoring/performance data stores. Additionally, real-time vector and column databases are becoming popular for fast feature generation and ML serving. These changes are driving the need for optimized architectures and design patterns that will address the challenges and requirements of AI and ML workflows.

Challenges at the Intersection of Architecture and ML

The relationship between architecture and ML is marked by several key challenges, as highlighted in recent discussions among industry practitioners and academics, such as the Dagstuhl seminar on the future of the topic. Some of these challenges are summarized here:

- **Data-centric architecture:** Data plays a pivotal role in both AI and non-AI systems, as well as within MLOps and DevOps frameworks. The emphasis on data-centric approaches underlines the need for architectures that can manage and leverage data effectively across different stages of the AI life cycle.

- **Evolution and adaptability:** AI systems are inherently autonomous and capable of evolution. The MLOps pipeline must not only enable but also harness this adaptability in a way that maintains trust and ensures alignment with the intended outcomes.

- **Observability and uncertainty:** The complex and often inscrutable nature of AI systems, coupled with their inherent uncertainties, poses significant challenges. Architectures must facilitate observability and manage uncertainty throughout the system and its pipelines, ensuring reliable and predictable operation.

- **Trust and trustworthiness:** Building and maintaining trust in AI systems requires linking objective evaluations of system quality with subjective user and stakeholder trust. This involves developing new evaluation techniques that account for the probabilistic and nondeterministic nature of AI, providing a foundation for trustworthiness.

- **AI-driven optimization and design:** AI is increasingly involved in deployment and runtime optimization, as well as in designing interfaces. Certain aspects of system operation and user interaction are being optimized automatically, while leveraging AI to improve efficiency, performance, and user experience. This trend toward AI-driven optimization and design reflects a broader shift in how systems are developed, deployed, and maintained, with AI playing a central role in both the architecture and the operation of modern systems.

15.3 AIWare or AI-as-Software

In the previous section, we discussed the impact of AI characteristics on the future of AI engineering, MLOps, and architecture, including the use of AI to solve some of the challenges in these areas. AI can certainly follow human instructions and help generate requirements, design, code, test suites, and infrastructure code. In fact, by late 2024 Google used AI to generate more than a quarter of all new code, which is then reviewed and accepted by engineers, according to CEO Sundar Pichai. This raises the question of whether AI might eventually write all of the code, replacing human developers and DevOps/ML engineers. Some argue that the hottest programming language is now English, or even jokingly suggest that the current AI wave is a revenge of the English major against STEM professionals.

Historical analogies to the current development movement include the rise of higher-level programming languages, which relegated assembly language programming to a niche specialty, and the advent of fourth-generation query languages, which reduced the demand for database specialists. In these cases, the role of software developers evolved, but the need for some form of code and specialists in software development persisted. In fact, the number of developers worldwide has steadily increased. A similar phenomenon is likely to occur as AI-generated software becomes more common.

However, what if we no longer need a significant amount of traditional software code to be written, even by AI following human instructions? That scenario would lead to the emergence of AI-as-Software, also known as AIWare.

Historically, AI components have been depicted as minor elements within the larger context of software systems, designed to perform specific tasks based on models learned from data. Early models, such as decision trees, provided human-understandable logic and decision paths for some AI components. More recently, narrow ML models, such as those used for face recognition, fraud detection, and content analysis, have been employed despite being more difficult to fully understand. These models play a partial role within a larger system, where they are integrated through traditional code for business logic and connected to the non-AI portions of the system.

However, with the advent of more general-purpose models boasting billions of parameters, business logic is no longer external to the model but rather embedded within its parameters and weights. Many business functions and logic that were previously handled by non-AI components are now being absorbed into the model, manifesting as inscrutable weights. This shift toward end-to-end AI, in which all functions are encapsulated within a single black box, as parameters/weights rather than distinct narrow AI components explicitly chained together by traditional business code logic, represents a new direction.

One question is how data is persisted in AIWare. This might be done through long-term memory, or it might be done through structured databases. The latter approach might be an intermediate step, starting with human database engineers designing schemas, consistency constraints, and deciding on access rights. If development proceeds in this direction, such technological choices will likely be opaque to users, and eventually automated by the AI itself.

While software once "ate the world," in this future, AI is "eating the software."

Example Cases: Tesla and Gemini-Reasoning

The recent release of Tesla's fully autonomous driving software offers a glimpse into one possible future. Autonomous driving software was traditionally a blend of AI and non-AI components, including small AI modules for lane/object/space detection, object tracking, and some AI planning, alongside numerous non-AI components. These might have included encoded traffic rules and control and safety components, all meticulously written and tested, connected by glue code. However, Tesla introduced a single large neural network model as the core of its system. This model, trained on millions of hours of footage from highly rated Uber drivers, embeds all logic—covering obstacle detection, traffic rules, planning, and control—within its billions of parameters. No explicit programming for traffic rules or separate subcomponents existed; thus, AI nearly constitutes the entire software, eliminating the need for traditional code generation based on specific requirements and instructions.

Another perspective argues against the assumption that certain software aspects, such as the UI, must always be designed by humans (assisted by AI) and wrap around the powerful AI models. The Gemini-Reasoning demo[1] suggests that this approach is not necessarily essential. When a father asked Gemini to devise an outdoor birthday plan for his animal-loving daughter, the AI system first self-deliberated over the appropriate UI format, deciding on a rich interface with graphics and drop-down menus. It then self-generated a UI skeleton tailored to the query and answer, before populating it with the actual AI-generated answer, all within a sophisticated but fully self-designed and generated UI at runtime. This demonstrates the AI system's capability in conducting requirements analysis, design, and content generation autonomously and at runtime. In some instances, it created UI code for rendering; in others, it functioned as the software itself, presenting information without generating traditional code.

In the future, a user might simply ask a general-purpose AI system to "act" like any software, such as a browser or a to-do management system. The AI system would then function as that software, tailored to the user's needs, without the need to go through the process of writing one.

---

1. www.youtube.com/watch?v=v5tRc_5-8G4

15.4 Trust in AI and the Role of Human Engineers

The shift toward AI-generated software and AI-as-Software inevitably raises concerns about trustworthiness. Without traditional development processes, such as human-driven requirements analysis, design, coding, and testing, ensuring the reliability and safety of these systems becomes challenging. However, just as trust in compilers and narrow ML components has grown over time, it is conceivable that trust in both AI-generated software and end-to-end AI systems could also develop, provided appropriate new safeguards are in place. Even in the most drastic envisioning of an AI-as-Software world, there will still be essential roles for human engineers.

15.4.1 System-Level Guardrails

Architects play a central role in defining human-understandable guardrails around AI systems. These guardrails serve as boundaries within which AI operates, ensuring that the systems align with human rights, desires, and legal frameworks, even if the internal workings of the AI system remain opaque. However, for guardrails to be effective, they need to be present at all interfaces of an AI system that can create an impact—such as UIs, APIs to other systems and tools, database connections, and more.

15.4.2 Design of Multi-Agent Systems

The future may be populated with either general-purpose AIs capable of performing many tasks or specialized AIs focusing on specific functions and coordinating with each other and humans. This highlights the need to carefully design agent-to-agent and agent-to-human interactions, define their roles and qualities, and determine the connectors between them while ensuring their operations remain reliable. These design considerations will be critical for the effective operation of multi-agent systems.

15.4.3 Understanding and Quality Control of AI Models

Despite the internal complexity of many AI models, efforts are being made to decipher their structures to better control quality and behavior. This opens up avenues for targeted in-model quality control and optimization through components, connectors, and structures, offering roles for those skilled in both software engineering and architecture.

15.4.4 Specialization of FMs and Learning Outside the Model

While the construction of large FMs may involve fewer individuals, the specialization and fine-tuning of these models for specific applications remain significant tasks. Once the FM-based AI systems are deployed, continuous learning may be desired. Much of this learning may happen outside the model—not by feeding data back into model training, but rather through better prompts, in-context learning, and guardrails. This necessitates expertise in LLMOps and FMOps, focusing on adapting and enhancing FMs for particular needs.

15.5 Summary

AI engineering, as an emerging discipline, continues to evolve.

One driving force is the development of the DevOps field, which has grown from simply automating tasks across the development and operations divide and providing fast feedback to offering enhanced observability, root-cause analysis, and what-if scenarios. These advancements help humans better understand complex systems and make more informed decisions across the DevOps spectrum.

Another significant factor is the nature of AI itself. AI-based software systems come with unique characteristics that demand improved approaches to address them. At the same time, AI systems can support these approaches by generating software artifacts—from requirements and design to code and test suites—and by assisting with DevOps and MLOps processes.

However, the most profound change might be the advent of AI-as-Software, where complex AI models encapsulate most functions and business logic within their parameters. In this scenario, neither AI nor humans would write software in the traditional sense. Instead, AI *is* the software.

No matter what the future holds (though it is likely to be a blend of these developments), it will require AI engineers, software architects, and MLOps engineers to develop new tools, methods, and philosophies to navigate the evolving landscape. This future may involve providing human-understandable guardrails outside AI models, refining general-purpose AI into specialized applications, enabling learning outside the model, and managing the intricate relationships between humans and AI, as well as between AI systems themselves. The horizon has never been broader or more exciting for us humans.

15.6 Discussion Questions

1. What is the difference between DevOps 1.0 and DevOps 2.0? Use a few examples to discuss this distinction.

2. How do you build trust in code generated by AI?

3. In a world where AI is the software, what are your views on the role of human engineers?

15.7 For Further Reading

For DevOps 2.0, check out this podcast with one of the movement's leaders, Adam Jacob: www.arresteddevops.com/the-new-devops/.

For insights into the future of AI-generated coding for complex AI-based systems, see Cheng et al.'s work on Prompt Sapper [Cheng 24], a production tool leveraging LLMs for building AI chains.

To explore the use of FMs in designing advanced AI agents, refer to the following publications: [Lu 24B], which provides a reference architecture for responsible generative AI; [Liu 24], which offers a catalogue of architectural patterns for FM–based agents; and [Zhou 24], which presents a taxonomy of architecture options for such agents.

For a thought-provoking perspective on whether LLMs will become the operating systems of the future, see the article on *Medium* [Protege 24].

To explore the complex issue of trust in AI systems, refer to the publication by NIST, which delves into the challenges and considerations around trust in AI [NIST 19].

For details about the concept of framed autonomy, please refer to [Dumas 23].

References

[Ahern 04] Ahern, D. M., Clouse, A., & Turner, R. (2004). *CMMI distilled: A practical introduction to integrated process improvement.* Addison-Wesley.

[Akiba 19] Akiba, T., Sano, S., Yanase, T., Ohta, T., & Koyama, M. (2019, July). Optuna: A next-generation hyperparameter optimization framework. In *Proceedings of the 25th ACM SIGKDD International Conference on Knowledge Discovery & Data Mining* (pp. 2623–2631). ACM.

[Ameisen 20] Ameisen, E. (2020). *Building machine learning powered applications: Going from idea to product.* O'Reilly Media.

[Amershi 19] Amershi, S., Begel, A., Bird, C., DeLine, R., Gall, H., Kamar, E., Nagappan, N., Nushi, B., & Zimmermann, T. (2019, May). Software engineering for machine learning: A case study. In *2019 IEEE/ACM 41st International Conference on Software Engineering: Software Engineering in Practice (ICSE-SEIP)* (pp. 291–300). IEEE.

[Avizienis 04] Avizienis, A., Laprie, J. C., Randell, B., & Landwehr, C. (2004). Basic concepts and taxonomy of dependable and secure computing. *IEEE Transactions on Dependable and Secure Computing, 1*(1), 11–33.

[Bass 22] Bass, L., Clements, P., & Kazman, R. (2022). *Software architecture in practice* (4th ed.). Addison-Wesley.

[Bass 19] Bass, L., & Klein, J. (2022). *Deployment and operations for software engineers* (2nd ed.). Self published. https://www.amazon.com/Deployment-Operations-Software-Engineers-Engineering/dp/B09XT6L7T5

[Bass 15] Bass, L., Weber, I., & Zhu, L. (2015). *DevOps: A software architect's perspective.* Addison-Wesley.

[Beck 20] Beck, N., Martens, C., Sylla, K. H., Wegener, D., & Zimmermann, A. (2020). *Zukunftssichere Lösungen für maschinelles Lernen.* https://publica.fraunhofer.de/entities/publication/be431a0b-ae8e-4644-9b0b-429249bcd8f0

[Bird 20] Bird, S., Dudík, M., Edgar, R., Horn, B., Lutz, R., Milan, V., Sameki, M., Wallach, H., & Walker, K. (2020). *Fairlearn: A toolkit for assessing and improving fairness in AI.* Microsoft, Tech. Rep. MSR-TR-2020-32.

[Brownlee 16] Brownlee, J. (2016). *Machine learning algorithms from scratch with Python.* Machine Learning Mastery.

[CCPA] California Office of the Attorney General. (n.d.). *California Consumer Privacy Act (CCPA).* https://www.oag.ca.gov/privacy/ccpa

[Cheng 24] Cheng, Y., Chen, J., Huang, Q., Xing, Z., Xu, X., & Lu, Q. (2024). Prompt sapper: A LLM-empowered production tool for building AI chains. *ACM Transactions on Software Engineering and Methodology, 33*(5), 1–24.

[CMUSEI CMM] Carnegie Mellon University Software Engineering Institute, Paulk, M. C., Curtis, B., Chrissis, M. B., & Weber, C. V. (1994). *Capability maturity model for software: Guidelines for improving the software process.* Addison-Wesley.

[Dumas 23] Dumas, M., Fournier, F., Limonad, L., Marrella, A., Montali, M., Rehse, J. R., Accorsi, R., Calvanese, D., De Giacomo, G., Fahland, D., Gal, A., La Rosa, M., Völzer, H., & Weber, I. (2023) AI-augmented business process management systems: A research manifesto. *ACM Transactions on Management Information Systems (TMIS), 14*(1), 1–19.

[Fielding 00] Fielding, R. T. (2000). *Architectural styles and the design of network-based software architectures.* University of California, Irvine.

[FraunhoferIAIS AIAssCatalog] Fraunhofer Institute for Intelligent Analysis and Information Systems (IAIS). (n.d.). *AI assessment catalog.* https://www.iais.fraunhofer.de/en/research/artificial-intelligence/ai-assessment-catalog.html

[Gamma 95] Gamma, E., Helm, R., Johnson, R., & Vlissides, J. (1995). *Design patterns: Elements of reusable object-oriented software.* Pearson Deutschland.

[Géron 22] Géron, A. (2022). *Hands-on machine learning with Scikit-Learn, Keras, and TensorFlow.* O'Reilly Media.

[Goldberg 17] Goldberg, Y. (2017). *Neural network methods in natural language processing.* Morgan & Claypool Publishers.

[Goodfellow 16] Goodfellow, I., Bengio, Y., & Courville, A. (2016). *Deep learning.* The MIT Press.

[Huyen 22] Huyen, C. (2022). *Designing machine learning systems: An iterative process for production-ready applications.* O'Reilly Media.

[IISA 2023] Industry Innovation and Science Australia. (2023). *Barriers to collaboration and commercialisation.* Commonwealth of Australia. https://www.industry.gov.au/sites/default/files/2023-11/barriers-to-collaboration-and-commercialisation-iisa.pdf

[Kampik 24] Kampik, T., Warmuth, C., Rebmann, A., Agam, R., Egger, L. N., Gerber, A., & Weidlich, M. (2023). *Large process models: Business process management in the age of generative AI.* arXiv preprint arXiv:2309.00900.

[Kazman 22] Kazman, R. (2022, July 25). Tactics and patterns for software robustness. *SEI Blog.* https://insights.sei.cmu.edu/blog/tactics-and-patterns-for-software-robustness/

[Kläs 20] Kläs, M., & Jöckel, L. (2020, September). A framework for building uncertainty wrappers for AI/ML-based data-driven components. In *Computer safety, reliability, and security: SAFECOMP 2020 Workshops: DECSoS 2020, DepDevOps 2020, USDAI 2020, and WAISE 2020, Lisbon, Portugal, September 15, 2020, Proceedings 39* (pp. 315–327). Springer International Publishing.

[Kläs 18] Kläs, M., & Vollmer, A. M. (2018, September). Uncertainty in machine learning applications: A practice-driven classification of uncertainty. In *Computer safety, reliability, and security: SAFECOMP 2018 Workshops, ASSURE, DECSoS, SASSUR, STRIVE, and WAISE, Västerås, Sweden, September 18, 2018, Proceedings 37* (pp. 431–438). Springer International Publishing.

[Lewis 21] Lewis, G. A., Ozkaya, I., & Xu, X. (2021, September). Software architecture challenges for ML systems. In *2021 IEEE International Conference on Software Maintenance and Evolution (ICSME)* (pp. 634–638). IEEE.

[Lewis 20] Lewis, P., Perez, E., Piktus, A., Petroni, F., Karpukhin, V., Goyal, N., Küttler, H., Lewis, M., Yih, W-t., Rocktäschel, T., Riedel, S., & Kiela, D. (2020). Retrieval-augmented generation for knowledge-intensive NLP tasks. *Advances in Neural Information Processing Systems, 33*, 9459–9474.

[Liu 24] Liu, Y., Lo, S. K., Lu, Q., Zhu, L., Zhao, D., Xu, X., Harrer, S., & Whittle, J. (2024). *Agent design pattern catalogue: A collection of architectural patterns for foundation model based agents.* arXiv preprint arXiv:2405.10467. https://arxiv.org/abs/2405.10467

[Lu 23A] Lu, Q., Zhu, L., Whittle, J., & Xu, X. (2023). *Responsible AI: Best practices for creating trustworthy AI systems.* Addison-Wesley.

[Lu 24A] Lu, Q., Zhu, L., Xu, X., Liu, Y., Xing, Z., & Whittle, J. (2024, April). A taxonomy of foundation model based systems through the lens of software architecture. In *Proceedings of the IEEE/ACM 3rd International Conference on AI Engineering-Software Engineering for AI* (pp. 1–6). IEEE.

[Lu 23B] Lu, Q., Zhu, L., Xu, X., & Whittle, J. (2023). Responsible-AI-by-design: A pattern collection for designing responsible artificial intelligence systems. *IEEE Software, 40*(3), 63–71.

[Lu 24C] Lu, Q., Zhu, L., Xu, X., Whittle, J., Zowghi, D., & Jacquet, A. (2024). Responsible AI pattern catalogue: A collection of best practices for AI governance and engineering. *ACM Computing Surveys, 56*(7), 1–35.

[Lu 24B] Lu, Q., Zhu, L., Xu, X., Xing, Z., Harrer, S., & Whittle, J. (2024, June). Towards responsible generative AI: A reference architecture for designing foundation model based agents. In *2024 IEEE 21st International Conference on Software Architecture Companion (ICSA-C)* (pp. 119–126). IEEE.

[Lu 24D] Lu, Q., Zhu, L., Xu, X., Xing, Z., & Whittle, J. (2024). Towards responsible ai in the era of generative ai: A reference architecture for designing foundation model based systems. *IEEE Software.*

[Majors 22] Majors, C., Fong-Jones, L., & Miranda, G. (2022). *Observability engineering: Achieving production excellence.* O'Reilly Media.

[NIST 20] Rose, S., Borchert, O., Mitchell, S., & Connelly, S. (2020). *NIST Special Publication 800-207: Zero trust architecture.* National Institute of Standards and Technology. https://doi.org/10.6028/NIST.SP.800-207

[NIST 19] Stanton, B., & Jensen, T. (2019). *Trust and artificial intelligence.* National Institute of Standards and Technology. https://www.nist.gov/publications /trust-and-artificial-intelligence

[NIST 23] National Institute of Standards and Technology. (2023). *NIST AI Risk Management Framework (AI RMF) 1.0.* https://doi.org/10.6028/NIST.AI.100-1

[OECD AIPrinciples] OECD. (n.d.). *OECD AI principles.* https://oecd.ai/en /ai-principles

[Paaß 23] Paaß, G., & Giesselbach, S. (2023). Foundation models for natural language processing: Pre-trained language models integrating media. *Springer Nature*, 436.

[Protege 24] Protege IGDTUW. (2024). Part 1: Introduction to LLM OS. *Medium.* https://medium.com/@protegeigdtuw/part-1-introduction-to-llm-os -1cfec39689f7

[Shamsujjoha 24] Shamsujjoha, M., Lu, Q., Zhao, D., & Zhu, L. (2024). *Towards AI-safety-by-design: A taxonomy of runtime guardrails in foundation model based systems.* arXiv preprint arXiv:2408.02205. https://arxiv.org/abs/2408.02205

[Shankar 22] Shankar, S., Garcia, R., Hellerstein, J. M., & Parameswaran, A. G. (2022). *Operationalizing machine learning: An interview study.* arXiv preprint arXiv:2209.09125. https://arxiv.org/abs/2108.13557

[Shankar 21] Shankar, S., & Parameswaran, A. (2021). *Towards observability for production machine learning pipelines.* arXiv preprint arXiv:2108.13557. https://arxiv.org/abs/2209.09125

[Sze 20] Sze, V., Chen, Y. H., Yang, T. J., & Emer, J. S. (2020). *Efficient processing of deep neural networks.* Morgan & Claypool Publishers.

[TensorFlow Guide] https://www.tensorflow.org/tutorials/quickstart/beginner

[TensorFlow Tutorials] https://www.tensorflow.org/tutorials

[Touvron 23] Touvron, H., Lavril, T., Izacard, G., Martinet, X., Lachaux, M. A., Lacroix, T., & Lample, G. (2023). *Llama: Open and efficient foundation language models.* arXiv preprint arXiv:2302.13971.

[Tran 20] Tran, N., Schneider, J. G., Weber, I., & Qin, A. K. (2020). Hyperparameter optimization in classification: To-do or not-to-do. *Pattern Recognition, 103*, 107245.

[Vassilev 24] Vassilev, A., Oprea, A., Fordyce, A., & Anderson, H. (2024). *Adversarial machine learning: A taxonomy and terminology of attacks and mitigations.* No. NIST Artificial Intelligence (AI) 100-2 E2023. National Institute of Standards and Technology.

[Vaswani 17] Vaswani, A., Shazeer, N., Parmar, N., Uszkoreit, J., Jones, L., Gomez, A. N., & Kaiser, L. (2017). Attention is all you need. In *Advances in neural information processing systems.* Curran Associates. https://papers .nips.cc/paper_files/paper/2017/file/3f5ee243547dee91fbd053c1c4a845aa -Paper.pdf

[Weber 24] Weber, I., Linka, H., Mertens, D., Muryshkin, T., Opgenoorth, H., & Langer, S. (2024) FhGenie: A custom, confidentiality-preserving chat AI for corporate and scientific use. In *ICSA '24: IEEE International Conference on Software Architecture, Software Architecture in Practice (SAIP) track.*

[Wicker 18] Wicker, M., Huang, X., & Kwiatkowska, M. (2018, April). Feature-guided black-box safety testing of deep neural networks. In *Tools and Algorithms for the Construction and Analysis of Systems: 24th International Conference, TACAS 2018, Held as Part of the European Joint Conferences on Theory and Practice of Software, ETAPS 2018, Thessaloniki, Greece, April 14–20, 2018, Proceedings, Part I 24* (pp. 408–426). Springer International Publishing.

[Wiki Transformer] Transformer (deep learning architecture). (2024, September 8). In *Wikipedia.* https://en.wikipedia.org/w/index.php?title=Transformer_(deep_learning_architecture)&oldid=1244693922

[Wiki Word2Vec] Word2vec. (2024). In *Wikipedia.* https://en.wikipedia.org/w/index.php?title=Word2vec&oldid=1244273377

[Xia 24B] Xia, B., Bi, T., Xing, Z., Lu, Q., & Zhu, L. (2023, May). An empirical study on software bill of materials: Where we stand and the road ahead. In *2023 IEEE/ACM 45th International Conference on Software Engineering (ICSE)* (pp. 2630–2642). IEEE.

[Xia 24A] Xia, B., Lu, Q., Zhu, L., & Xing, Z. (2024, July). An AI system evaluation framework for advancing AI safety: Terminology, taxonomy, lifecycle mapping. In *Proceedings of the 1st ACM International Conference on AI-Powered Software* (pp. 74–78).

[Zaharia 24] Zaharia, M., Khattab, O., Chen, L., Davis, J. Q., Miller, H., Potts, C., Zou, J., Carbin, M., Frankle, J., Rao, N., & Ghodsi, A. (2024, February 18). The shift from models to compound AI systems. *BAIR Blog.* https://bair.berkeley.edu/blog/2024/02/18/compound-ai-systems/

[Zheng 24] Zheng, L., Chiang, W. L., Sheng, Y., Zhuang, S., Wu, Z., Zhuang, Y., & Stoica, I. (2024). Judging LLM-as-a-judge with MT-bench and chatbot arena. *Advances in Neural Information Processing Systems, 36.*

[Zhou 24] Zhou, J., Lu, Q., Chen, J., Zhu, L., Xu, X., Xing, Z., & Harrer, S. (2024). *A taxonomy of architecture options for foundation model-based agents: Analysis and decision model.*

[Zhu 22] Zhu, L., Xu, X., Lu, Q., Governatori, G., & Whittle, J. (2022). AI and ethics—Operationalizing responsible AI. *Humanity driven AI: Productivity, well-being, sustainability and partnership,* (pp. 15–33).

Index

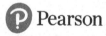